THE BERLIN NOVELS OF
ALFRED DÖBLIN

THE BERLIN NOVELS OF ALFRED DÖBLIN

Wadzek's Battle with the Steam Turbine,
Berlin Alexanderplatz,
Men without Mercy,
and
November 1918

DAVID B. DOLLENMAYER

University of California Press
Berkeley · Los Angeles · London

University of California Press
Berkeley and Los Angeles, California

University of California Press, Ltd.
London, England

© 1988 by
The Regents of the University of California

Library of Congress Cataloging-in-Publication Data

Dollenmayer, David B.
  The Berlin novels of Alfred Döblin.
  Bibliography: p.
  Includes index.
    1. Döblin, Alfred, 1878–1957—Criticism and
interpretation.   I. Title.
PT2607.035Z66   1988   833'.912   87-25527
ISBN 0-520-06000-8 (alk. paper)

Printed in the United States of America

1   2   3   4   5   6   7   8   9

For Linda

Contents

Acknowledgments

I would like to express my thanks to Professors Catherine Chvany, Kathryn Crecelius, and Robert E. Jones of MIT, Professor Heidi Thomann Tewarson of Columbia University, and to Judith Dollenmayer, who read parts of the manuscript and made good suggestions for its improvement. I also honor the memory of Professor Krystyna Pomorska, whose interest in Futurism was a source of inspiration. A special debt of gratitude is owed to Professor Heinz D. Osterle of Northern Illinois University for two thorough, critical, and immensely helpful readings of the entire manuscript.

A fellowship from the Old Dominion Foundation gave me some precious time to begin work on Döblin.

Parts of the book have appeared in different form in *The German Quarterly*, *The Germanic Review*, and the *Jahrbuch für Internationale Germanistik*.

Finally, this book would not have been possible without the constant encouragement and infinite patience of my wife, Linda Pape.

Abbreviations

Complete bibliographical information for these and other works by Döblin is given in "Works Cited," pages 203–4.

ASLA	*Autobiographische Schriften und letzte Aufzeichnungen*
AzL	*Aufsätze zur Literatur*
BA	*Berlin Alexanderplatz. Die Geschichte vom Franz Biberkopf*
BMG	*Berge Meere und Giganten*
Briefe	*Briefe*
DHF	*Drama. Hörspiel. Film*
E	*Erzählungen aus fünf Jahrzehnten*
EJ	*Alexanderplatz Berlin: The Story of Franz Biberkopf,* trans. Eugene Jolas
IüN	*Das Ich über der Natur*
JR	*Jagende Rosse, Der schwarze Vorhang, und andere frühe Erzählwerke*
MWM	*Men without Mercy,* trans. Trevor and Phyllis Blewitt
November	*November 1918: Eine deutsche Revolution.* Vol. 1, *Bürger und Soldaten;* vol. 2, *Verratenes Volk;* vol. 3, *Heimkehr der Fronttruppen;* vol. 4, *Karl und Rosa*
P	*Pardon wird nicht gegeben*
RP	*Reise in Polen*
SLW	*Schriften zu Leben und Werk*
SPG	*Schriften zur Politik und Gesellschaft*
UD	*Unser Dasein*

W   *Wadzeks Kampf mit der Dampfturbine*

WL   *Die drei Sprünge des Wang-lun. Chinesischer Roman*

Woods   *November 1918: A German Revolution,* trans. John
             E. Woods. Vol. 1, *A People Betrayed;* vol. 2, *Karl
             and Rosa*

WV   *Der deutsche Maskenball von Linke Poot. Wissen und
             Verändern!*

Zeitlupe   *Die Zeitlupe. Kleine Prosa*

Introduction

Alfred Döblin belongs in the pantheon of great German writers who were born in the final quarter of the nineteenth century, began writing before the First World War, flourished during the Weimar Republic, and went into exile during the Third Reich. Like Kafka, he was a Jew from a lower-middle-class mercantile family. Like the poet Gottfried Benn, he had a parallel career as a practicing physician. Like Thomas Mann, whom he despised, and Bertolt Brecht, whose friend he was, he spent his exile in the exotic refuge of southern California and returned to Europe soon after the war was over. Like the Austrian novelist Joseph Roth, he turned to Catholicism late in life under the pressures of exile.

In his life and works, Döblin mirrors the turbulence and fecundity of German letters in the first half of the twentieth century. Before the First World War he had already established himself on the Berlin literary scene with his contributions to the journal *Sturm,* one of the central organs of German Expressionism. Early stories like "Die Ermordung einer Butterblume" (The Murder of a Buttercup) are masterpieces of Expressionist prose, a genre most Expressionists neglected in favor of poetry and theater. Beginning with *Die drei Sprünge des Wang-lun* (The Three Leaps of Wang-lun), completed just before the First World War, Döblin developed a new style that he called "epic" fiction. During and after the war, he continued to write monumental epics of social upheavals and mass movements.

Like most Berlin writers between the wars, Döblin's political sympathies were left of center.[1] Although he became increasingly disillusioned with party politics and resigned from the Social Democratic Party in 1928, he continued to be an active member of various left-liberal writers' organizations and, after 1928, of the prestigious Prussian Academy of Sciences. His masterpiece *Berlin Alexanderplatz,* published in 1929, was an immediate best-seller and Döblin's only commercial success. Forced into exile in 1933, he spent bitter years in

I

Paris and Hollywood, cut off from his German-speaking public and from the Berlin he loved so much. In 1945, largely forgotten in his native country, he returned to Germany as an officer of the French army of occupation. Embittered by his inability to place his works with German publishers and by the conservative restoration he saw developing in West Germany, he emigrated a second time in 1953 and settled in Paris. His last novel was published in East Germany in 1956, the year before his death.

Alfred Döblin's reputation with the reading public, both in his own time and today, rests largely on the novel *Berlin Alexanderplatz*. "Whenever they mentioned my name," he wrote in 1955, "they added *Berlin Alexanderplatz*."[2] It was an especially ironic fate for so prolific a writer, a fate he struggled unsuccessfully to overcome. Unlike Robert Musil and *The Man without Qualities*, Döblin did not regard *Berlin Alexanderplatz* as his magnum opus, but rather as one link in a chain of works, each of which he described as growing out of questions left open by its predecessor (*BA* 506). The open and problematic ending is indeed one of the most striking characteristics of Döblin's works, a reflection of his own discomfort and inability to find satisfactory and conclusive answers to the urgent social and moral questions he raised. For Döblin is a writer with a deep sense of unease both about himself and his place in society and about modern man and society in general. His novels arise from and reflect that unease.

The popularity of *Berlin Alexanderplatz* is based to some extent on the misconception that it is a document of Berlin in the turbulent, seething twenties. It is that, but it is also much more. The montage technique that informs every page of the novel was immediately recognized as a major formal achievement by critics like Walter Benjamin,[3] and we will see that while the montage does serve a documentary purpose by mounting things like contemporary hit songs and advertisements directly into the fictional text, it also has the more important purpose of suggesting the integration and unity of a reality that at first appears chaotic. In its encompassing of everything from vulgar *Schlager* to mythological and biblical references, the montage pieces together universal meaning out of the often sordid reality of Berlin in the twenties.

Berlin was for Döblin both his real home and the archetypical metropolis, a microcosm of the entire world. In an early autobiographical sketch he describes himself as a "Berliner with vague notions of other cities and regions" (*ASLA* 13). Even after seven years of exile from Germany, in a letter of 1940, his pen slipped, writing "Berlin" when he meant "Paris" (*Briefe* 240). He never really recovered from being banished from his native soil. Yet for such a confirmed *homo urbanus* and the author of the most famous city novel in German, there is a curious dualism running through the list of seventeen novels he published during his lifetime. Less than half of them are set in contemporary Berlin. The others range geographically from the jungles of South America to the river valleys of China, and chronologically from the seventeenth to the twenty-seventh century. Döblin himself drew attention to this dualism in his afterword to a 1955 edition of *Berlin Alexanderplatz:*

> How curious: I had spent my whole life in the East End of Berlin, had attended the Berlin public schools, was an active socialist, a public health system doctor—and I wrote about China, about the Thirty Years War and Wallenstein and finally even about a mythic and mystic India. My friends entreated me to write about Berlin. I hadn't turned my back on Berlin on purpose. It just happened that way. I could give freer rein to my imagination that way. All right then, I could do something different. You can also write about Berlin without imitating Zola.
>
> (*BA* 507)

Döblin here suggests two related reasons, one formal and one psychological, for the dualism evident in the settings of his novels. First, he has avoided writing about his contemporary environment because he does not want to be misunderstood as perpetuating the tradition of nineteenth-century naturalism by "imitating Zola." If he eventually came to call his own fictional method—and indeed his worldview—*Naturalismus,* he meant something quite different from Zola's *naturalisme.* Döblin, himself a doctor who practiced first psychiatry and then internal medicine, was much more skeptical than Zola had been in the previous, more positivistic generation that science and the scientific method would eventually be able to answer completely all questions about human life and the universe. Even in a quite fiercely "naturalistic" text like the early story "Von der himmlischen Gnade" (On Heavenly Mercy), there are anomalous and jarring narrative intrusions from other, metaphysical and satiric levels that throw naturalism into question. For Döblin, fiction was never a carefully controlled experiment in social reality, but rather an "epic work," chronicling mass movements and social upheavals rather than registering the nuances of individual psyches. The epic work, for instance, scorns the amatory complications that in Döblin's view comprise the plot structure of the average realistic novel (not that relations between men and women are unimportant in his works; indeed, we will see that the struggle to come to terms with sexuality and women occupies a central place in Döblin's oeuvre). There is also a streak of utopianism in most of Döblin's novels, although the explicit utopias in his works—the society of the future in the science-fiction fantasy *Berge Meere und Giganten* (Mountains Seas and Giants) and the Paraguayan Jesuit Republic in *Amazonas*—end in disaster.[4]

Along with his view of the novel as an epic work goes the psychological aspect of Döblin's aesthetic theory and practice. He says in the afterword to *Berlin Alexanderplatz* quoted above that he had neglected Berlin in order to give his imagination freer rein. Like many other authors, he used the metaphor of pregnancy and birth to describe the creative process. He wrote to Martin Buber in 1915 apropos the novel *Wadzeks Kampf mit der Dampfturbine* (Wadzek's Battle with the Steam Turbine), "I never have a conscious intention. I always write completely involuntarily, and that's not just a turn of phrase. This book was written in a single stretch from August to December 1914, and that fact also proves to me that the book has no birth defects: I never make any progress by thinking" (*Briefe* 80). Döblin here describes his method as almost automatic writing, and although one cannot take him completely at his word in the above passage, his novels do often have the formless, surging incoherence one would expect from such a technique. It was thus that he hoped to confront reality most directly, to divest himself of consciousness and merge with his object: "I am not I, but rather the street, the streetlights, this or that occurrence, nothing more" (*AzL* 18).

At its best, this technique does indeed set free Döblin's imagination to create visions of extraordinary dynamism and power. At its worst, it results in flabbiness, obscurity, and banal tedium (almost all of Döblin's works could stand some cutting). But it also means that the writer's own subconscious is very near the surface of his text. We will see how certain themes and patterns of action, particularly with regard to sexuality and women, recur obsessively throughout Döblin's long career.

If turning his back on Berlin meant that Döblin could give freer rein to his imagination, then the converse is also true, that writing about the contemporary metropolis imposed limits on his imaginative hypertrophy. The monstrous biological fantasies of *Mountains Seas and*

Giants present the most extreme example of Döblin's unbridled imagination, while the 1935 city novel *Pardon wird nicht gegeben* (Men without Mercy)[5] is his most austere, controlled work, his closest approach to a traditional novel.

There was thus a life-long tension in Alfred Döblin the novelist between his tropically fertile imagination and the cold exigencies of the social and political reality in which he lived. Of course, no literary work is written in a temporal and social vacuum, and even the novels Döblin set in distant times and exotic places implicitly refer to the society in which they were written.[6] In fact, both *The Three Leaps of Wang-lun* and *Mountains Seas and Giants* (1924) have dedicatory prefaces in which the narrator speaks from his contemporary urban environment before launching his story. Nevertheless, it is in what I will call the "Berlin novels" that Döblin's concern with contemporary society is most explicitly evident. It is in them that the dilemma that underlies all his works, the struggle between the contradictory impulses of passive acceptance of fate and active resistance to oppression, is directly related to the crises of urban and industrialized Germany in the first half of the twentieth century. In describing how he came to write the mammoth tetralogy of the German revolution, *November 1918,* Döblin clearly expresses the opposition between the two sorts of novel he wrote: "After satisfying my thirst for adventure in the South America book, I returned to my native shores. I thought of Berlin, the distant city, and began to examine in my mind how everything had come about, as I had in 1934 in *Men without Mercy*" (*AzL* 394).

The theme of Berlin, with its explicit concern for contemporary society, is present in Döblin's earliest surviving work and recurs throughout his oeuvre. The social and political questions it raises became more and more urgent during the course of the Weimar Republic. *Berlin Alexanderplatz* is surely the most perfect expression of the city theme and Döblin's greatest achievement as a novelist. It is a city novel of the stature of Joyce's *Ulysses* and Dos Passos's *Manhattan Transfer.* But his other Berlin novels also deserve our attention, not only because they help us understand the achievement of *Berlin Alexanderplatz,* but for their own sake. They are engaging, disturbing works of a great and unique prose stylist, and at the same time documents of the dilemma of a progressive writer caught between the ideological fronts that would tear the Weimar Republic apart.

Döblin was a constant experimenter with form, and his four Berlin novels are distinctly, even radically different from each other. They chart both Döblin's social concern and the development of the formal means to express that concern in fiction. His first Berlin novel, *Wadzek's Battle with the Steam Turbine* (written 1914), despite its provocatively Futuristic title, is a difficult, introverted, darkly comic work with a narrative focus that never allows the reader any distance from the psychotic viewpoint of its hero, the industrialist and engineer Franz Wadzek.[7] In *Berlin Alexanderplatz*, written thirteen years later, the narrator establishes an ironic distance from his narrative. He is now a *monteur* who relativizes and universalizes the story of Franz Biberkopf by surrounding it with fragments from other lives and other levels of reality. In *Wadzek*, Berlin remains a shadowy background for the psychotic drama of the central figure. In *Berlin Alexanderplatz* it becomes itself a central figure of the novel and a microcosmic reflection of a universal order.

But the cautious optimism evident at the end of *Berlin Alexanderplatz*—the hope for a positive synthesis of individual and collective—was shattered in 1933. The ambiguous provenance of the marching feet that end Döblin's greatest novel was soon to be resolved as fascist reality. In the two Berlin novels Döblin wrote in exile, there is a definite shift of intention in reaction to the disastrous end of the Weimar Republic. Döblin is more overtly concerned with social and political questions, more sharply, pessimistically focused on the relation between the individual and society, more solicitous of understanding from his readers. *Men without Mercy*, the first novel he wrote in exile, is remarkably economical in length and conventional in technique compared to his other works. Later in life, he would depreciate his work on it as "skirmishing around in a little Berlin novel" (*AzL* 392), but in fact it is his most conscious attempt to explore the interconnections between familial and social oppression and to espouse liberation in both realms. It is also the first Berlin novel in which he focuses on revolution as a possible means to that end. Revolution then becomes a central theme of Döblin's final Berlin novel, the tetralogy *November 1918* (1939–1950). It is a gigantic work of multiple narrative strands in which the narrator chronicles the failure of the German revolution in many voices, satirizing its ineptitude, mourning its murdered idealists, scourging its enemies and betrayers. What sets it apart from Döblin's other Berlin novels is the Christian faith of both its central character, Friedrich Becker, and its narrator, a faith that reflects

Döblin's own religious crisis and conversion during the long and discontinuous composition of the novel. We will see what the implications of that conversion are for the central opposition in Döblin's thought between passive acceptance and active resistance. We will also see how the obsessively recurring and problematic image of women in Döblin's works culminates in *November 1918* in his fictionalization of the historic Rosa Luxemburg.

Of all his contemporaries in the vibrant literary culture of the Weimar Republic, Döblin is perhaps the most difficult to summarize. He was tremendously prolific and stylistically uneven. Some of his novels are so different from each other as to seem the products of two completely different writers. The present study does not pretend to do justice to his entire work. Its intention is to see Döblin in the longitudinal perspective of his Berlin novels; to demonstrate how they use the urban milieu as a common focal point for the personal, the political, and the sexual; and to learn what they have to tell us about the possibilities of a progressive German novelist in the catastrophic first half of our century.

I

The City Theme in Döblin's Early Works

Alfred Döblin first encountered Berlin under the cloud of a severe trauma. He was born in 1878 into a Jewish family in the provincial Pomeranian port of Stettin (now Szeczin in Poland) as the next-to-youngest of five siblings. When Döblin was ten years old, his father, the proprietor of a tailor shop, abandoned his family and ran off to America with one of his seamstresses. This early experience of abandonment was to affect profoundly Döblin's subsequent life and work.[1] In his first extended autobiographical essay, the "Erster Rückblick" (First Glance Back) of 1928, he describes his family as "driven out of a little paradise" (*SLW* 111). Döblin's mother, the practical daughter of a successful commercial family, took her five children off to Berlin where they received help from her two brothers, both prosperous businessmen in the capital. Döblin describes his arrival in Berlin in 1888 as a kind of rebirth: "I was actually only pre-born in Stettin" (*SLW* 110). Thus, his experience of the metropolis is connected with birth, Döblin's habitual metaphor for literary creation.

The external result of Max Döblin's betrayal and abandonment of his family was their removal to Berlin. The internal consequences for Alfred Döblin are more difficult to assess. The difficulty is compounded by Döblin's personal reticence: "Psychically I'm a touch-me-not and only approach myself from the distance of epic narrative" (*SLW* 37). "First Glance Back," which Döblin wrote on the occasion of his fiftieth birthday in 1928, is revealing but also self-consciously stylized. He presents himself as having inherited his artistic temperament from his father, an amateur artist and musician. His mother, by contrast, "was sensible, from a merchant family," and called his father a "cultured lackey." Döblin adds laconically, "A cruel phrase. A sad story, this mercantile pride in money in my mother's family" (*SLW* 121). All his artistic talent was thus perceived to come from the father-betrayer, while his mother, who had saved the family, stood for solidity, good sense, and loyalty, but also for repression of creativity. No

8

wonder Döblin hid his early writings from his family and published them under pseudonyms. They represented a betrayal of his mother. Peter Gay uses the phrase "revolt of the son" to describe the intellectual mood of Expressionism and the early years of the Weimar Republic.[2] But in Döblin's case, this archetypal revolt was frustrated by the literal absence of his father. His mother was the oppressive authority figure in his youth, but overt rebellion against her was blocked, even in the fifty-year-old essayist, by a guilt-ridden need to be loyal.

Surely in the familial disaster of his early childhood lie the roots of the problematic sexuality that informs all of Döblin's work. Almost all his early stories, collected in 1913 under the title *The Murder of a Buttercup*, concern themselves with the demonic power of sexuality. In both men and women, the sexual drive invariably leads to murder, suicide, or madness.[3] At the age of forty, after seven years of outwardly contented marriage, Döblin was still obsessed with and troubled by his relationship to female sexuality. In an unfinished autobiographical sketch, he admits to having been ignorant of female anatomy as late as the first semester of his medical studies, when he was twenty-two (he had already fallen several years behind in school because of the family's move to Berlin).

It seems probable that this sketch was written as an act of penance and self-examination after the death on January 19, 1918, of the young nurse Frieda Kunke, Döblin's lover and the mother of his illegitimate son.[4] Döblin had met her in 1907, when he was twenty-nine and she sixteen. They were both working at the Berlin Municipal Insane Asylum in Buch. Frieda Kunke was a gentile from a working-class background. Two years later Döblin met the medical student Erna Reiss, the daughter of a well-to-do Jewish businessman. Although he became engaged to Erna Reiss in February 1911, he continued his love affair with Frieda Kunke, and their illegitimate son was born in October 1911. Döblin married Erna Reiss shortly thereafter, in January 1912, and their first son was born in October. In January 1918, Frieda Kunke died of tuberculosis.[5]

What is striking is Döblin's clear repetition of the pattern established by his own father: a socially acceptable marriage to a tyrannical mother-figure, a love affair with a much younger, working-class woman.[6] In Döblin's case, however, the order in which the relationships come is reversed, and it would appear that he intentionally sought out a mother figure as his wife in order to escape both the social and sexual irregularity of his attachment to Frieda Kunke. She was never mentioned in any of his autobiographical writings. The constellation of his mother and his father's "little modiste" (*Schneidermamsell; SLW* 20), repeated in his own wife and Frieda Kunke, seems to have determined the polarity of domination and submission so typical for the women in his fiction. We will find this polarity and the related theme of the *pater absconditus* recurring and being transformed throughout Döblin's career as a writer.

□

The earliest surviving piece of Döblin's fiction is the story fragment entitled "Modern. Ein Bild aus der Gegenwart" (Modern: An Image from the Present). "Story" is a not entirely satisfactory designation for this remarkable work of the eighteen-year-old *Gymnasium* student, for "Modern" is an essay on the status of women in Wilhelmian society, framed by an illustrative fictional narrative about a young woman in danger of sinking into prostitution.

In the fictional component, the unemployed seamstress Bertha wanders the streets of Berlin looking for work. She almost surrenders to the sexual advances of her boyfriend, but her provincial Catholic piety saves her. The manuscript breaks off amid her agonized thoughts of contrition and her fears that she will not be able to continue resisting temptation, with a strong suggestion that she will drown herself to escape her dilemma.

In spite of its occasionally florid style and the histrionic pathos of its concluding pages, "Modern" contains the seeds of Döblin's mature prose style.[7] The panorama of Berlin street life that opens the story, for instance, is already cinematic in its flow. Panning like a camera, the narrator's eye picks out seemingly random but characteristic details until it reaches the central character, who first appears as just another face in the crowd. The movement of this crowd of pedestrians is described by the dynamic, restless verbs that are from the first a trademark of Döblin's prose: *fluten, drängen, vorbeirauschen, vorübereilen, stoßen, trotten, wogen* (surge, jostle, rustle away, hurry by, shove, trot, billow). The first and last words specifically suggest water, one of Döblin's central images.

The young author also displays a mastery of details used not just to provide realistic local color, but to introduce, for instance, the central motif of sexual challenge and temptation. As an elegant lady studies a display of hats in a shop window, a young man looks over her shoulder: "With an expression of satisfaction he blew the smoke of a cheap cigar into the lady's face, who immediately rustled away in indignation. Pretty shop girls with supple bodies hurried past, arm in arm. They shoved and jostled giggling, unabashedly staring every gentleman in the face" (*JR* 7). It is the effect of the big city's overt sexual temptation on the provincial heroine that interests the narrator. In both her outward circumstances (poverty, unemployment, vulnerability) and her inner life (the irresistible sexual drive in conflict with the dictates of religion), Bertha illustrates the theses of the essay that Döblin inserted into the middle of the fictional narrative.

This essay on the role of women in contemporary society is longer than the entire narrative. Considering that Döblin was eighteen at the time, it is no surprise that the essay is highly derivative, borrowed sometimes almost word for word from August Bebel's immensely popular and influential *Die Frau und der Sozialismus* (Woman and Socialism), first published illegally in 1879 and reissued continuously during Bebel's lifetime.[8] Döblin attacks the institution of bourgeois marriage as a purely monetary arrangement and proclaims the naturalness of the sexual drive in both men and women: "What you call animalistic is the only natural thing in our society" (*JR* 15). A tirade of sarcasm directed at what passes for contemporary sexual education ends by attacking the seductiveness of female fashions in a way that suggests the personal desires and frustrations underlying the essay: "The skirt on the hips, that's going to throw the hips into bold relief, and the corsets, a wasp waist is always interesting—never mind about abdominal illnesses and such nonsense; and then the high heels, to make the fall even harder . . ." (*JR* 16). If Döblin takes from Bebel the scientific, evolutionary view of man as "the highest of animals" (*JR* 16), sharing instincts and drives common to all animals, he argues the point with the vehemence of an adolescent overcompensating for his own sexual uncertainty and inexperience. Moreover, instead of adopting Bebel's purely positive view of man's natural instincts, Döblin betrays a good deal of ambiguity toward "nature." On the one hand, it is a benevolent *Mutter Natur* (*JR* 23), but it is also called the "terrible ruler Nature" (*JR* 22).

The essay contemptuously dismisses the question of the role of aristocratic and bourgeois women as "the ladies' issue" and devotes itself to the "women's issue, which is much, much more serious"—that is, the role of working-class women. While the bourgeois wife is idealized, the working woman is exploited: "And so she accepts for starvation wages any and all employment, harder than a man's, naturally for much lower wages, after all, she's only a—woman!" (*JR* 17). Yet it is also among the proletariat that the inchoate ideal of a socialist society is already discernible as present necessity: "She must earn, support her husband, nourish her family, feed her children, with no chance to be a mother and housewife. But she is a woman, the *companion* of her husband with equal duties and responsibilities" (*JR* 17, emphasis in original).

The central indictment of the essay, for which the story of Bertha is the fictionalized illustration, is that capitalist society forces thousands of working-class women into prostitution. It not only follows Bebel in citing statistical evidence of the miserable wages paid to women and of the number of prostitutes in Berlin, but also in pointing out the roots, social and instinctual, of prostitution: "An implacable law of nature says that you must obey your sexual instinct! And our society says that you must get married! And to be able to marry, you must possess money to support a family. If you have no money, and you want to 'love'—then—there's prostitution" (*JR* 18). The essay ends with a grandiloquent call for free love and marriage as a private pact, for an end to capitalism, and with the assurance that "a new world will blossom, better and more beautiful than the present one, a world in which all will have an equal duty to work, equal joy from their work, and no joy without work and no work without joy. Indeed, may work itself be a joy!!" (*JR* 19–20). Presciently, however, Döblin modulates back into the second half of his fictional narrative with the insight that social reform must be accompanied by a change in individual psyches: "as long as women do not *feel* themselves to be the equals of men, they will continue to be inferior to men, will continue to let men humiliate and degrade them" (*JR* 20, emphasis in original).

If the socialism in the essay is derivative, the form of the entire work is not derivative at all. The attempt to join fiction and essay, however clumsily executed, shows a tendency toward montage, or the direct juxtaposition of heterogeneous elements, which gains increasing importance in Döblin's work. We see Döblin at the very beginning of his career already trying to break the bonds of traditional narrative, even though the fictional part of the work remains quite conventional, and in fact is itself not free of the penny-dreadful bathos it satirizes at one point. Juxtaposition is present not just at the level at which story and essay are joined, but also more subtly in narrative details like the rhetorical counter-voices Döblin builds into his essay in order to destroy them: "What do we care about this rabble who throw themselves at the first man they see?!—" (*JR* 19). From the first, he suppresses smooth narrative transitions in favor of abrupt juxtapositions that heighten the psychological immediacy and veracity of the fiction. For example, in the following passage, Bertha has just sat down on a park bench to rest:

> Magnificent trees stretched high their branches; the fountains play amidst the green grass, glittering and dissolving to mist in the sunlight.
> And the fountains play and the green leaves, they rustle—rustle—rustle.
> Ah youth, youth!
> Flooded with light the sky rises before her, the village with its bake oven, the stalls and pond. There, the priest in his cassock, with such a mild and peaceful face—oh, if she should now have to make confession! There is her mother too, her dear mother, and there are the boys; how the rascals call to her, "Bertha, Bertha!" The biggest of the three scamps pinched her in the arm. She wanted to slap him, she raised her arm with the parasol—
> "But girl, hey, Bertha, get up! Now she's even falling asleep in broad daylight! Hey listen, for God's sake! Let's go! Gee, you're still a little sleepy!"
> And her girlfriend helped her up . . .
>
> (*JR* 9–10)

The transitions from waking, to dream, to abrupt reawakening are accomplished without overt narrative guidance. Döblin instead carefully manipulates the tense of narration in order to suggest the process within Bertha's brain. The original preterite of narration ("stretched") changes to present in midsentence ("play") as she gradually nods off. The abrupt end of her dream is anticipated by the return to the preterite while still within the dream ("pinched"). A gradual change in narrative tone replaces explicit narrative comment on the contrast between her village past and her urban present. The thrice repeated "rustle" eases us out of the city and into the dreamworld of Romantic poetry. The exclamation "Ah youth, youth!" is of indeterminate origin. Is it Bertha's internal sigh, the narrator's comment, or simply a disembodied epitaph for the idyllic life that is gone forever? There is no clear-cut answer. Finally, when the dream is interrupted, the absence of any phrase such as "Liese said" reproduces for the reader Bertha's own experience of being rudely snatched from her dream. Later in life Döblin would answer an interviewer's question "Which stylistic phrase do you hate most?" quite simply: "He said."[9]

Clearly, the fiction in "Modern" serves Döblin's social commentary. He has chosen a single, unexceptional life from the metropolis in order to illustrate a social thesis. But it is more the fictional than the essayistic component that points toward the future. The glowing socialism of the essay disappears from his work and does not reemerge until 1918, under the impression of the German revolution. "Modern" is atypical in its progressive attitude toward women, and in hindsight, one can discern even in this early work a disturbing sexual ambiguity beneath the socialist polemics. The sex drive is natural, yet also terribly implacable: "man is the highest animal and there is no difference between a pregnant cow lowing miserably as she calves and the mother who gives birth amidst terrible pains" (*JR* 16). If for Bebel the emphasis is on "highest," for Döblin it is on "animal." There is no indication of any basis for a relationship between men and women other than the erotic drive imposed by the "terrible ruler Nature."

The city in "Modern" is seen in Marxist terms as a place of corruption and exploitation of the working class. Industrial and technical progress in the service of capitalist society will almost inevitably force Bertha into prostitution: "That prostitutes should be so numerous in Berlin is easily explained by the rise of its machines, etc., etc., its industry, each of whose increasing improvements makes a multitude of workers superfluous and thus prostitutes the female workers" (*JR* 18). This purely negative and Marxist-deterministic attitude toward the city is thus connected to the ambiguous but implacable sexual instinct. During the next eighteen years, Döblin's attention as a writer turned away from the social question and naturalistic urban setting central to "Modern" and toward an almost obsessive preoccupation with psychosexual themes.[10]

□

Between the turn of the century and *The Three Leaps of Wang-lun*, completed in 1913, Döblin made two early attempts in the novel form. *Jagende Rosse* (Galloping Horses), written in 1900 while he was still in the last year of *Gymnasium* but unpublished until 1981, is the plotless, lyrical outpouring of a narrative "I" addressed to a longed-for but unattainable "thou." Dedicated "To the Memory of Hölderlin in Love and Devotion" (*JR* 26), the work is stylistically indebted to that great poet's epistolary novel *Hyperion*.[11] In 1902–3, Döblin wrote *Der schwarze Vorhang* (The Black Curtain), which was published in installments in Herwarth Walden's Expressionist journal *Der Sturm* in 1912 and in revised form as a book in 1919. Its hero, the schoolboy Johannes, has a tortured relationship with a girl, Irene, whom he murders before committing suicide.

These two novels, along with the stories "Adonis" and "Erwachen" (Awakening) of 1901, contain almost no trace of either the metropolitan theme or the social concern so central to "Modern." Both *Galloping Horses* and "Adonis" have vaguely rural settings,[12] and when the lyrical "I" of the former attains a final affirmation of life, Döblin uses conventional images of a natural existence, close to the earth, to express it: "Reborn to suffering and yearning, [life] turns to the soil, to the earth, to the fields; there it breaks out and expands in the air of heaven and dissipates in change and transformation, to grow again between sky and sea and earth" (*JR* 82). Such natural cycles were to be one of the main themes in the pantheism[13] Döblin espoused in such writings on natural philosophy as *Das Ich über der Natur* (The I over Nature; 1927) and *Unser Dasein* (Our Existence; 1933).

What is remarkable is the contrast between such lyrical, Hölderlin-inspired nature imagery and the naturalism of "Modern." The only thing the earlier story has in common with these works is the issue of sexuality: the adolescent sexual ferment beneath the socialist rhetoric of "Modern" now surfaces with a vengeance. Bebel's critique of capitalist society as the exploiter and degrader of women disappears. The ideal of woman as the social and sexual equal of man is replaced by the timeworn psychological and religious opposition of female sensuality and male spirituality.[14] Woman's susceptibility to exploitation is now reinterpreted as her instinctive readiness to sacrifice herself to the man.

The traces of fear of sexuality and women discernible in "Modern" become centrally important in these works. Women are presented as alien beings, usually hostile and often fatal to the troubled male heroes. The first-person narrator of the story "Awakening" criticizes women's lack of inner life: "The eyes, yes the eyes; they are still the

eyes that have never looked inward" (*JR* 102). In the story "Adonis,"
the hero is a psychotic torn between the sensual, maternal attraction of
a woman and the intellectual pull of his former teacher, a monk. In the
end, he and the woman drown themselves together. The eternal opposition between the sensual and the spiritual could not be more clear.

The narrative "I" of *Galloping Horses* goes so far as to deny women
their humanity even in the sexual act he shares with them: "I only love
what is beneath me. Even when I love human females, I'm practicing
sodomy" (*JR* 69). Sexuality is still regarded as a natural drive of the
human animal, but it is naturally demonic, undermining and destroying the metaphysical unity all these heroes seek. Johannes, the hero of
The Black Curtain, "could not comprehend that the human being was
not sufficient unto itself, that it split into man and woman, was eter-
nally pushed beyond its own borders, driven toward an alien being.
Everyone bears sexuality's mark of Cain: a fugitive and a wanderer
shalt thou be; thou shalt—love" (*JR* 128). He feels himself both attracted to and repulsed by Irene, and their sadomasochistic relationship ends in a gruesome murder-suicide: Johannes bites her in the
throat before killing himself.

The instinctual drives that the polemicist of "Modern" wanted to
liberate from the taboos of bourgeois social convention are now seen
as dark, implacable forces out of man's control and far beyond the
reach of society. There is in effect no society in these works; their only
social dimension is the scorn of the narrator in *Galloping Horses* for
the human rights "Modern" so stoutly defended. The "law of nature"
now simply reduces mankind to its basest instincts: "Gorging and tip-
pling, those are their sacred 'rights of man,' that was my right. They
move in filth, that is their element; in whinnying lust they engender
filth, blowflies that couple wherever they are, in any foul air" (*JR* 44).
Notice that the narrator does not exclude himself from his indictment;
the self-loathing in these works is most evident in this first-person
narrative.

Between the derivative "Modern" and *The Black Curtain*, Döblin
finds an original if disturbing voice as a writer. He turns radically inward, abandoning social and urban themes for a prose of psychosis,
inner torment, and violence against both the self and others. In order
to return to social themes and the public novel, he had to resolve his
tormented view of sexuality. We shall see how he found a provisional

solution to this problem by the time he wrote *The Three Leaps of Wang-lun*.

□

Between *The Black Curtain* and *The Three Leaps of Wang-lun*, Döblin's fictional output was limited to short stories, partly because of the demands of his medical training. For the most part, these stories continue to exploit the sexual and psychological themes of *The Black Curtain*. The best of them have a satiric edge that exposes bourgeois pretensions and proprieties to ridicule. This avant-garde scorn for the bourgeoisie, a pose Döblin cultivated his entire life, made him naturally receptive to Filippo Tommaso Marinetti and his Futurist cohorts when they burst onto the Berlin cultural scene in 1912.[15] In March of that year, *Der Sturm* had prepared the ground by publishing both Marinetti's "Manifesto of Futurism" (originally published in *Figaro* in 1909) and a separate manifesto of the Futurist painters. The painters then exhibited in Herwarth Walden's *Sturm* gallery in April and May, and Marinetti came to Berlin for the occasion.

Both Futurist manifestoes reject the art of the past, especially as it is enshrined by bourgeois society: "Set fire to the libraries! Divert the canals in order to flood the museums!"[16] Both proclaim a new aesthetic of speed and dynamism and declare Futurist art to be the art adequate to the modern world.[17] They reject individual man as the central subject matter of art, praising instead the modern machine: "Just as interesting as the pain of a man is for us the pain of an electric lamp twitching under electric cramps in the most heart-rending colors."[18]

Döblin was tremendously excited by the Futurists' paintings. He wrote an enthusiastic review of the exhibition for *Der Sturm*.[19] When he met the painters and Marinetti during their visit, he remarked to the latter, "If only we had something similar in literature" (*AzL* 9). In July, Döblin began writing his first mature novel, *The Three Leaps of Wang-lun*.

Herwarth Walden, meanwhile, continued to champion the cause of Futurism in Germany. In October 1912, *Der Sturm* published Marinetti's "Technical Manifesto of Futurist Literature" and in March 1913, the "Supplement to the Technical Manifesto," both of which elaborate the stylistic implications for literature of the general principles enunciated in the first manifesto.[20] On the basis of these stylistic pronouncements, Döblin had second thoughts about Futurism and published his "Futuristic Verbal Technique: Open Letter to F. T. Marinetti." This open letter explicitly ended his year-long flirtation with the Italian movement: "Cultivate your Futurism. I'll cultivate my Döblinism" (*AzL* 15).

What was it that made Döblin first extol Futurism and then reject it barely a year later?[21] It is clear from his review, "Die Bilder der Futuristen" (The Pictures of the Futurists), that he was initially attracted to these paintings by their rejection of mimetic realism in favor of subjective, expressive dynamism. The painter, he writes, "is not an imitator, but an innovator. Animation is everything" (*Zeitlupe* 9). Beyond this rather general enthusiasm, Döblin discerns no particular Futurist program: "It is not a direction, but a movement" (*Zeitlupe* 11). In Marinetti's "Technical Manifesto" and "Supplement," there was much with which Döblin could agree because it conformed to his own emerging narrative, the new "epic" style of *Wang-lun:* the rejection of levels of style; advocacy of intuition and the unconscious in artistic practice; and hostility to the psychological analysis characteristic of nineteenth-century realism: "The 'I' in literature must be destroyed, and that means all psychology."[22]

But when Marinetti proposes specific stylistic rules in order to achieve the goals of Futurism, Döblin rebels against the Italian's reductive monomania. In order to reshape literature as an intuitive, irrational art, Marinetti feels an "impetuous need to free words from the prison of the Latin period."[23] Verbs should appear in infinitive form in order to free them from the tyranny of the narrator's control. Adjectives and adverbs are abolished because they retard and add undesirable nuance to the dynamic flow. Mathematical and musical symbols will replace punctuation. Nouns should be juxtaposed to each other in chains of analogy, unconnected by conjunctions. Not surprisingly, given Marinetti's worship of war, his fierce misogyny, and his elitism, the examples he offers are "man—torpedo boat, woman—harbor, crowd—surf."[24]

The core of Marinetti's new style is the theory of analogies, that is, pairs or chains of nouns whose interrelation both writer and audience grasp intuitively, without the mediation of "like" or "as." The more unexpected and farfetched these analogies, the more profound will be their effect. The "Supplement" of March 1913 ends with a text by

Marinetti in French entitled "Bataille: Poids + Odeur" (Battle: Weight + Smell) which actually follows the rules laid down in the "Technical Manifesto." It consists almost entirely of such analogic pairs, with an occasional mathematical symbol thrown in.

Döblin begins his "Open Letter to Marinetti" by reaffirming his allegiance to the general stylistic aims that he understands them to share:[25]

> It's clear to both you and me, Marinetti: we desire no embellishment, no decoration, no style, nothing superficial, but hardness, cold and fire, softness, the transcendental and the shocking, without wrapping paper. . . . We both reject whatever is not direct, not immediate, not saturated with objectivity [*gesättigt von Sachlichkeit*] . . . naturalism, naturalism; we still fall far short of being naturalists.
>
> (*AzL* 9)

Döblin uses two terms that were to become centrally important in his mature works: *Sachlichkeit* and *Naturalismus*.[26] *Sachlichkeit* is a difficult word to translate adequately into English; it can mean both "objectivity" and "sense of reality" but also "impartiality," "detachment," and "pertinence." The root noun *Sache* (physical object, thing) suggests external, physical reality as opposed to inward, psychic states. *Sachlichkeit* is the main ingredient of what Döblin now calls naturalism. He would repeatedly make clear over the next twenty years that he used this term not to refer to the literary movement of the late nineteenth century, but rather to a recurrent impulse toward a nondecorative art that attempts to convey reality as directly as possible: "Naturalism is no historic 'ism,' but the torrent that of necessity breaks in on art again and again" (*AzL* 18).

Having stated the general principles he believes they share, Döblin proceeds to attack Marinetti for narrowness and dogmatism in their application. On the one hand, he writes, Marinetti has fallen victim to a "tiny, tiny mistake" by confusing reality and materiality (*AzL* 11). The Italian is in effect propounding a new but impoverished theory of mimesis: "We are supposed to imitate only the bleating, puffing, rattling, howling, snuffling of earthly things, to try to achieve the tempo of reality, and you call this not phonography, but art, and not just art but Futurism?" (*AzL* 10).[27] On the other hand, the "telegram style" of "Bataille," far from making literature more *sachlich*, actually makes it more abstract by distilling it into analogical lists. With specific reference to Marinetti's pairs "général îlot" and "ventres arrosoirs têtes foot-ball éparpillement,"[28] Döblin writes:

Your battle is chock full of images, analogies, similes from beginning to end. Fine, but that doesn't look very modern to me, it's just good old reliable literature; I'll grant you all your images,—but let's have that battle! Be direct, Marinetti! Yes, it's easy to call the general an "island," to let heads fly like footballs and let ripped-open bellies gush like watering cans. Frivolity! Antiquated! Museum! Where are the heads? What about the bellies? And you claim to be a Futurist? That's the worst kind of aestheticism! Things are unique; a belly is a belly and not a watering can. That's the ABC of the naturalist, the genuine, direct artist. It is the task of the prose writer to forego images.

(AzL 12–13)

In place of Marinetti's skeletal analogies, Döblin posits gesture as the means to approach reality: "A general can and must be plastically presented by means of a movement. He must be presented in this way; everything else is empty talk" (AzL 14).

A text as dogmatically conceived as "Bataille" was grist for the mill of Döblin the stylistic critic. But the "Döblinism" announced at the end of the "Open Letter" is as yet only negatively defined as a reaction to the excesses of Futurism. Two months later, in the essay "An Roman-autoren und ihre Kritiker: Berliner Programm" (For Novelists and Their Critics: Berlin Program), Döblin presented the first positive statement of the principles that would inform his prose for the next twenty years.

The essay first declares loyalty to the modern world in tones that still have a Futurist ring: "Old Pegasus, outstripped by technology, has in his bewilderment been transformed into a stubborn jackass. I maintain that every good speculator, banker, soldier, is a better poet than the majority of contemporary authors" (AzL 15). He also writes of the "strict, cold-blooded methods" that will be necessary to render the modern world accurately. But in place of the bullying, elitist Futurist rhetoric, he now introduces the idea of the writer in a social context, "pledged to a common path and a common enterprise": "Writing is not chewing your nails and picking your teeth, but a matter of public interest" (AzL 15). From now on, he will regard literature as, among other things, a public act with social and ethical consequences.

In the course of writing The Three Leaps of Wang-lun, for which the "Berlin Program" is a theoretical pendant, Döblin takes the Futurist dictum of the elimination of the "I" far beyond its merely formalistic meaning. The public writer can no longer write lyrical novels about isolated psyches, as Döblin had done in his earlier works. He now seeks a more objective, more *sachlich*, and more public style, one of

> genuine novelistic prose with the principle: the subject of the novel is reality liberated from soul [*die entseelte Realität*]. The reader in complete independence presented with a structured process: let him evaluate it, not the author. The façade of the novel cannot be other than stone or steel, flashing electrically or dark, but silent.
>
> (*AzL* 17)

In order to liberate reality from "soul," Döblin calls for a *Kinostil*, a motion-picture style in which images pass by "in extreme concentration and precision" (*AzL* 17). The author, no longer an analyst and interpreter of his characters but only an observer, eschews the role of omniscient narrator. Indeed, Döblin demands total self-abnegation: "I am not I, but rather the street, the streetlights, this or that occurrence, nothing more. That is what I call the style of stone" (*AzL* 18).

Döblin's encounter with Futurism thus had the positive effect of forcing him to articulate clearly the principles of the new prose style he would use so effectively in *Wang-lun*. But if he ultimately rejected Futurism on stylistic grounds, we have seen that he continued to think of himself as sharing certain general avant-garde assumptions with Marinetti. Moreover, he went out of his way to express his continuing admiration for Marinetti's 1909 novel *Mafarka le Futuriste:* "In your 'Mafarka' you often give perfect expression to massive, unrefined feelings. You are rhetorical, but your rhetoric is not a lie" (*AzL* 9).[29] Indeed, even six years later, Döblin quotes with approval from the polemical preface to *Mafarka* in order to contrast it to Otto Flake's *Die Stadt des Hirns* (*AzL* 32). Thus Döblin is not rejecting the ideology of Futurism, but rather Marinetti's means for realizing it.

Let us return to the first "Manifesto of Futurism" and to *Mafarka* to see more specifically what elements of that ideology attracted Döblin. Both manifesto and novel were published in 1909. Marinetti had apparently already written the novel in 1907–8,[30] so that it may be assumed to have influenced the content of the manifesto. In both, Futurism appears to have been initially not so much a stylistic as a thematic revolt. In contrast to later texts like "Bataille: Poids + Odeur," the novel does not reject conventional syntax and grammar, although its style is distinguished by extravagant and sometimes outrageous imagery. Similarly, the eleven numbered theses of the manifesto contain

no specific stylistic formulae for Futurist art; they are instead provoca-
tive challenges to established notions of the beautiful and to institution-
alized art: "A racing car, its body packed with great pipes like serpents
with explosive breath, a howling automobile . . . is more beautiful
than the 'Winged Victory of Samothrace.'"[31]

But beyond this famous *enfant terrible* provocation to aesthetic
conventionality and tradition, a program emerges which, as Armin Arnold has pointed out, owes much to Nietzsche's *Zarathustra*.[32] What
Arnold does not point out is that the program also propounds the psychological preconditions for fascism.[33] Its irrationality modulates
naturally into aggression and brutality: "Just as literature up to now
has celebrated contemplative passivity, ecstasy and slumber, we now
intend to celebrate aggressive movement, feverish sleeplessness, the
gymnastic step, the dangerous leap, the slap, and the punch."[34] And
later: "art can only be violence and cruelty."[35]

This diction of violence culminates in the glorification of war and
contempt for women, subsumed under one number in Marinetti's list
of desiderata: "We shall praise war—the world's sole hygienics—militarism, patriotism, the destroying gesture of the anarchists, the beautiful thoughts that kill, and contempt for womankind."[36] A subsequent manifesto clarifies the logic of this coupling: women are the
embodiment of pacifism, naturally timid and opposed to war: "It is
certain that our nerves demand war and despise women! Of course,
for we fear their tendril-like arms, entwining our knees on the morning
of farewell!"[37] It was indeed a woman who embodied the idea of pacifism in Europe at the time Marinetti was writing: Bertha von Suttner,
whose novel *Die Waffen nieder!* (Lay Down Your Arms) had appeared
in 1889 and who had been awarded the Nobel Peace Prize in 1905.

But in his preface to *Mafarka*, Marinetti defends the misogyny of
his manifesto on different grounds: "And yet it is not the animal value
of woman that I dispute, but her sentimental importance. . . . I want
to vanquish the tyranny of love, the obsession with the unique woman,
the great romantic moonlight that bathes the façade of the bordello."[38]
He represents his misogyny as an integral part of his rejection of the
art of the past, an anti-Romantic revolt against love as the dominating theme of most nineteenth-century art. Marinetti's antifeminism
may thus appear at first blush to be purely aesthetic. In fact, in a manifesto entitled "Zerstörung der Syntax—Drahtlose Phantasie—Befreite
Worte—Die futuristische Sensibilität" (Destruction of Syntax—Wire-

less Fantasy—Liberated Words—The Futuristic Sensibility) whose German translation was published in *Der Sturm* in May 1913,[39] he announces that technological change has already brought about "full equality of man and woman, with only a slight difference in her social rights."[40]

Marinetti here sounds almost like a feminist, although no feminist would have claimed in 1913 that women enjoyed anything approaching equal rights, much less proclaimed them a *fait accompli*. The psychological equality the Futurists actually had in mind was outlined by Valentine de Saint-Point, Marinetti's appointed leader of the Futurist "Action Féminine,"[41] in her "Manifesto of the Futurist Woman," whose German version appeared in *Der Sturm* in May 1912:[42]

WOMEN MUST NOT BE GRANTED ANY OF THE RIGHTS DEMANDED BY THE FEMINISTS. TO GRANT THEM WOULD NOT BE TO INITIATE THE LONGED-FOR FUTURISTIC TRANSFORMATION, ON THE CONTRARY, IT WOULD MEAN SUPERFLUOUS ORDER. . . .

Women, you have believed in morality and false prejudices for too long; return to your sublime instincts, to savagery, to cruelty.

While men battle and wage war against each other, you produce children as a bloody tribute to war and heroism; think of the demands of destiny. Let them grow and blossom, not for yourselves, for your enjoyment, but in unbounded freedom.[43]

In this text too, one hears clear echoes of Nietzsche. But in Marinetti's novel *Mafarka le Futuriste* there are no heroic women bearing the warriors of the future. On the contrary, women are useful only for their "valeur animale," as in the mass rape of captured Negresses in the first chapter:

[The soldiers] had laid out all the Negresses, wriggling and bruised, in the mud, and they were taking aim with their black, sooty rods, more twisted than roots.

One saw the sleek, glossy bellies of the young women and their little breasts the color of roasted coffee writhing with pain under the heavy fists of the males, whose bronze backs rose and fell tirelessly amid the lively slap-slop of the green slime.

Some chanted funereal songs; others furiously sank their teeth into the manes of their mistresses, then paused, their mouths filled with bloody hairs, and knelt for a long time, staring into those mournful eyes rolled up in pain, terror, and lust.

Because from time to time the women would jerk under the recoil of a forced spasm, with a pleasure all the keener for being involuntary. The agile black legs with their delicate ankles thrashed convulsively, like a piece cut off a snake's body, and wound themselves one after the other, with the sound of a whip cracking, around the back of the male.[44]

The scene continues in this vein for four more pages before Mafarka intervenes and disperses the mutinous soldiers. What is noteworthy here is not so much the predictable and smug assurance that women actually enjoy being raped. It is rather the insidious aestheticization of violence, the pleasure of a gourmand in describing the precise colors of the ravished bodies in terms of food: "their little breasts the color of roasted coffee" (later in the passage, the hips of the youngest girl are described as "varnished and sugared, the color of beautiful vanilla").[45] The imagery dehumanizes the women by focusing interest on isolated body parts—bellies, breasts, eyes—and this dissection culminates in a simile of maiming, the writhing legs "like a piece cut off a snake's body."

Women, indeed, are ultimately not even estimated for their "valeur animale," but rather hated and feared for their sexuality, which threatens to sap the vital energies of men. In a characteristic passage, Mafarka has two dancing girls thrown to the sharks because they have excited him sexually: "Like butterflies and flies, you have invisible proboscises for sucking out the strength and perfume of the male! . . . All the poison of hell is in your glances, and the saliva on your lips has a gleam that kills . . . yes, it kills as well as and better than daggers."[46] The novel's preface declares programmatically that the hour is near when the Futurists, unwilling to accept the lot of being "miserable sons of the vulva," ". . . will engender prodigiously, by a single effort of their exorbitant will, giants of infallible deeds." Marinetti announces "that the spirit of man is an unused ovary. . . . It is we who fertilize it for the first time!"[47]

This Futurist immaculate conception is more than mere metaphor: the novel culminates in Mafarka's construction of a gigantic winged son, Gazourmah, "beautiful and free of all the defects that come from the maleficent vulva and predispose to decrepitude and death!"[48] Clearly, Mafarka goes far beyond Zarathustra's advice to women, "Let your hope be, 'May I bear the Superman!'"[49] Both father and son repel the advances of Coloubbi, the ultimate woman, a seductive mother/lover figure whose sexuality is a deadly threat. She expires after Gazourmah's final rejection and her death unleashes the cataclysmic destruction of the earth, a "bataille tellurique"[50] above which Gazourmah mounts serenely on his giant wings.

Döblin thus found his view of women only confirmed in Marinetti's *Mafarka*. Even in the "Open Letter" that marked his break with Futurism, he assures Marinetti that he is fully in agreement with what he calls his "anti-eroticism" (*AzL* 15). In addition, I suggest that he found prefigured in *Mafarka* the possibility of overcoming the obsession with the demonic, destructive power of sexuality characteristic of his works before 1912.

In *The Three Leaps of Wang-lun*, written during his encounter with the Futurists, Döblin found a formula, as it were, with which he would lay the demon of sexuality: the idea of a rape followed by "sacred prostitution."[51] In the absence of their leader Wang-lun, the male sectarians of the "Truly Weak" are not able to maintain their vow of chastity. Incited by Wang's second-in-command, Ma-noh, they fall upon their sister sectarians in a mass rape possibly suggested by and worth comparing to the "Viol des Négresses" in *Mafarka:*

> How the women's hill began to tremble.
> Cries and shrieks leapt a thousandfold across the valley and echoed from the far hill.
> Terror grew ever greater; amid the sharp voices a deep rumbling, cracking, bellowing could be heard.
> Wide-eyed horror tried to escape from the shadows of the catalpa and was yanked back.
> After long, raving minutes, pieces of white and colored clothing spattered from the top of the hill, fell into the moss, rolled down soundlessly.
> A strange quiet fell over the hill, interrupted by long, spasmodic cries, penetrating cat-like whimpers, the music to breathless helplessness that bites itself in the finger, lets the soul shrivel as if in vinegar, to the frenzy of despair that draws bodies into its maelstrom.
>
> (*WL* 145–46)

Döblin, whose misogyny is less insouciantly automatic than Marinetti's, has managed to make this rape almost incorporeal. Here the violence is more thoroughly aestheticized than in *Mafarka;* it is an Expressionist *tour de force* of acoustical images—only the *sounds* of a mass rape. In the process, both rapists and raped have lost all individuality, are nothing but collective noises, "cries and shrieks leapt a thousandfold" and "a deep rumbling, cracking, bellowing." On the other hand, the collective terror of the women becomes personified: "Wide-eyed horror tried to escape. . . ." If Marinetti's Negresses ultimately surrender willy-nilly to their lust, Döblin's sectarians, both men and women, go a step further: they are joyfully reconciled to their sexuality once the rape has been accomplished. Individuals are gradually reconstituted from the fragments of color and sound into which they had been broken during the rape:

> For a long time, nothing moved on the women's hill. Then white and colored dots began to shimmer between the tree trunks. Running of men black as shadows, mixing of colors, handfuls of sounds, talking, fragments of calls, a swell of noise. Bright sisters embraced each other as they came gliding down the hill. The brothers hip by hip. A jubilant cloud, saturated in light, descended into the valley.
>
> (WL 147)

Ma-noh, with a new feeling of power, adopts sexuality as a doctrine and renames the sect "the Broken Melon." When Wang-lun returns, he recriminates with Ma-noh for having violated the principle of celibacy. Wang, however, has brought with him a great battle-sword, the sign that he has compromised the principle of Wu-wei in a different way and is ready to use force to protect the sect from the persecution of the Emperor. Neither man has been able to maintain the Taoist ethic. It is simultaneously an ethical and a political question that lies at the center of *Wang-lun:* what is the proper response to oppression—passive acceptance or active resistance? Wang-lun metaphorically takes "three leaps" back and forth between these two positions, perishing in the final battle for Peking without having definitively chosen either one. Thus, although the extravagant language and exotic setting of *Wang-lun* betray the Futurist influence, Döblin has moved decisively away from the Futurists' amoral, aestheticized aggression and love of violence. Wang-lun's ideal is clearly pacifist and he takes up arms with extreme reluctance. The novel, in fact, first clearly formulates what would remain Döblin's central and unresolved moral dilemma: activism versus passivity. As Leo Kreutzer has written, "the irreconcilability of opposites . . . becomes a sort of basic pattern in Döblin's life and thought." [52]

The "sacred prostitution" of the sect, however, is for Döblin at least a provisional escape from the obsession with the destructive power of sexuality which dominates his early works. Although sexuality still means a disruption of the ideal unity, it now can have a redemptive purpose. Once they have been raped, the sisters of the Broken Melon continue to sacrifice their bodies in order to protect the sect: "The sisters armed themselves to erect a wall of gentleness around the Broken Melon. . . . The younger beauties were the sacred prostitutes. They said that no one would hinder them from treading the smooth path to the Western Paradise, not now, when they were ready to share everything, everything with everyone" (WL 174–75).

With the concept of sacred prostitution, Döblin has moved beyond the dilemma of sexuality in his early stories, where it is simultaneously natural and destructive. But his solution, as we shall see, is to establish an obsessively recurring pattern whose psychological roots lie in the disaster of his childhood. Women can now serve as redemptive figures, but at the price of self-sacrifice for the sake of a male hero, which usually means being literally or metaphorically raped. Moreover, the positive image of the sacred prostitute seems to be accompanied almost automatically by its negative: woman as solipsistic monster. Jost Hermand and Frank Trommler have drawn attention to the cliché character of such polar images of women, based on "the time-honored division into whore and madonna types."[53] It is noteworthy, however, that Döblin's particular variation of this cliché totally excludes the sexually pure madonna ideal. The positive, redemptive pole for him is the prostitute, a figure we will see recurring obsessively in his work.

□

Before turning to Döblin's first Berlin novel, let us look briefly at the story "Von der himmlischen Gnade" (On Heavenly Mercy), first published in *Der Sturm* in September 1914, and probably written soon after the completion of *Wang-lun*. The story is one of Döblin's first works since "Modern" to be set in contemporary Berlin. Its language reflects the new style Döblin described in the Berlin Program. The pathos and polemics of "Modern" have given way to the "style of stone" of an impersonal and self-effacing narrator.

The plot of "On Heavenly Mercy" is purposely aimless and alogical. It concerns the Nasskes, an old and impoverished couple who commit a casual robbery and are caught and imprisoned for a brief period. Upon their release, the husband hangs himself, apparently out of spite. The milieu is the barren edge of the modern city whose inhabitants are more like brutalized peasants than city dwellers. They represent the lumpen proletariat whose poverty has ground them down to almost subhuman status. An important change occurs in the way Döblin portrays working-class characters: In "Modern," he spliced essay and fiction into an indictment of capitalist society and the human toll it takes. In "On Heavenly Mercy," by contrast, the poverty of the Nasskes appears absolute. No causes are sought; only effects are dispassionately presented. If there is an indictment here, it is totally implicit.

Poverty has killed the Nasskes' emotional lives and turned them into machines: "They had gotten out of the habit of talking. Their bones performed their service tirelessly, machines that had been started up once and for all; they carried their hearts, doing their sluggish and hesitant ticktock, the wheezing lungs; and their heads teetered on their withered necks" (*E* 140). Their dialogue is reduced to primitive instrumental utterances and brief, spiteful exchanges. When the old man hangs himself, his wife's reaction is brutally matter-of-fact: "Annoyed, she shuffled into the kitchen; after a while she chirped back, 'I'm supposed to cut him down, that good-for-nothing? A dead person like that is disgusting.' Later, after the corpse had been laid on the mattress, she said to Rutschinski, 'Get that out of here. Get a move on'" (*E* 146).

The fierce, unblinking *Sachlichkeit* of the story conforms to the narrative ideals of the Berlin Program, yet two contrasting narrative modes interrupt the primary narrative at critical points. One is a wickedly parodied Romanticism. The "blooming chestnut tree" across from the Nasskes' shack is in itself a Romantic icon, but one they expressly take no notice of, passing it "sightlessly." The goldfinch who hops about among its branches, however, leaves the reader in no doubt about a Romantic invasion of the story, for after a preliminary "Kivitt, kivitt, tsvrr" it unexpectedly breaks into song: "Green is the May. With a bouquet of lovely flowerets bedecked are hill and vale. The bubbling of cool brooks is heard by every little forest bird" (*E* 139).[54] There is wonderful shock value in the sudden intrusion of this snatch of supernatural rhymed kitsch into the naturalistic narrative. Without comment, the narrator simply juxtaposes these two apparently irreconcilable visions of the world. That irreconcilability is underlined by the old man's total deafness to the poetry in the finch's song: "'We don't have to listen to these pieces of shit.' The old man picked up a stone, threw it over the fence into the tree. The bird flew away" (*E* 139–40).

The song does not exist in his world. It is a purely narrative event, and when it is over, the story continues as if nothing out of the ordinary had happened in the text. At the very end of the story, the same goldfinch reappears (it is clearly the same, since the narrator uses the definite article), this time sitting in a beech, another tree from the Romantic forest: "The goldfinch sang, 'Let nature's bloom dispel man's gloom, his soul rejoice and flower in this glad time and gentle clime, enjoy the springtime hour. And pray to God above to send his mercy and his love'" (*E* 147).[55] The montage of these snatches of a pious, optimistic Romanticism that recalls the texts of the poet Matthias Claudius has been interpreted as holding out a hope of transcendence or of the "permanency of natural existence."[56] Yet the juxtaposition is so abrupt, the contrast so extreme, the finch's lyric so shallow compared to the Nasskes' degradation, that it is hard to see how God "sends his mercy" in this story, despite its title. Indeed, the title seems almost cynical when the reader discovers that it is derived from the finch's song rather than from the primary narrative.

There is, however, a second intrusive narrative mode that must be taken more seriously as an indication of another level of reality. It consists of a lyrical metaphor for death, first occurring at the very beginning of the story: "No country is so peaceful as the one that leads into death. Life arches above one's head like a bridgespan, and below it flows the water, carries the boat, takes it further" (*E* 139). The metaphor returns and is elaborated at the moment old Nasske hangs himself. The antitranscendental primary narrative, the "style of stone," has just pictured him as "a long, light package on a rope" (*E* 145), then: "The bridgespan glided away overhead; a rapids lifted the boat, dropped it into a pool; the boat went down smoothly and freely, a feather in the wind, sank" (*E* 145–46). While this metaphor is impossible to untangle logically, its import is clear. Life is fragile and brief, while death is the absolute reality underlying it. While the superficial optimism of the finch seems to deny death, this metaphor not only asserts its reality, but celebrates it as ultimate peace.

Yet even the transcendence suggested by the river metaphor does not seem the ultimate, reconciling "meaning" of the story. Both it and the finch's songs are simply juxtaposed to the primary naturalistic narrative without transition or narrative comment. They are, moreover, carefully spaced and alternated within the story. The river metaphor opens the story, followed shortly by the singing goldfinch. The metaphor recurs after Nasske's suicide, while the goldfinch has the last word of the story. Partly because of this placement, the two modes seem to cancel each other. Döblin's narrator is playing with the form of the story itself, emphasizing these intrusions by locating them at particularly important structural points, yet denying us the key to their importance. In spite of the symmetrical, closed form they suggest,

Döblin uses them to keep the story open. Unwilling to accept the stark brutality and hopelessness of the primary narrative as absolute, he is nevertheless unable to subsume it under a redeeming metaphysical order. The montage preserves the jarring clash of irreconcilables without glossing it over.

There remains, however, an attempt at a sort of redemption within the story, and it involves, not surprisingly, the figure of a prostitute. The pimp Rutschinski rents the second floor of the Nasskes' house and occupies it along with his girlfriend Emma. The narrator focuses attention not on the active Rutschinski, but on the passive Emma. The longest continuous episode in the work, in fact, concerns Emma and is completely tangential to the Nasskes' story.

Emma, "a blond former nursemaid" (*E* 142), represents a step beyond the situation of Bertha in "Modern." Bertha's "redemptive" characteristics—her religiosity, search for legitimate work, resistance to temptation—are apparently absent in Emma. As with all the other characters in "On Heavenly Mercy," Emma's inner life is opaque to the reader, following the principles of the Berlin Program.

Rutschinski sends her out to earn some extra money for the imprisoned Nasskes, and she is brought into the local first-aid station the following morning, drunk, filthy, and bleeding from a beating. What has happened is unclear, but apparently Emma was beaten by a customer she was trying to recruit as a lawyer for the Nasskes. The narrator is not so much interested in causes as in the scene at hand: "Emma was snoring on the floor. Mucus hung from her mouth and was already forming a puddle on the linoleum. She exuded the smell of schnapps and tobacco smoke" (*E* 143). Her helpless, semiconscious figure is contrasted to the antiseptic atmosphere of the station and to Walter, the medical attendant on duty, "an older man in a white-and-red striped blouse with bared arms. He was wearing steel-frame spectacles; he had lost the hair from the middle of his skull, but on the sides it was bushy and grew malevolently toward the front, black and gray" (*E* 142). In a narrative so completely restricted to externals, it is no surprise that this figure is as brutal as his description would suggest. In the style of stone, appearance *is* character, so that his hair can grow "malevolently."

Emma is for him "the female," "a new case" (*E* 143). He spits contemptuously on the floor in front of her and roughly holds smelling salts under her nose. He is agitated by and obviously interested in the open seductiveness of her clothes, and when she violates the sanctity of his antiseptic medicine cabinet, he becomes brutal:

> "Look at what this slut is wearing. Boots up to her knees." Her net stockings of blue silk were exposed to view. With a jerk she pulled her head out of his arm, crouched down, then crawled like a dog on all fours to the dressing table, while her hair hung down over her swollen face. She pulled herself up, panting, with him right behind her with the wash cloth. She staggered over to the wall, pulled at the latch of the medicine cabinet, pressed her face against the glass, smearing it. He yanked her sideways, "Hey you, get your mitts off there."
>
> (*E* 143)

His expressions of disgust approach a climax as he unconsciously mimes a rape:

> He forced her down with his broad torso, pressed her knees down, held her against the table top with his encircling arms. He ground his teeth; his bald head was moist and shiny with sweat. "Let go of my shirt, you filthy pig. You should be ashamed of yourself, acting like this. You should be ashamed, you should be ashamed!"
>
> (*E* 144)

Finally, when she scratches his face while struggling to escape the smelling salts, he punches her twice in the mouth.

There is a disturbing ambiguity in the tone of Emma's encounter with the medical attendant Walter. As has already been noted, it contributes nothing at all to the advancement of the plot, yet is the longest single episode in the story. While the attendant is implicitly condemned for his brutality, the narrator presents his mishandling of Emma in such detail and at such length that one begins to suspect a certain voyeuristic enjoyment on his part.[57] Emma is a quadruple victim: exploited by Rutschinski, beaten by a customer, further mishandled by the authorities whose job is supposedly to help her, and also "victimized" by the narrator. The narrative victimization is partly the ritual that allows her to become a redemptress (it is she who earns the money, tries to recruit a lawyer, and comforts the widow Nasske at the end), but partly also an excuse to describe her brutalization in graphic detail. The style of stone creates an "objective" framework for such exploitation. Narrative affect has not really been eliminated, only channeled into the descriptive details.

"On Heavenly Mercy" is a laboratory demonstration of the principles enunciated in the Berlin Program: rejection of psychological analysis and rational causality; elimination of the subjective, authorial narrator; restriction to the notation of processes and movements. The story's lumpenproletarian characters lend themselves particularly well to these techniques. Yet the story is not simply a nihilistic mirror of their brutal lives. The jarring juxtaposition of irreconcilable narrative modes breaks through the illusion of a unified reality created by conventional narrative. A few years later Döblin formulated this idea in the often-quoted dictum, "If you can't cut a novel into ten pieces like an earthworm and each piece moves independently, then it's no good" (*AzL* 21). In *Wadzek's Battle with the Steam Turbine,* written shortly after "On Heavenly Mercy," Döblin continued his assault on traditional narrative fiction by attacking the idea of the hero.

2

Wadzek's Battle with the Steam Turbine

From the first appearance of Döblin's second published novel, *Wadzek's Battle with the Steam Turbine,* in 1918, most readers have found it a strange and disturbing work. Martin Buber, to whom Döblin had sent the typescript, could find no connection between *Wadzek* and its predecessor *The Three Leaps of Wang-lun* (*Briefe* 76–79). Most critics who reviewed the book also had to admit their perplexity.[1] The bewilderment of the reviewer for *Geschichtsblätter für Technik, Industrie und Gewerbe* (a journal of industrial and technological history), who was doubtless misled by the novel's title into reading it in the first place, is fairly typical. He "searched in vain for a good thought, a subtle psychological insight."[2] To be sure, there were a few positive voices early on, above all that of the young Bertolt Brecht, who in his diary praised the antitragic character of the work and called it "altogether a powerful book."[3] But basically, this novel has remained an anomaly to critics and scholars alike.

It is difficult to fit *Wadzek* developmentally between *Wang-lun* and *Wallenstein*—two long, epic novels of historical societies in upheaval, works in which Döblin by his own admission took "pleasure in grandiose phenomena" (*AzL* 388). *Wadzek*'s modern urban setting, small cast of characters, and claustrophobic narrative make it seem the work of another author altogether. If one compares *Wadzek* to the later and more famous *Berlin Alexanderplatz,* however, one can discern thematic parallels which suggest that *Wadzek* is a first attempt to give fictional expression to problems that would be much more thoroughly treated in Döblin's masterpiece.[4]

Wadzek's Battle with the Steam Turbine is Döblin's only novel whose title does not correspond to its contents. It is not about the individual's battle against enslaving technology, as one would expect, although that may have been Döblin's original intention.[5] By his own account, he began with a Futuristic theme, but the book took matters into its own hands (we have already seen how Döblin describes his method of composition as similar to automatic writing): "I planned the technology of a gigantic Berlin, but it became something on a very human scale, that is, the first part of that story, how technology expels a person, a *comical* book" (*Briefe* 77, emphasis in the original). Even this characterization of the novel is not quite right, for Wadzek willfully withdraws from the world of industrial and technological competition rather than being expelled by it. But it is important to note that Döblin's initial intention was to write a "gigantic" novel like *Wang-lun* or *Wallenstein,* but set in contemporary, industrial Berlin. He is even supposed to have done extensive background research at the factories of Siemens and Halske and the AEG (the Berlin General Electric Company).[6] As we will see, it is the psychopathology of the central character and his family—"something on a very human scale"—that overwhelmed this original intention.

Wadzek is divided into four books, each of which is subdivided into unnumbered episodes. We meet Franz Wadzek in the role of engineer and industrialist only in book 1, and even then only briefly. Wadzek's competitor Jakob Rommel has defeated him by producing a new steam turbine (Wadzek produces piston-driven machines), and also by secretly buying up shares in his company. Wadzek first tries to enlist the help of his former protégée, Gabriele Wessel or Gaby, who is now Rommel's mistress. She agrees to get a list of the stock certificates Rommel plans to buy in exchange for an introduction to Wadzek's daughter Herta.[7] When this plan fails, Wadzek, aided by his friend Schneemann (an engineer who works for Rommel), desperately attempts to impede his rival by intercepting and changing the text of a letter from Rommel to the agent who is purchasing shares for him.

When this attempt is also foiled, Wadzek insanely decides to barricade himself in his suburban villa in Reinickendorf on the edge of Berlin, along with his wife, daughter, and ally Schneemann, there to await attack by the authorities—or rather, by the whole society. This slapstick "siege" comprises the long second book. The longer the besieged household awaits this completely illusory attack, the more Wadzek becomes entangled in his delusion. Finally one night, he fires on supposed attackers (who are only poaching wild birds in his front yard), is interrogated with Schneemann at the local police station, then reprimanded and released. Profoundly downcast, he returns to Berlin.

The third book begins with a series of darkly symbolic, highly enigmatic scenes. Wadzek breaks off with the "traitor" Schneemann, discovers renewed passion for his enormously fat wife Pauline, but then also renews contact with Gaby Wessel.

In the fourth book, after Pauline throws a disgustingly drunken costume party with two women cronies, Wadzek leaves his family, fleeing to America with Gaby aboard an ocean liner.

☐

It was already clear to Brecht in 1920 that a basic theme of *Wadzek* was a critique of the related concepts of tragic fate and heroism: "The hero [i.e., the central character] refuses a tragic fate. One shouldn't fob off tragedy on mankind . . . [*Wadzek*] leaves man modestly in partial darkness and doesn't proselytize."[8] In his December 1915 letter to Martin Buber, who found the novel incomprehensible, Döblin himself mentions the "apparent tragedy" and the "fate" against which Wadzek struggles, and then "the affectionately comic fundamental feeling" that underlies and relativizes them (*Briefe* 80).

The theme of heroism emerges early in the first book after Wadzek pays a humiliating, futile, and senseless visit to his industrial competitor Rommel in an attempt to borrow money and end their rivalry. He gains only a sweaty collar for his pains, and that damp collar becomes a motif to remind the reader (and Wadzek) again and again of his humiliation. Wadzek goes straight from Rommel to the patent office, where he looks up heroic figures from the history of technology in order to fortify himself for the coming battle: "He read about Watt and Stephenson. He got more and more excited. He sunk his teeth in and didn't let go" (*W* 24).

In the course of the second book, Wadzek's sense of heroic mission hypertrophies into a delusion of grandeur and a persecution complex; both evaporate in the sober reality of the Reinickendorf police station at the end of the illusory siege. The comedy of this scene, like the comedy in *Don Quixote,* lies in the confrontation between an imperturbably mad heroic ideal and the antiheroic and corrupt reality of everyday life. Döblin himself uses the analogy of Quixote, calling both Wadzek and the Don "weaklings" in his letter to Buber (*Briefe* 80). Otto Keller has remarked about Franz Biberkopf in *Berlin Alexanderplatz* that "His heroic posture is . . . a constant contrast with the actual state of affairs, so that a satirical disjunction arises between pretension and re-

ality. Biberkopf becomes another Quixote, tilting at windmills."⁹ This
statement is equally valid for Wadzek—indeed, his windmills are far
more illusory than Biberkopf's.

The structure of *Wadzek*'s plot mirrors the critique of heroism, its
stages clearly reflected in the titles of the four books: "The Conspiracy" (heroic battle against fate); "The Siege of Renickendorf" (persecution complex and retreat after the initial defeat); "Knocked to the
Ground and Shattered" (stroke of fate); "Let's Pull Ourselves Together
and Go Home" (a new and more hopeful beginning). It is significant
that the heaviest blow to Wadzek is not defeat at the hands of his business rival Rommel. That is already a foregone conclusion at the beginning of the novel, for Wadzek realizes very early that Rommel's engine
Model 65 is in fact superior to his own R4 (W 30).¹⁰ The real stroke of
fate is Wadzek's realization at the end of the second book that no one
has persecuted and besieged him, that he has been heroically tilting at
windmills. The crisis in the middle of the novel is precipitated precisely
by the destruction of his heroic image of himself.

This critique of heroism is anticipated at the beginning of the novel
by a kind of cautionary tale, contained in the biography of Schnee-
mann.¹¹ The narrator makes clear at the first introduction of Schneemann that he is important as a type: "There were many men like him
in the city," and "Like all men of his type, he had a clever, suffering
wife and several children" (W 12). The parallels to Wadzek are obvious: Schneemann begins as an engineer and inventor who "suffered
from ideas" (W 12). A powerful industrial firm steals his invention
and crushes him. He curses his native city, Stettin (which was also
Döblin's native city), and settles in Berlin where he "grew a skin of sul-
len obstinacy" (W 13). In just the same way, Wadzek decides to go to
Reinickendorf and "refuse, refuse" (W 76) after his business defeat at
the hands of Rommel.

Following his own defeat, Schneemann has withdrawn into a petit-
bourgeois family idyll. His heroic self-image survives only in his
dreams, in which he "stands there like an ancient Roman with his
shield on his left arm, his short sword grasped in his right fist, awaiting
the assault" (W 13). He has chosen Wadzek as his substitute hero. The
dynamics of their relationship are defined by their inversely varying
moods; when Wadzek is enthusiastic and full of fight, Schneemann is
fearful, and vice versa. Schneemann's constant impulse is to take shelter in the security of his family circle. "I'm a decent man" (W 72), he

protests, when Wadzek wants to draw him into the battle against Rommel. He believes himself already in possession of that conventional decency to which Franz Biberkopf aspires at the beginning of *Berlin Alexanderplatz*. The portrait of Schneemann as a petit bourgeois is completed by his fondness for quoting scraps of Goethe out of context, his political conservatism, and his admiration for the military: "He discovered in Berlin his passion for the army, in which he himself had not served on account of his corpulence" (*W* 13).

In his letter to Buber, Döblin characterizes Schneemann as Wadzek's "comparative" (*Briefe* 80), and that suggests two things. First, Schneemann is offered from the beginning as an object of comparison to Wadzek, and second, he is literally Wadzek's comparative degree: more Wadzek than Wadzek. He is one developmental stage ahead of Wadzek, and therefore not just a comparison but also a warning. In the late essay "Epilog," in which Döblin surveys his past work, he characterizes *Wadzek's Battle with the Steam Turbine* in the following way: "In *Wadzek*, man struggled breathlessly in pursuit of technology; he kicked, screamed, stumbled, and fell flat on his face. Then came someone else, ran, raced, gasped" (*AzL* 387). Although this passage has been interpreted as referring to Wadzek and Rommel,[12] it makes more sense when applied to Schneemann and Wadzek. The word "struggled" in the preceding quotation is an inadequate translation of one of Döblin's most characteristic words, *zappeln*. It denotes helpless, convulsive motion and combines the ideas "dangle," "wriggle," and "struggle." Such a word seems much more fitting for the compulsive antics of Wadzek and Schneemann than for the ponderous giant Rommel.

Schneemann's role as Wadzek's predecessor and *Doppelgänger* is underlined by his name: Snowman, a pale figure liable to melt away under the heat of reality. Wadzek plays repeatedly with his friend's labile name. He calls him "King Schneemann" and "Weissmann" or Whiteman (*W* 28) and later "Schneemann alias Polar Bear" (*W* 220). The narrator also plays with the name, atomizing Schneemann in the act of enjoying a glass of beer into "numerous little beer-drinking Snowmen" (*W* 120). Even Schneemann himself tries to withdraw from the Reinickendorf adventure with the words, "The Snowman has snowed his last" (*W* 147). At another point in the often slapstick second book, the obese Schneemann insists that the same Loden coat will fit him and the small, nervous Wadzek: "You've got the same build.

There are small differences, but they don't count. The chest and shoulder measurements are the main thing. Ask your tailor if that isn't the main thing in a coat. You're a militiaman like me." They then stand chest to chest and back to back, but cannot reach agreement and accuse each other of "subjectivity and prejudice" (W 83).

Döblin gives their strange relationship unmistakably homoerotic undertones, especially during a scuffle that erupts after Wadzek taunts Schneemann with the threat of going to prison with him: "He pressed the resisting man against himself, tried to hook his knees around his legs, and choked the man into himself, into his throat, so that nothing would remain of Schneemann and nothing of Wadzek. And now, now he wanted to murder him completely" (W 74). The similarity to the medic's pinning down of Emma in the story "On Heavenly Mercy" is striking. There too an act of violence masks a sexual act. The diction of this passage from *Wadzek,* distorted by its emotional vehemence, has Wadzek figuratively incorporating Schneemann by eating him, thus becoming one with him. At least since *The Black Curtain,* sex in Döblin's work simultaneously symbolizes lost metaphysical unity and the despairing attempt to regain it. At the drunken costume party in the fourth book, the festivities are similarly described as "cannibalistic" (W 284), with similar homoerotic undertones. Frau Kochanski, the dipsomaniacal tavernkeeper who is one of Pauline's cronies, jumps "wildly onto the overstuffed lady, clamped her slim legs around one of Pauline's columnar ones, shinnied up, sank into the swamp. 'Let me hug you, Fatty Pauline. You're [i.e., Pauline and the third friend, Frau Litgau] both swine. We're all pigs in the sty together'" (W 286–87).

□

Schneemann is thus both Wadzek's double and an exemplum whose function is to warn Wadzek of a wrong path, but the question remains: which is the right path? How is Schneemann's example to be interpreted? At the beginning of the novel, Wadzek's world is divided between his business and his family, and he strives to keep the two separate, especially since the family sphere is a woman's world. In the first episode of book 1, he declares to Gaby, "It is the mental capacity of women, the undifferentiated mental capacity that I always have to contend with. Business is one thing, family relations another" (W 12). This is an expression of the double standard inherent in bourgeois culture that Döblin, under the influence of Bebel, pilloried in "Modern." Yet we have seen how the contempt for the "undifferentiated mental capacity" of women informs what Döblin himself wrote after "Modern." In Wadzek's remarks about business and the family, the problematic image of women is again connected to the structure of modern industrial society as in "Modern."

In Wadzek himself, the split between family life and business corresponds to a split between his feelings and his intelligence. The novel uses the terms "heart" and "idea," a pair of polar opposites that emerges early on, in the second and third episodes of book 1. Wadzek boasts to Schneemann that he is prepared to sacrifice his daughter to his business interests. He refers to "human sacrifices" and embellishes his supposed heroism with a quote from *Wilhelm Tell*, whose hero was forced to put his son in mortal danger (Wadzek prefers Schiller to Schneemann's Goethe). Schneemann replies, "As for my daughter, I wouldn't have the heart to . . ." (W 14). But Wadzek brushes Schneemann's objections aside with the rhetorical question, "Hand on your heart, Schneemann, would you doubt the morality of your daughters when all is said and done?" (W 15). The realm of the heart is not even recognized as legitimate; it exists only as a shadow in banal and hackneyed phrases: "Hand on your heart, Schneemann. . . ." The polarity between idea and heart has a clearly sexual aspect from the beginning: the main female characters—Wadzek's wife Pauline, his daughter Herta, and Gaby—are creatures of feeling, but not of thought. Apropos his decision to "sacrifice" his daughter, Wadzek declares, "My wife's got nothing to say about it. The patriarchal standpoint is the correct one" (W 15).

There is a mythical prefiguration[13] lurking beneath the surface of the text at this point, alluded to by phrases like "human sacrifices" and "My wife's got nothing to say about it." The parallel is Agamemnon's sacrifice of his daughter Iphigenia as recounted in Aeschylus's *Oresteia*. It is Herta herself, the sacrificial Iphigenia figure, who later draws explicit attention to the parallel in conversation with Gaby: "An evil fate hangs over our house. Agamemnon is nothing compared to us," and "the next time you see him [i.e., Wadzek], he'll be in the bathtub" (W 40). In the *Oresteia*, Agamemnon sacrifices his daughter to Diana in order to succeed in the heroic and masculine pursuit of war. He dies a shameful and unworthy death when Clytemnestra murders him in the bath to avenge her daughter. Gaby's demand of an introduction to

Herta as the price of her help in Wadzek's struggle with Rommel similarly injects the realm of the family, of the "heart," into the masculine
world of business. His punishment, as we shall see, will not be murder,
but rather the destruction of his heroic, masculine image of himself.
Herta quotes his laments to Gaby: " 'They're castrating me; that's right,
castrating.' Do you have an encyclopedia? I'd like to see what they're
doing to Father." [14]

Following Wadzek and Schneemann's discussion of the sacrifice of
Herta, in which the word "heart" figures so prominently in their
clichés, the third episode shows Wadzek for the first and last time as a
captain of industry in a pitiless capitalist world. He stands embattled
before a general meeting of his stockholders, defending his ideas.
Here, in the masculine realm of business competition, "idea" is developed as the opposite of "heart." Wadzek is self-confident, mocking,
sarcastic. His eyes, later almost always described as "beautiful" and
"unforgettable," with "great blue pupils" (W 59), are here "his shrewd
little eyes" (W 16). Wadzek is in this episode pure intelligence, a hero
of ideas: "He would continue to develop his ideas, he explained, his
ideas and no one else's" (W 16). He then tells his stockholders, "Stay
out of our struggle, the struggle of ideas" (W 17).

But both the concept "heart" (or feeling) and the concept "idea" (or
intelligence) remain curiously abstract in this novel because of its presentation of character. We have already seen how the empirical psychology of the Berlin Program allows the narrator no privileged insight
into the psyche of his figures; he must content himself with the record-
ing of processes, that is, of the chains of their perceptions and affects.
Wadzek's Battle with the Steam Turbine shows that such a narrative
technique also has implications for the intellectual dimension of the
figures. If it works well for the brutalized lumpen proletarians in "On
Heavenly Mercy," it is more problematic in the case of the bourgeois
entrepreneur Wadzek. There is almost no trace of the thought processes or actual intellectual problems of an engineer and industrialist
in the novel. It is as if Wadzek were only pantomiming such a person.
For this reason, the competition between Rommel's Model 65 steam
turbine and Wadzek's R4 piston engine can later on easily hypertrophy
into a "battle of the individual against the monopolies, against the
trusts" (W 172). Yet Wadzek should not be misconstrued as a social
hero. [15] The struggle in *Wadzek* has little to do with capitalist competition. It is purely psychological and metaphoric, like the struggle be-

tween Shlink and Garga in Bertolt Brecht's *Im Dickicht der Städte* (In the Jungle of the Cities), a work that surely reflects the influence of Döblin's novel.

□

For much of the novel, Wadzek is in fact a psychotic, like the central characters of so many of Döblin's early novels and stories.[16] On a first encounter with so strange and unsettling a novel, it is easy to conclude that all the characters are at least slightly batty. The reviewer of the *Geschichtsblätter für Technik, Industrie und Gewerbe* described the novel's characters as "some of them imbeciles, the others psychopaths."[17] But to say this is to be misled by the narrative method, the "style of stone" that only registers surface perceptions and ignores any inner life that might connect those perceptions in a logical way. If the narrator occasionally ventures into Wadzek's mind, it is only by way of metaphor: "This is how things were within him: the rattling of bars, a lion's cage opened at the height of his pharynx, then something raged and bellowed out across the iron-clad floor, up and down" (W 68).

This disjunct narrative prevails from the first episode of the novel, in which Gaby comes home and finds Wadzek waiting for her. Objects, persons, and actions are sharply focused but isolated. Wadzek's first appearance is typical: "A bouquet approached her out of the semi-darkness; Wadzek said in his normal voice, 'Good evening, good evening, dear lady'" (W 7). The bouquet and Wadzek simply follow one another paratactically, while their relation to each other has been suppressed. When such suppression is practiced not just in an easily understood detail like this, but consistently throughout the novel, it forces the reader to experience the same deep insecurity and disconnectedness that beset Wadzek.

Here is the first extended description of him:

> Wadzek sauntered around the room. He bounced, whipped around all the free-standing furniture in the room, muffled his voice, crowed. He had a childlike, long face with an unkempt reddish-blond beard. Walked up to chairs, whatnots, sniffed them, always as if he were their friend, relative, in-law. He trotted around in his street clothes, his hands buried to the elbows in his pockets, in order to dispel any impression of formality. He seemed only to be comfortable under the protection of some object, seldom stepped into the center of the room. If he had lost contact with something, he would discreetly slip back to it. When

Gabriele had induced him to sit down, he turned on his chair, sought contact with the fringe of the tablecloth.

(W 7)

The description opens with a series of contradictions. The first sentence seems to establish a man at ease with his surroundings, but "sauntered" (*schlenderte*) is immediately contradicted by "bounced" and "whipped" (*wippte, schnellte*). No sooner has he muffled his voice than he crows. Although at first he is described as a friend and even relative of the things around him, his deep alienation from the world soon manifests itself in the senseless desperation with which he clings to individual objects. Gabriele, on the other hand, is perfectly at her ease—it is her house, after all—so the jagged, paratactic narrative reflects Wadzek's perception of the world, not hers. Part of the threat of women in all of Döblin's works is that they are connected to the material world, to "nature," and at ease in it.

Other characters in the novel, in particular Wadzek's bright, edgy daughter Herta, diagnose him as mad. She calls the villa in Reinickendorf a "madhouse" (W 92) and later says to Gaby, "I tell you, he's quite mad" (W 212). Indeed, Wadzek himself intermittently recognizes his own psychosis. He knows perfectly well, for example, that stealing Rommel's letter will do no good (W 54), but feels compelled to do it. Just before snatching it, he mutters to himself, "I'm suffering from some condition" (W 61) and afterwards, he fights against "the rising tide of a psychotic attack" (W 63).

Given the deeply disturbed relation to the world that underlies the entire narrative, it is no surprise that thematic and symbolic material like the heart/idea dichotomy floats on its surface in a rather insubstantial way.[18] Such themes are nevertheless important to follow, because they supply the structure that Döblin insisted was there in the novel (*Briefe* 80). Let us see how it works.

□

Wadzek's first "reading" of the moral of his life is that one must not give up and devote oneself to the heart, like Schneemann, but rather must battle heroically against fate. This interpretation dominates the first two books, during which Wadzek pays hardly any attention to his family and is ever ready to sacrifice them to his cause. He is Agamemnon, single-mindedly pursuing his masculine aims: "We are kings, the equals of kings, when we're working. Everything else must be subjugated, must serve us: family, house, daughter. Whether they like it or not" (*W* 14).

But this interpretation is clearly false from the beginning, and Wadzek's heroic battle for "ideas" is doomed to failure. Gaby's demand in the first episode connects the family sphere to the business sphere, heart to idea. For their part, Wadzek's wife Pauline and Herta mock and undermine the adventure in Reinickendorf. In the police station, at the end of the second book, both Wadzek's heroic ideal and his idea of tragic fate are utterly destroyed. Kurgeweit, the younger of the two policemen on duty, sizes up Wadzek and Schneemann perfectly: "Here's how things stand: they're trying to be big shots. They're a better class of people" (*W* 176). The slang phrase for "being a big shot," *sich dicke tun,* is, as we shall see, exactly the one used by a morphine addict in *Berlin Alexanderplatz* to deflate the pretensions to tragedy of a young friend who has lost his job: "You shouldn't be a big shot about your destiny. I'm against fate. I'm no Greek, I'm a Berliner" (*BA* 57).

While Wadzek's heroic interpretation of Schneemann's exemplum prevails in the first two books, the opposite interpretation becomes operative in the third book: one should emulate Schneemann, give in, live for one's family. Thus *Wadzek,* too, raises the dualism of resistance and acceptance that is central to *Wang-lun.* In spite of much inner resistance, Wadzek finally surrenders to contrite adulation of his wife.

A scene in the novel's third book has attracted the attention of all interpreters of the novel, for although clearly symbolic, its symbolism is obscure.[19] In this scene, Wadzek first calls a large wardrobe mirror "the hole in the world" (*W* 191) and then shatters it with his elbows. The scene marks a critical point in Wadzek's change from activity to passivity, from the pantomime of an embattled industrialist to the pantomime of a contented family man. It is important that the glass mirrors not only Wadzek, but also his "comparative" Schneemann; they stand side by side before it. Wadzek uses the mirror to compare the fallen tragic hero (himself now or Schneemann in his Stettin days) with the smug petit bourgeois, who regards himself "with intimate familiarity" (*vertraut; W* 191): "This on the left, you see, in the mirror, now moving its mouth and talking, is you—in Stettin. You yourself, Schneemann, not me. . . . A wave of the hand, hocus-pocus, there you stand today, powerful, fat, before and after" (*W* 192). When Wadzek first spits at and then shatters his own image in the mirror, he is taking symbolic leave of his ideal, heroic self-image. Now he throws Schneemann out. He no longer needs him as a cautionary example, because he is about to become a Schneemann himself. Logically enough, Schneemann shortly thereafter disappears from the novel.

The first interpretation of Schneemann's exemplum has been proved wrong, but this second one cannot be correct either. It is nothing but an admission of defeat, the reverse of heroism. Now "the mighty Frau Wadzek" sits reading the newspaper (W 226), now she sits "heroically triumphant over her prey" (W 228). In *Wadzek*, as in Kafka's "Metamorphosis," reading the newspaper is a quintessentially male occupation, the symbol of patriarchal dominance.[20]

Döblin's rigidly polar image of women is nowhere so clear as in Pauline and Gaby, the two principal women in *Wadzek*. It is difficult to think of a woman in literature more repellent than Pauline Wadzek. Although the first full-scale description of her does not occur until the second book, the reader already knows of her corpulence. But he is unprepared for the ferocious loathing of the description now unleashed by the narrator. It is worth quoting *in extenso* in order to convey its full force, and to show the obsessive attention to physical detail characteristic of the entire novel:

> Frau Wadzek was a head taller than her husband. She was built like a pyramid, as it were, or better yet, like a cone; for while her head, including its masses of hair, was of normal size, her shoulders narrowed as though in expectation of a graceful, delicate personage further down, and in fact were followed by a narrow, collapsed chest resembling a deflated tire. But only then came her breasts, which in their bulkiest parts seemed to have slipped downwards, causing a pouchlike protrusion from the front elevation. And their unlooked-for swelling (had these organs been transferred to her back, one would have regarded their possessor as a hunchback or as the bearer of a half-filled water bag)—this unexpected swelling continued in a straight line both forwards and to the sides in contours that must have belonged to Frau Wadzek's stomach. For a while, the abdomen continued to extend along the lines initiated by the breasts and described the frontal volume of a taut bladder. What followed further down eluded direct observation. The brown skirts, laced tightly in the vicinity of the lower deposition of the breasts, were forced as a result of unknown circumstances to ruffle out like crinolines, after they had overcome the vault of the belly. The proportions in the rear, from the shoulder blades downwards, also grew increasingly generous; no element needed to be ashamed of any other. Frau Wadzek possessed a flattened face with a somewhat protruding chin; the woman usually shoved her lower jaw forward, especially during attempts at re-

flection. In the course of a long married life she had succeeded in finding a point of support on her body for her stout arms, namely the not clearly visible but nevertheless extant trough between the bottom of the sacks of her breasts and the upper end of her hemispherical stomach. Her crossed arms floated at rest on the inflated belly, half covered by the warm padding above them. No one, upon mere reflection, could have found a better resting place for her arms. Now while Frau Wadzek's tumultuous skirts floated around her when she walked, or more precisely, when the mass of her person was displaced in space, this evenly undulating image underwent a transformation at the moment that it came to rest. Then the relationships of equilibrium were changed: the center of gravity was transferred into the vicinity of her resting arms, somewhat above the conjectural site of her navel. From this point downwards, the lower masses fell diagonally forwards, forming together with her skirts a slanting plane, which was usually distinguished by a blue and red striped apron.

(W 108–109)

Like the description of the medical attendant Walter in "On Heavenly Mercy," this passage demonstrates that the objectivity of the style of stone does not preclude narrative judgment of characters. Such judgment is simply transferred from overt narrative comment to an attitude inherent in the description of perceptual phenomena. It is not just that Pauline's inner life is not shown: she *has* no inner life, or at least none beyond her "attempts at reflection." Her conversation throughout the novel consists almost entirely of hackneyed expressions of indignation. As for her exterior, it is not just described but systematically dehumanized—in another passage her figure in a darkened corridor is characterized as "something extensive, something blackly superhuman" (W 123). The controlling metaphor is that of a monumental edifice: she is a "pyramid" with a "front elevation," her belly a "vault," her arms find a "point of support." She is reduced to a series of geometric lines and planes, like some monstrous Expressionist portrait.

It could be objected that here we simply see Pauline from Wadzek's perspective. Yet Wadzek is not particularly hostile to her at this point: his mood is the "melancholy of leave-taking" (W 109). More important, Pauline continues to be described in this way even after their reconciliation in the third book. The narrator returns to the image of her arms resting in their "trough," for example, with tiresome tenacity (W 111, 133, 232), and always refers to her with unconcealed sarcasm and scorn. Her characteristic activity is vomiting, which she does in each of the last three books (W 138, 183, 291).

Pauline's habitual indignation at Wadzek's failure to respect and appreciate her is only one manifestation of her complete solipsism. In Reinickendorf, for example, she has "an overflowing feeling of pity for herself" (W 133). Later she "prayed aloud to 'her dearest, dearest Lord God'" (W 227), and after Wadzek has abandoned her and Herta has suffered a nervous breakdown, she "bore with dignity, indeed, with a certain austerity the fate that God had sent—not to her, but to two others who had once been close to her" (W 321).

Although she neglects her own daughter, Pauline's single selfless act in the entire novel is motherly: she rescues a boy from her husband's literally murderous fury (W 102). And it is to a smotheringly protective mother figure rather than to a wife that Wadzek becomes reconciled in the third book. The first book already hints at his ambivalence toward Pauline, his desire both to command and to submit. As he leaves his house for his interview with Rommel, he "looked around to see if she would call him back, not let him go to Rommel" (W 19). Later he complains to Schneemann, "My wife let me go; you can't trust anybody" (W 25). Yet when she *does* try to restrain him from a similar act, he "bellowed in fury, knocked her arm away, slammed the door behind him" (W 68). Wadzek's relationship to Pauline is characterized by alternation between contempt and mindless, slavish devotion. His surrender to her doubtful charms is explicitly the result of shattering his self-image in the mirror (W 227). Now he is "a prisoner" (W 227) and "totally contrite" (W 228).

Gaby Wessel is Pauline's polar opposite. She is described repeatedly as beautiful, with dark blonde hair and large breasts. She is a fashionable woman, and Anthony Riley has noted that one description of her in the novel is borrowed from an illustration in the "Fashion and Society" section of the *Berliner Zeitung* of September 27, 1913 (W 348). Döblin saved the clipping with the *Wadzek* manuscript, and it suggests his continuing fascination with the feminine fashion against whose seductiveness he railed in "Modern." Here is how Wadzek reproachfully describes Gaby's walk in the novel's first episode:

> There is without doubt something about your walk calculated to make men uneasy. . . . You place one foot forward—slowly, much too slowly to our way of thinking—draw the right foot after it, while your upper body sways forward, not in a straight line, but like my hand here, if you imagine my fingers to be your legs. Like a ripe fruit, or a fruit dish. As if you intended to tip and spill out your contents. I might also say you

were like a basin of water, a basin with goldfish, almost brimming over
at each step.

(W 9)

As in the description of Pauline Wadzek, human motions here are first
described as mechanical movements. But while the narrator's description of Pauline persists in dehumanizing geometrical and architectural
metaphors, Wadzek, himself an engineer, modulates from a scientific
demonstration into more poetic and conventionally beautiful images—a bowl of fruit, a basin of water. Preserved among Döblin's
early notes for the novel, however, is a narrative description of Gaby
that is much closer in spirit to the description of Pauline: "muscles with
their padding of fat, arms, large breasts, a laced-in belly with winding
intestines, a rib-enclosed barrel with the slippery machinery of the
lungs, blood vessels" (W 347–48, note to p. 31). Although Döblin did
not make use of this passage in the final version of the novel—doubtless
in order not to obscure the polarity between the two women—it suggests that Pauline and Gaby are, so to speak, sisters under the skin.
Their polarity in the end represents simply two sides of a composite
picture of woman; it is not surprising that they never meet. Gaby, in
contrast to Pauline, is given a chance to respond to her description,
which she does in a perfectly comprehensible way: "Take your hands
off the table, please. You're being ridiculous" (W 9). She emerges in
both description and dialogue as a human being, perhaps the most
"normal" figure in the novel, while Pauline is reduced (or inflated) to
an inhuman monstrosity.

If Pauline is solipsistic and devouring, triumphing over her "prey"
at the moment Wadzek submits (W 228), Gaby is meek and gentle
(sanftmütig; W206), defenseless to the point of masochism. She is the
only character whose past is extensively narrated, another factor that
contributes to the impression of her humanity (W 203–205, 207–
208, 250–52). But that past consists of a series of willing submissions
to sexual exploitation. Of her relationship with Rommel, for instance,
Gaby says, "I am nothing better than Rommel's mistress. I chose that
for myself" (W 10). Nor does she choose it out of social or finan-
cial necessity, like Bertha in "Modern" and Emma in "On Heavenly
Mercy." Gaby is the daughter of a naval officer, and thus comes from a
good family, as Rommel emphasizes when trying to persuade her to
marry him (W 34–35). She associates Rommel with the principal of
her school who made an obscene remark to her when she was thirteen

(*W* 252). A manuscript passage deleted from the printed version goes so far as to suggest that Gaby associates love with rape: "Incidentally, she didn't call this joy she derived from other people 'love,' since she strangely enough used that word for a long-since superannuated feeling for an older man she had known in her eighteenth year, a man who later unfortunately got what he wanted from her in a very violent way" (*W* 361, noted to p. 325). Thus Gaby's biography from childhood has been shaped by her submissive relations to men. She has chosen the life of a kept woman, the modern parallel to the "sacred prostitution" in *Wang-lun.* She ultimately chooses the failed and beaten Wadzek over the successful Rommel.

Although Pauline and Gaby represent the extremes of solipsism and self-sacrifice, they share certain qualities as women, and this suggests again that they are really two halves of a composite image. Both live purely on instinct and emotion, whether selfishly or selflessly. Theirs is the realm of the heart. Neither is allowed to participate in the world of business, the world of ideas where the battle between Wadzek and Rommel is waged. Both men find it impossible to discuss business with their consorts (*W* 18, 250). When Wadzek later does attempt to explain his ideas to Pauline, she cannot understand them (*W* 232–33).

The portrayal of women in *Wadzek* is thus rigidly binary. They are either monstrously solipsistic and dominating or selflessly submissive and defenseless. This polarity of dominance and submission is related to the polarity of activity and passivity in which Döblin's male heroes struggle. The difference is that the men, like Wadzek and Wang-lun, alternate between one state and the other and are therefore more complex and interesting. They are the center of their respective novels, because it is they who change and thus provide something to narrate. The polarity in Döblin's image of women is static; each female figure is either the one type or the other. Moreover, each female pole is weighted with narrative value judgments. Gaby's masochistic submission is clearly valued positively, Pauline's solipsism negatively. If Wadzek's flight with Gaby at the end of the novel was meant as an escape from the constraints of both polarities, we will see that it is not fully convincing. But in order to deal with the end of the novel, we must consider the Schneemann parable once more.

□

In the last two books of the novel, a third interpretation of the Schnee-mann story emerges—a third resolution of the heart/idea dichot-omy. Its outlines are contained in two speculative passages in which Wadzek, contrary to his usual behavior, actually engages in something approaching rational thought. Significantly, in both cases Wadzek is attempting to explain himself to women. First, he uses the metaphor of a ship to explain to his wife and daughter his newly emerging attitude:

> Wadzek said that he wanted to serve humanity in a critical way. He had been in many ways enlightened by recent events, had learned things. It didn't matter, he continued, at which point in a development one stood, whether more at the front or further back. The helmsman is important; the stoker is important; the passenger is important; the ship is impor-tant; the ship owner is important. As he had said, you mustn't neglect anything. Contempt doesn't pay, no question about it. Delusions of grandeur—well, the name said everything. But for the individual it was necessary to be flexible, that is, to scramble adroitly to his place.
>   Herta interrupted him: then the shoeshine boy on the ship was also important. Not only him, said Wadzek emphatically, but also his wife, who isn't even traveling on the ship, but is at home cooking lentils and bacon, washing her children, drying them off, and so on.
>   And the beggar knocking at her door? Herta stubbornly persisted.
>   If a beggar would even knock at the door of such an obviously poor household, was the reply. But if he did, then one would certainly have to say that even this beggar was important for the ship. . . . The main thing were the interrelations: the water on which it sails, it too is of impor-tance for the ship, and the wind. They were difficult considerations, and he wasn't completely finished with them. The basic mistake, at any rate, was persisting to be a stoker and not looking at the whole. Obstinacy in one's own interpretation and stubbornness, pig-headedness. That was the dumb thing. Tack! Tack to the right, tack to the left!
>
>   (W 235–36)

After he leaves his wife, Wadzek develops a related metaphor in con-versation with Gaby. He praises birds and fish over plants and flowers, because the former

> had to accommodate themselves to the wind, had to adapt to every in-fluence of the weather; because [plants] can't do that, because they can't move, that's why they freeze in the winter. Leaves fall off, blossoms fall off even earlier. "Have you ever seen a human whose arms fall off in the winter? Or a bird whose wings fall off? They simply fly south. One has to orient oneself. It's false praise to say someone is rooted to the land. If I were a member of the nobility, I would put a weathervane in my coat of arms. The principle of adaptation is the most important one; one has to renew oneself."
>
>   (W 304)

These passages suggest the possibility of reconciling the dichotomy between heart and idea, of escaping the inevitability of a tragic fate. Wadzek now criticizes his former position as one-sided, as "working in a vacuum, hypothetical activity" (*eine Tätigkeit ins Blaue hinein, eine ideelle Tätigkeit;* W 237).

The young Brecht must have had these passages in mind when he praised the novel in his diary. But they give the impression of being foreign bodies within the novel, because they are the only passages in which a thought is actually developed intellectually. And they remain mere metaphor, pure theory, because they are not converted into action. They have no consequences for the novel's outcome. Wadzek does not in fact become a lecturer on technology and morality at a private technical college, as he plans (W 237–39), but rather flees to America aboard an ocean liner whose propeller is driven by—supreme irony—one of Rommel's steam turbines.

Wadzek's flight with Gaby is not the result of his new ideology of flexibility and interconnectedness, but rather Döblin's aesthetic escape hatch, suggested by the similar flight of his own father. That new ideology might indeed have made it possible to return to his original intention of writing a novel about the interaction of technology and the individual. But that intention was overwhelmed by the familial constellation—the Agamemnon complex, if one will. Wadzek boasts to Gaby that he has foiled Rommel's attempt to make him into a tragic hero, forgetting he had chosen that role for himself: "He's not going to make me into his Macbeth" (W 335). America is for Wadzek only a new field to conquer, a capitalist's dream, a regression to his old heroic pose: "You've got to have elbow room, have the right to fight force with force, to cast down and destroy what gets in your way. We'll have plenty of that over there" (W 334).

In its sexual aspect too, the end of the novel is a grotesquely comic regression to the polarity of domination and submission. Wadzek and Gaby are about to make love for the first time as the novel ends. After a previous unsuccessful attempt foiled by his inhibitions and habits of command ("You've twisted everything. I don't want love; I'll forgo tenderness. I want obedience"; W 325), the novel closes with Wadzek's declaration, "You see, everything is functioning" (W 336). Its comedy is heightened by the fact that Wadzek addresses Gaby with the formal *Sie* after having just offered her the familiar *du*. This engineer's approach to intimacy as a well-functioning machine cannot be interpreted as a resolution or a happy end.[21] Aboard a real ship, the metaphorical ship that showed the interdependence of all things is forgotten. The experimental field in which Wadzek's inchoate morality of flexibility and adaptation could have been tested is not America, but "gigantic Berlin." But then it would have had to be the Berlin of *Berlin Alexanderplatz,* not the rather vague urban backdrop of *Wadzek.* Only once in this first Berlin novel is there a hint at the rich fictional possibilities of the city. In the fourth book, just before deciding to escape to America, Wadzek and Gaby are riding in a horse-cab through the Friedrichstrasse:

> Between the stone masses of the buildings, the façades of the Friedrichstrasse, agape with windows. Buried between the steep, straight walls the whole length of the Friedrichstrasse. The granite slabs of the sidewalk press their edges against each other, impenetrable to the rain. The blackish-brown asphalt from the pits of Ragusa and Caserta, dumped streaming onto the street, stamped onto the gray cement foundation, flattened by hot steamrollers. The horsehooves echo over it. People between the buildings, above the granite slabs, people beside the wagon wheels, people on the traffic islands. Over the wet back of the asphalt, of the giant stage, the carriages roll. The chassis of light automobiles, approaching like invaders [*wie ein Einfall*], sway on tires inflated to bursting; from invisible exhaust pipes bluish-gray clouds are exhaled backwards; they spew poisonous gases into the air: suffocating carbon monoxide, stinking acrolein. The thundering towers of the omnibuses wobble past. Around their upper decks run advertising posters, visible from afar: Manoli Cigarettes, Luhn's Soap, Nivea Creme, The Best Lightbulb from the General Electric Company. The air around these stamping edifices vibrates. The weight of their hundreds of tons, window panes, wooden frames, sheet metal sides, trembles. Swaying from side to side they press the asphalt with tires as thick as arms. Above the heads of the teeming animals and men, above their excited skulls, their fluttering mufflers, above the chaos of whispers, screams, men hawking papers and cursing, police whistles: the cones of alabaster-white light beneath tiny black hats. The chasm between the buildings strung with metal wires, arc-light after arc-light, a swaying, endless burden of flame. On the street corners cast-iron candelabra mounted on blocks of stone. The human waves break on them, divide.
>
> (W 314–15)

Nothing like this rich passage appears elsewhere in the novel. Set off by its switch to present tense in the midst of the novel's otherwise consistent use of narrative preterite and by its reference to the scene as a stage, it is a shortened version of a passage in Döblin's original manuscript that bears the title "Evening Over Berlin," an indication that it was conceived as a sort of Expressionist prose poem.[22] Baudelaire, the author of prose poems in *Le Spleen de Paris*, is the only lyric poet mentioned in Döblin's letter to Marinetti. Clearly, the passage has been installed into the text as a set piece, with no immediately apparent connection to Wadzek and Gaby;[23] the narrative of their cab ride simply resumes in the preterite when this city poem ends after something less than two pages.

The passage anticipates the use of the city in *Berlin Alexanderplatz*. Many techniques and urban details used here are more fully exploited in the later novel: the atomizing, scientifically exact description of everyday phenomena, the quotations of advertisements, the flowing tides of pedestrians. At the same time, the echoes of Futurism are clearly audible in the dynamic verbs alternating with verbless noun phrases, and in the animal images used to describe machines.

The human figures that swarm and flow among the objects are ambiguous. Döblin at least hints that a measure of human enjoyment is possible in this environment: "The valley of this street is filled with the murmuring of these people, with their delighted strolling arm in arm, shoulder to shoulder. They peer right and left into the steamed-up windows, smile, hurry by" (W 315). On the other hand, the prose poem ends in an all but explicit indictment of a materialistic, acquisitive society: "The buildings jammed full from top to bottom, like bookshelves. Behind the windowpanes: objects, let loose upon mankind. The busy creatures wade past them, are held fast, tear themselves free, slip into side streets" (W 315). The city, although viewed in sharp detail in this passage, seems in the end alien to humankind. People are viewed in the collective, as they are in much of *Wang-lun*, and thus appear controlled and driven by a sinister environment.

Thirteen more years would pass before Döblin fully used the metropolis and its thousands of parallel human stories as a counterweight to his hero Franz Biberkopf. In *Wadzek*, such balance is blocked by the psychotic point of view of the central character, which makes a real confrontation with urban and industrial reality impossible. For Döblin himself, the affect-laden family theme overwhelmed his original intention to write an urban novel. As Roland Links has written, "the horizon of the author—at least within the novel—reaches no further than that of his hero."[24]

But it is noteworthy that already in *Wadzek* Döblin uses the image of the city as a coral colony, an image to which he returns in the im-

portant essay of 1924 entitled "Der Geist des naturalistischen Zeitalters" (The Spirit of the Naturalistic Age). As Wadzek rides the streetcar toward his fateful meeting with Rommel early in the novel, the
narrator describes the passing scene: "The life of the city went on without end; behind empty construction sites, new shops and restaurants
arose, storage yards for coal, iron; the city was growing like a coral
colony" (*W* 19). In the essay of 1924: "The cities are the principal resi-
dence and seat of the human group. They are the coral colony for man,
the collective being" (*AzL* 74). Döblin's image of the coral colony
changed significantly in the intervening years: whereas in *Wadzek* the
growth of the city is a technological and industrial process seemingly
independent of man, the essay defines the cities as an explicitly human
achievement, "quite clearly expressions of the human social instinct"
(*AzL* 71). One can, however, discern in the ship metaphor and in the
description of the Friedrichstrasse in *Wadzek* the germ of a collective
city that would come to maturity in *Berlin Alexanderplatz,* a city
whose very existence relativizes the theme of individual fate and mocks
the idea of heroism.

3

Berlin Alexanderplatz

Döblin's literary life during the Weimar Republic was intense and varied. Besides novels, he wrote plays, a verse epic, two books of philosophical speculation, a book on contemporary Poland, plus occasional journalism and theater reviews. His imaginative works were accompanied and illuminated by a steady stream of essays. The record of Döblin's complex and often contradictory political and social ideas and how they influence his fiction is contained mainly in the essays he wrote for such liberal journals as the *Neue Rundschau* and the *Neuer Merkur.* They reflect a gradual change in Döblin's political, philosophical, and aesthetic views that had a profound effect on the novel *Berlin Alexanderplatz.*

Scholars who have attempted to sort out Döblin's politics have generally come to the conclusion that they were at best confused.[1] What is clear is that from 1919 on, Döblin considered himself a progressive writer on the side of the working class. His basic political sympathies lay with the workers' and soldiers' councils that were formed early in the German revolution of 1918–19 and then bypassed and suppressed by the majority Social-Democratic government under Friedrich Ebert. "A comradely association of free men," Döblin wrote in 1919, "forms the natural basic cell of all society, the small community; there one must begin. . . . That's what Prince Kropotkin had long known and taught, what he learned from the Swiss watchmakers in the Jurabund, in political jargon: syndicalism, anarchism" (*SPG* 92).[2] But his interest in anarchism was never that of an activist, only of an observer and sympathizer. This is the pose Döblin adopts in a series of occasional "glosses" he wrote in 1919 and 1920 on the contemporary political and cultural scene. He wrote under the pseudonym Linke Poot (Left Paw) for the journal *Die Neue Rundschau,* where he was serving as editor. In these articles, Döblin attacks the Weimar state and its Social-Democratic leadership as a thin veneer beneath which the old power structure of officers and junkers remains: "Gemany, the Imperial Republic" (*WV* 22).

By 1921, however, in a speech entitled "Staat und Schriftsteller" (The State and the Writer), Döblin has accepted the new German state, at least as a theoretical ideal to be striven for, and urges his fellow artists to activism in its support. An ideal image of the Weimar Republic emerges as a new societal order, spiritualized through its artists and writers, trying to break out of the old, capitalistic and imperialistic mold. To the latter definitely belong the negative images of the city that arise at the end of the speech and echo the Friedrichstrasse passage in *Wadzek:* "Amid the roar of the factories, amid the window displays that entice and disquiet the people, amid the partisan wrangling, I wanted to speak to writers—without resignation, but rather full of hope" (*AzL* 61). In another 1921 essay, "Der Epiker, sein Stoff und die Kritik" (The Epic Writer, His Subject-Matter, and the Critics), Döblin defends his choice of the Thirty Years' War as the subject of his novel *Wallenstein* by presenting an even more incisive image of the contemporary writer and his spiritual isolation in modern industrial and consumer society:

> The cities have destroyed everything. Everyone sits at his desk and writes away; he can take delight in the scratching of his pen. Nothing holds the human masses together. They only touch each other. The fact that they speak a common language is only superficial. The nations have developed into immense conglomerations in which—besides other diseases—industry rages; the inventive spirit, unbridled, uncontrolled, absorbing absolutely everything, has led the mutually dependent European nations to the ideal of the inner-spring mattress and toothpaste.
>
> (*AzL* 335)

Döblin here sees the cities as the focus of the restoration of both the old capitalistic, exploitative order and the "partisan wrangling" that prevented the parties of the Left from establishing a new order after the war.

In his next major novel, Döblin was to present a prognosis for the "disease" of industrialism and uncontrolled technology. *Mountains Seas and Giants,* written between 1921 and 1923 and published in 1924, is a fantasy set in the twenty-third to twenty-fifth centuries A.D. Humanity, organized into supranational regions and city-states, perfects its technological mastery of the natural world. Hunger is abolished, for example, through the artificial synthesis of food. The hubris of the technocrats, however, leads them to attempt the deglaciation of Greenland in order to gain new land. The attempt has terrifying consequences, freeing from the glacial ice prehistoric monsters which reproduce in frenzied hypertrophy and attack the European continent. In the end, groups of "settlers" are left to begin again under primitive conditions. Nature, supposedly brought under total control by technology, rebels and overwhelms human society.

As Döblin gradually turned away from leftist party politics in the early twenties, bitterly disappointed at the failure of the Weimar state to achieve a genuine renewal of Germany, he evolved instead a new attitude toward the natural world. We have seen that in his earlier works, nature is identified with woman and thus alien and hostile to man. In the Expressionist story "The Murder of a Buttercup," for instance, the central character casually beheads a flower during a forest stroll and is soon obsessed by the idea that he has "murdered" it—or rather, murdered her—for he gives it the name Ellen.

It is by no means the aesthete's appreciation of the surface beauties of nature to which Döblin, the quintessential *homo urbanus,* is now converted. He describes how some ordinary stones picked up on a Baltic beach during a vacation induce a sort of epiphany leading to the composition of *Mountains Seas and Giants:* "The stones on the Baltic shore touched me. For the first time, really for the first time I returned hesitantly—no, unwillingly—to Berlin, the city of houses, machines, human masses to which I was otherwise totally devoted. I felt the desire to stay even longer in the midst of nature, and for once to be surrounded by such things as these" (*AzL* 347). We will see that nature ceases to be associated with women as the realm of emotions. It is now appropriated for intellectual man as part of a dynamic, ordered universe.

The novel *Mountains Seas and Giants* marks the turning point in Döblin's view of nature. It begins with a dedication that connects it specifically to contemporary reality. It is as if Döblin needed this reassurance before his imagination carried him into the distant past or future. *Wang-lun* had been dedicated to the Taoist Liä-Dsi, the preacher of passivity in the face of life's unalterable flux. *Mountains Seas and Giants* is dedicated to the flux itself, in the shape of the "thousand-foot thousand-arm thousand-head" Nature, which now is positively reinterpreted. The narrator plunges into a world alive with dynamic forces, a world in which the cultivated nature of a park on the edge of Berlin forms a seamless continuum with the entire universe:

> I walk on the soft, springy ground at the low-lying end of the Schlach-tensee. Over there the tables chairs of the Old Fisherman's Cottage, haze above the water and the reeds. I'm walking on the floor of the air. En-closed in this moment with myriads of things in this corner of the world. Together we are this world: soft ground, reeds, lake, chairs, tables of the Fisherman's Cottage, carp in the water, gnats above it, birds in the gar-dens of the villas of Zehlendorf, cuckoo's call, grasses, sand, sunshine, clouds, fishermen, poles, lines, hooks, bait, children singing, warmth, electric tension in the air. How blindingly the sun rages up there. Who is that? What a mass of stars rage beside it; I can't see them.
>
> The dark, rolling, roaring power. You dark, furious, intertwined— you gentle, delightful, unimaginably beautiful, unbearably heavy, un-ceasing powers. Trembling grasping flickering thousand-foot thousand-spirit thousand-head.
>
> *(BMG* 10)

This ecstatic hymn to the natural world, with its characteristic strings of nouns and adjectives, is the declaration of a pantheistic worldview that decisively influences Döblin's production from now on. At the same time that Döblin was withdrawing in disappointment from the cut and slash of party politics in the Weimar Republic,[3] he was turning toward a speculative natural philosophy characterized by an overriding biological metaphor. He bypasses, as it were, the con-crete questions of political power and how it can be controlled and used, by moving into a universal context and rising above politics.

Döblin's new attitude found its most concentrated expression in *The I over Nature* and the important essay of 1924, "Der Geist des naturalistischen Zeitalters" (The Spirit of the Naturalistic Age). It is only seemingly paradoxical that the one represents an act of accep-tance of man's place and purpose in the totality of the universe while the other is a paean to the spirit of the modern industrial age, because now there is no longer any dualism between man and his works on one side and nature on the other. Both are subsumed under the biological metaphor which had come to dominate Döblin's thought. The string of nouns in the dedication to *Mountains Seas and Giants* already estab-lished a continuum from the narrator through inanimate objects and animate nature to the stars and sun.

"The Spirit of the Naturalistic Age," published in the same year as *Mountains Seas and Giants,* belongs in fact more to Döblin's writings on natural philosophy than it does among his essays on literature, where it was placed by Walter Muschg, the first editor of the Selected Works.[4] The essay is clearly a turning point in Döblin's thought.[5] He declares himself without reservation to be in favor of the scientific, technological, and industrial progress of our age, which he chooses to call "naturalistic." He rejects as specious the distinction between profound Germanic "culture" and superficial, Western, democratic "civilization" that Thomas Mann, for one, propagated in his *Betrachtungen eines Unpolitischen* (Observations of an Apolitical Man; 1918). How radically Döblin rejects this distinction can be seen in his positive use of images of the city and capitalistic phenomena like advertising, which only a few years earlier had attracted his scorn. We have seen him in 1921 using the example of toothpaste to mock the supposed achievements of "the inventive spirit." Now he uses the same image for a diametrically opposite purpose: to praise the new spirit and the practical orientation that ignores outdated philosophical problems: "We have respectfully acknowledged the greatness and importance of the old problems and have then turned to the production of toothpaste" (*AzL* 68). Similarly, the unbridled advertising he castigated in 1921 now wins his explicit approval as part of the dynamism of the new age:

> From the standpoint of the old power and way of thinking, there is no greater challenge, nothing so naively shameless as the shops, window displays, department stores of a big city. Any private person is allowed to open a shop or an entire department store and display his products. No censorship is practiced here, as it is in literature and art, although they are much less dangerous because their realm is the conservative one of the spirit. The unpretentious tradesman can decorate his wares, arrange and illuminate them in a suggestive way. One glance shows what is going on here: needs are being met and new needs are being bred. Man is being modified in an intensely practical way. The technical spirit walks the streets, agitating and forming.
>
> (*AzL* 82)

How did Döblin accomplish this apparent about-face in his assessment of the modern, technological world? The very title "The Spirit of the Naturalistic Age" suggests the answer: the new age has a spirit, a spirituality, specific to it, just as did the preceding scholastic-humanistic age. The spirit of the naturalistic age is as yet in its infancy, difficult to discern, but undoubtedly there. We stand, writes Döblin, only at the beginning of the new age, whose roots lie in the first precise observations of nature in the Renaissance, and which emerged fully with the birth of modern technology in the mid nineteenth century. As yet, the new epoch manifests itself only technologically ("The spiritual consequences of Copernicus have not yet been drawn"; *AzL* 83), and even its chief representatives think of it as materialistic and still revere the old values: "One encounters very capable fathers abashed by their piano-playing daughters. Three measures of Schumann make them red with embarrassment" (*AzL* 67).[6] But the inchoate ethics of the new age are already discernible. They are founded on the collective nature of its achievements and will be "grandly social and friendly" (*AzL* 83).

The most striking thing about this essay is that the biological metaphor prevails throughout. Its effect is to distance us from specific social problems by seeing them as part of a larger, natural process. The motive force behind the naturalistic age, for instance, is defined as the "social drive" (*Gesellschaftstrieb*), which in the realm of both natural history and social history "makes use of the small groupings it has formed at earlier, lower levels as material for larger and larger groupings" (*AzL* 64). The formation of nations and cultures is seen biologically as "attempts at variation, at the formation of new human types" (*AzL* 65). Both industrial capitalism and imperialism are now explained as expressions of the related "drive for expansion" (*Ausdehnungstrieb; AzL* 74). As late as 1923, in an essay on Heine's modern relevance, Döblin had attacked imperialism as "a terrible spirit of expansion, an empty drive for purely spatial increase" and showed its direct connection to the capitalistic "drive to cull, snatch, absorb" (*Klaub-Raff-Saugtrieb; AzL* 278). Yet in "The Spirit of the Naturalistic Age," he writes: "The urge to enlarge, to expand, is an expression of the naturalistic spirit." To be sure, he admits that this impulse is as yet impure, still mixed with a local, "rural" patriotism left over from the previous age. A purely naturalistic imperialism would be "peaceful and supranational" (*AzL* 75) in keeping with the nature of technology, presumably an economic and scientific rather than a military imperialism. "Under these circumstances," however, "it is basically inevitable that gigantic wars will burst forth from the epoch of the young naturalistic-technological spirit" (*AzL* 75–76).

The biological metaphor simultaneously annuls Döblin's earlier understanding of imperialism as an outgrowth of capitalism and allows him to accept imperialistic war as inevitable. It also allows him to praise the young Soviet Union in the very next paragraph as the country most profoundly influenced by the naturalistic spirit.[7] He clearly sees that the Soviets worship technology as much as the capitalists do: "The real enemy of this revolution is not the bourgeois. The capitalist and the Soviets have a common enemy, the antinaturalist, antitechnologist, the humanist: Tolstoy" (*AzL* 76).

Although Döblin recognizes nationalism and racism (which he subsumes under the generic term "the rural") as a countercurrent to the stream of naturalism, he misjudges their danger, categorizing them under the overriding biological metaphor as vestiges of an older organism: "The ancient words 'race' and 'blood' concern the inhabitant of the metropolis. They are, to be sure, something different than a soap factory and a locomotive, but they have their own specific life, take part in the differentiation within the social animal, and are characteristic of that in him which is not yet completely fermented, an older stratum" (*AzL* 81).

In this essay the metropolis achieves an apotheosis as the natural home of the "social animal" man in the naturalistic age.[8] The technological achievements of this age are collective achievements and need the metropolis in order to flourish. This is exactly what the old, individualistic, humanistic spirit hates about the cities: "The new spirit makes of the cities its body and instrument. That is why the cities, and especially the big cities, are objects of Romantic antipathy" (*AzL* 71). Man within the great cities is above all collective man: "Everywhere there exists the battle between the whole individual man and the drive of the group to make him into the carrier of a certain function" (*AzL* 73). Again, the biological metaphor allows Döblin to reinterpret this otherwise depressing development into a positive phenomenon: "Only the collective being Man as a whole represents the superior species Man" (*AzL* 73). The parallel to the social animals suggests itself: "Cities stand in the same line of development as caves, beehives, termite nests" (*AzL* 71). In a summation of the importance of the city, Döblin harks back to the coral colony metaphor he first used in *Wadzek:*

> The cities are the principal home and seat of the human group. They are the coral colony for Man, the collective being. Is there any sense in opposing the country and the city?[9] One can find weaknesses and dangers in the cities, can take sides in the battle of instincts at work in the cities. But one cannot reject or even evaluate the cities themselves, the foci of the social instinct. One can only confirm the existence of such forces of nature and their manifestations.
>
> (*AzL* 74)

In *Wadzek*, the image of the coral colony expressed the uncontrolled growth of the physical city and emphasized its alienation from the hero. Here, the image has been both humanized and absolutized. The growth of the modern city is a product of collective human endeavor, but also a "force of nature" beyond the control of the individual.

Because of its utopianism, its ruthless attack on the humanistic spirit, and its suggestion of approval for the idea of the sacrifice of the individual for the good of society, "The Spirit of the Naturalistic Age" is a deeply ambiguous essay. By the late twenties, Döblin had managed in *The I over Nature* to reach a purely speculative solution to the activity/passivity dilemma that characterized his early works and thus to formulate a new conception of the individual as integrated into and important for the world. The same pantheistic and biological thinking in the essay "The Spirit of the Naturalistic Age" leads to a positive, optimistic, utopian reinterpretation of technology and the modern city, now manifestations of an overriding life force. While still presumably critical of capitalism, Döblin now accepts imperialism, war, and needs artificially induced by unbridled advertising as "natural" developments.

The influence of these philosophical positions on Döblin's imaginative writing is evident in the essay "Der Bau des epischen Werkes" (The Structure of the Epic Work). Written during work on *Berlin Alexanderplatz* and originally delivered as a lecture at the University of Berlin, it bears directly on Döblin's greatest novel. Two new elements especially reflect the change from the Berlin Program of 1913. First, the epic demands "exemplary actions and figures" of the sort created by Homer, Cervantes, and Dante (models, along with Charles de Coster, to whom Döblin again and again appeals in his essays on fiction): "There one finds powerful basic situations, elementary situations of human existence, being worked out" (*AzL* 106). Strengthened by the convictions he had reached in *The I over Nature*, Döblin now defines this exemplary sphere as a "suprareality" (*Überrealität, AzL* 103) above and beyond the realities of everyday life.

From this premise follows logically the second new element in Döblin's narrative theory, namely the reintroduction of an authorial narrator: "Is the author allowed to have his say in an epic work? May he jump into this world? Answer: yes, he may and he should and he must" (*AzL* 114). He now casts off the "iron curtain" (*AzL* 113) of pure, objective narration which he had demanded in the Berlin Program, but retains the basic avant-garde, antitraditionalist impulse as well as his lifelong formal eclecticism: "The epic work is not a rigid form. It must be constantly developed like drama, and specifically in constant opposition to tradition and its representatives" (*AzL* 113). Under the same rubric of narrative freedom, he argues for the formal pluralism within the individual work that characterizes *Berlin Alexanderplatz:* "Authors will wring their hands in dismay when I advise them to be decisively lyrical, dramatic, even reflective in their epic work" (*AzL* 113).

As for the form of the work of fiction, Döblin continues and amplifies his distinction between the novel and the epic. In contrast to the novelist, the epic author never begins with a predetermined plot, but rather with a half-formed idea, "*in statu nascendi*"—again the birth metaphor: "One works his way toward the theme by writing. *Thus the reader experiences the production process along with the author*" (*AzL* 123, emphasis in original). Moreover, the epic is by nature infinitely extendable, an open form. Here Döblin adduces as evidence the episodic structure of Cervantes: "Again and again, Don Quixote battles against new kinds of windmills, and that is enough for Cervantes, and so it is simply stuck on and purely fortuitous that Don Quixote also happens to die" (*AzL* 125).

In its advocacy of the exemplary hero, the authorial narrator, and open form, "The Structure of the Epic Work" is the theoretical reflection of Döblin's work on *Berlin Alexanderplatz.*

□

Franz Biberkopf, the central character of *Berlin Alexanderplatz,* represents a departure from Döblin's earlier novels. From *The Black Curtain* to the verse epic *Manas* (1927), his heroes had been exemplary in the traditional sense of having inherent importance as either intellectuals (Johannes in *The Black Curtain*), great leaders of historical mass movements (Wang-lun, Wallenstein), technocrats (Wadzek, Marduk in *Mountains Seas and Giants*), or mythic heroes (Manas). Indeed, these earlier heroes often have something superhuman about them.[10] Franz Biberkopf is a more realistic hero than any of these predecessors. Sociologically and intellectually, he harks back to figures from Döblin's shorter prose, figures like Bertha in "Modern" or the Nasskes in "On Heavenly Mercy."[11]

Unlike the latter, however, Biberkopf is more than just a random victim of modern industrial society. He is an Everyman in the new, ahistorical sense outlined in "The Structure of the Epic Work." The narrator emphasizes his importance in one of the street-ballad passages which introduce each book of the novel: "But this is no ordinary man, this Franz Biberkopf. I did not call him here for sport, but to experience his hard, true, and enlightening existence" (*BA* 47, *EJ* 49).[12] Biberkopf's importance is not inherent, but lies in the fact that the narrator has chosen him, "called him here," in order to demonstrate those "elementary situations of human existence" mentioned in "The Structure of the Epic Work." The narrator openly announces his active participation in the work. Exemplary hero and active narrator go hand-in-hand in the service of enlightenment. The story of Biberkopf's life has a didactic function both for him and for the reader, and in the course of the novel, the narrator will speak freely to both of them.

However, Biberkopf is exemplary in a universal, not a social or political sense. He is an erstwhile laborer and pimp who, after serving four years in prison for the manslaughter of his girlfriend Ida in a fit of jealousy, is released at the beginning of the novel to try to begin his life again. Döblin from the beginning isolates him sociologically and forestalls any interpretation of him as a typical proletarian. He said as much in answer to a newspaper poll of writers conducted in 1928 or 1929: "I am interested in the social problem of people who, for one reason or another, have been torn from their own inner sphere and cannot easily join another class, the problem of people who stand 'between the classes'" (*SLW* 180). In fact, we shall see that Biberkopf is at pains to divorce himself from any solidarity with working people, whether they be socialist, communist, or anarchist.

The plot of *Berlin Alexanderplatz,* that is, the story of Franz Biberkopf, is simply told. It has the straightforward, banal quality of "On Heavenly Mercy."[13] Biberkopf is released from prison at the beginning of the novel, determined to lead a "decent" life. The novel is articulated by three increasingly severe disasters that bring this attempt to naught. With book 1 functioning as a prelude, the remaining eight books of the novel fall naturally into four groups of two. In books 2 and 3, Biberkopf first works at various occasional jobs—street vendor, peddler of Nazi newspapers—before becoming a door-to-door salesman of shoelaces with the uncle of his new girlfriend Lina. When he boasts to this uncle, Otto Lüders, about his sexual conquest of a young widow during his rounds, Lüders himself goes to the woman and robs and threatens her. When Franz finds out about Lüders' betrayal of his confidence, he sinks into exaggerated despair at the existence of such duplicity in a world in which he is trying to be decent.

In books 4 and 5, Franz goes into hiding from his friends and begins a drinking binge that lasts several weeks. He recovers enough to walk the streets again, and his friend Meck introduces him to a circle of shady characters whom Franz takes at their word to be fruit dealers. Actually, they are a burglary ring, the Pums gang. Franz is especially drawn to one member of the gang, Reinhold. A sickly-looking stutterer who cannot stand alcohol, Reinhold nevertheless exerts a magnetic fascination on women and on Biberkopf. The two men enter into a pact in which Biberkopf agrees to take over Reinhold's girlfriends as he becomes tired of them. Biberkopf soon decides, however, that this "spirited white slavery" (*BA* 193, *EJ* 235) is indecent, and he tries to cure Reinhold by revealing his habits to his newest girlfriend. When Biberkopf unwittingly gets involved in one of the gang's burglaries, Reinhold takes the opportunity to avenge himself by throwing Biberkopf from the speeding getaway car into the path of a following automobile. Franz loses his right arm as a result.

In books 6 and 7, he slowly recovers from the accident. In his "Third Conquest of Berlin" (*BA* 261, *EJ* 324), he reestablishes contact with his old friends Herbert and Eva, whom he had avoided up to now because of their criminal activities (Herbert is a pimp, Eva a high-class prostitute, a former lover of Franz's and now Herbert's girlfriend). In a world which has battered him twice, Biberkopf abandons the attempt to be decent, but not the delusion that he can survive by his own strength: "But Franz Biberkopf goes through the streets, jogging along in his own little way. He does not give in, and asks for nothing more than to get really well again and strong in his muscles" (*BA* 260, *EJ* 322–23). He begins to fence stolen goods for a new friend named Willi. When Eva introduces him to a young girl from the provinces, he allows her to become a prostitute for him, and thus returns to the life of a pimp and petty criminal which he had led before his prison term.

This girl Mieze, an embodiment of purity and self-sacrifice, becomes the great love of Biberkopf's life, yet he is still not satisfied. In a self-imposed test of his own power and courage, he again approaches Reinhold and begins to commit burglaries with the Pums gang. He boasts to Reinhold of Mieze's love for him and agrees to conceal Reinhold in his apartment so that he can witness her devotion.[14] But instead, a terrible fight develops between the lovers in which Biberkopf almost kills Mieze, as he had killed Ida. Reinhold conceives the idea of taking full revenge on Biberkopf through Mieze. He lures her into the woods outside Berlin, tries to rape her, and then kills her.

In the final two books, Biberkopf is arrested for Mieze's murder. He goes into a catatonic stupor and is interned in the prison hospital in Buch, on the edge of the city. During his catatonia, he has a vision of death, in the course of which he recognizes his own guilt and hubris. He is then resurrected as a new man. At the end of the novel, exonerated of the murder, he finds a job as gatekeeper in a "medium-sized factory" (*BA* 499, EJ 632). He faces the future with a new caution and sense of reality, but also with the determination to stand in solidarity with his fellow men.

□

The story of Franz Biberkopf summarized above conveys at best an inadequate impression of the novel, for this is a work that owes its fascination and greatness primarily to the way it is told. We have seen that Döblin's affinity for the montage technique is evident even in his earliest attempts at prose.[15] In "Modern," both the interweaving of essay and narrative and, even more, the details of narrative technique such as the incorporation of counter-voices and the suppression of narrative comment, presage Döblin's future development. In the story "On Heavenly Mercy," the introduction of the goldfinch's song and the lyrical metaphor for death into an otherwise fiercely naturalistic narrative serve primarily to shock the reader with a sudden, unmediated intimation of other layers behind the bleak narrative foreground. These other layers, however, do not significantly modify that foreground, they only shake our faith in its absoluteness.

Armed with the new narrative freedom proclaimed in "The Structure of the Epic Work," Döblin in *Berlin Alexanderplatz* makes montage the central technique of his narrator. Montage is on the one hand the aesthetic technique adequate to the city theme that permeates the novel. The life of an industrial metropolis resists description as a "linear, discursive process."[16] On the other hand, the montage technique not only dominates the presentation of milieu in the novel, but also of character and action. In order to see just how remarkable this accomplishment is, let us examine the city as it is presented in montage.

Döblin had intended to call his work simply *Berlin Alexanderplatz.* His publisher Samuel Fischer, concerned for clarity and certainly also for sales, urged the inclusion of the subtitle "The Story of Franz Biberkopf" (*AzL* 390). The simplicity of the original title emphasizes the importance of the city itself for the novel, an importance which far transcends the role of a mere setting for the hero's story. The title *Berlin Alexanderplatz* implies that place, the exclusively urban space of the novel, is just as important as character, the traditionally central concern of the bourgeois novel. At the very least one can say that in this novel, with more success than in perhaps any other, the modern metropolis comes alive and asserts its uniqueness.[17] We cannot conceive of the story of Franz Biberkopf without the Alexanderplatz, while the reverse is not the case. Throughout the novel, Döblin is at pains to demonstrate that Biberkopf's story, although exemplary, is merely one of many within the city. The frequent encapsulated narratives are all potential novels, whether they be several pages in length or only one sentence: "In a little hotel over there in that dark street two lovers shot themselves early yesterday morning, a waiter from Dresden and a married woman, both of whom, however, had registered under false names" (*BA* 53, *EJ* 55). Most of these novels *in ovo* surface only to disappear immediately, and have only an indirect, comparative relation to Biberkopf's story. What relates them to it and to each other is primarily the space in which they occur, "Berlin, Center and East" (*BA* 209, *EJ* 257).[18] It is the city itself which makes these parallel narratives plausible.

The formal introduction of the city as a component of central importance occurs in the first chapter of book 2. Book 1 already takes us into Berlin—its first chapter is entitled "On Car 41 into Town" (*BA* 13, *EJ* 4)—but it is a city radically distorted by the perspective of a convict freshly released from prison.[19] Biberkopf's acute anxiety at being freed finds expression in the apparently paradoxical assertion, "The punishment begins" (*BA* 13, *EJ* 4), and in the chaotic flood of images that assaults him as he rides the streetcar into the city (*BA* 13–14, *EJ* 4–6). His desperate wish is to flee back to the completely prescribed life of a prisoner. Döblin's virtuoso use of montage to reveal psychology is already evident here, when he juxtaposes Biberkopf's search for a hiding place and his need to manage his own time with the official prison regulations concerning the inmates' time and space:

He thought, this street is darker, it's probably better where it's darker. The prisoners are put in isolation cells, solitary confinement and general confinement. In solitary confinement the prisoner is kept apart from the others night and day. In isolation cells the prisoner is placed in a cell, but during his walks in the open air, during instruction or religious service, he is put in company with the others. . . . I'm really a big duffer, a fellow ought to be able to traipse his way through hereabouts, five minutes, ten minutes, then drink a cognac and sit down. When the given signal rings, work must begin immediately. It can only be interrupted at the time set aside for eating, walking, and instruction. During the walk the prisoners must hold their arms stiff and swing them back and forth.

(*BA* 14–15, EJ 6–7)

Biberkopf's terror at being plunged back into the city causes a radical distortion in his perception: the crowds of people surrounding him seem lifeless, like the mannequins he notices in a store window, so lifeless that they are referred to collectively with the neuter singular pronoun:

Wax figures stood in the show-windows, in suits, overcoats, with skirts, with shoes and stockings. Outside everything was moving, but—back of it—there was nothing! It—did not—live! It had happy faces, it laughed, waited in twos and threes on the traffic islands opposite Aschinger's, smoked cigarettes, turned the pages of newspapers. Thus it stood there like the street-lamps—and—became more and more rigid. They belonged with the houses, everything white, everything wooden.

(*BA* 14, EJ 5–6)

Conversely, inanimate objects spring threateningly to life by virtue of the dynamic verbs which accompany them: "The cars roared and jangled on, house fronts were rolling along one after the other without stopping. And there were roofs on the houses, they soared atop the houses, his eyes wandered straight upward: if only the roofs don't slide off, but the houses stood upright" (*BA* 15, EJ 7).

Thus it is Biberkopf's overwhelming ochlophobia and agoraphobia which define the city and set the tone in book 1. The hallucination that the roofs are slipping off the buildings—the symbolic expression of his fear of total chaos—will recur throughout the novel when he thinks back on this first crisis (*BA* 99–100, 126, 140, 246, 250, 277, 492–93; EJ 117, 150, 165–66, 304, 309, 345, 624). Although he has physically arrived in Berlin, he is "Still Not There" (*BA* 17, EJ 10), as the title of the second chapter avows, because he cannot yet draw the line between himself and his surroundings. He is not yet capable of perceiving the city objectively. Book 1 thus concerns the preconditions for his psychological reentry into Berlin: first, the reestablishment of his identity with the help of some Jews who befriend the terror-stricken man,[20] and second, the compulsive reassertion of his masculinity through the rape of Minna, the sister of the girl he has murdered. The preliminary character of book 1 is also attested to by the fact that it is the only book whose primary tense is the traditional narrative preterite, rather than the present which the narrator otherwise prefers.[21]

Having brought Biberkopf from Tegel to Berlin, from the edge of paranoia to "normalcy," Döblin is ready to introduce the city as an autonomous component of equal importance to the hero. At this point, the beginning of book 2, the technique of montage takes full command of the narrative. To be sure, montage occurs throughout the novel. We have already cited an example from book 1, and one can find others on almost every page. The technique predominates, however, in those chapters that concentrate on Berlin itself and mention Biberkopf either only in passing or not at all. The importance of such chapters to Döblin's overall conception is evident in their placement: four of the novel's nine books (2, 4, 5, and 7) begin with such chapters. In addition, book 8, while it does not begin with an urban montage, ends its first chapter with a montage passage (*BA* 397–400, *EJ* 500–503).

Montage is, of course, a term borrowed from film, and although Döblin does not use the term himself in his essays on novelistic theory,[22] he does acknowledge repeatedly his debt to film. We have seen him advocating a *Kinostil* in the Berlin Program, sixteen years before *Berlin Alexanderplatz*. In his review of Joyce's *Ulysses*, written while he was at work on *Berlin Alexanderplatz*, he assesses both film and the daily press as a challenge to the traditional novel: "The movies have invaded the territory of literature; newspapers have grown powerful, are the most important and widespread form of the written word, the daily bread of all men" (*AzL* 288). Finally, in "The Structure of the Epic Work," Döblin welcomes the recent use of film, or "picture narration" (*Bilderzählung*), in the live theater, as one means of breaking down the barriers between stage and audience (*AzL* 113). While he does not mention Piscator or Brecht in "The Structure of the Epic Work," it has been demonstrated convincingly by Dietrich Scheunemann that cross-genre influences were of great importance to Döblin at this point in his life. It is also to Scheunemann's credit that he directs attention to a specific film, Walther Ruttmann's 1927 documentary "Berlin, the Symphony of a Great City," which used montage to convey the hectic and many-layered life of Berlin and likely had an influence on Döblin's novel.[23]

It was Walter Benjamin who first explicitly used the term montage to characterize the style of *Berlin Alexanderplatz*. In his 1930 review of the novel,[24] Benjamin not only identifies the technique, but sees in it the key to Döblin's attempt to reestablish the old connection between the epic artist and his public: "The material of the montage is, after all, by no means random. Genuine montage is based on documents." The technique of montage, according to Benjamin, thus lends the epic work both authenticity and authority. It is a formal technique which anchors the work in the life of the people and as such fulfills the same function as "the formulaic verses of the old epic." Both Benjamin and Scheunemann stress that the use of montage does not mean the elimination or even the weakening of the narrator: "Epic means both the open, basically unending series of independent images which, taken singly, are unmotivated, and at the same time the appearance of a narrator who is organizing the narrative, expressing opinions, and informing the reader about the purpose and goal of his undertaking."[25] But even in the full-dress urban montages, where the narrator's role is limited to that of monteur, there are indirect ways in which narrative opinion is conveyed. Let us examine the first such montage, in chapter 1 of book 2, in its dual function as documentation of and judgment upon the city.[26]

The hero himself appears only in the title of the chapter, "Franz Biberkopf Enters Berlin" (*Franz Biberkopf betritt Berlin;* BA 49, EJ 50). The transitive verb suggests his newly won integrity and mastery of his environment, with the alliteration providing mock solemnity. The first book of the novel presented Berlin from Biberkopf's radically limited perspective. Now the city appears *in propria persona*, in a montage of aural and visual images gathered around the Rosenthaler Platz.

While the montage is, by its very nature, composed of extremely heterogeneous elements, their grouping in this chapter, although it may initially seem to reflect nothing more than the jumble of impressions which confront one in the midst of a busy city, is not simply

fortuitous. The chapter has several organizing principles. First, it progresses temporally from daytime (the bustle of activity on the Rosenthaler Platz, *BA* 51–54, EJ 53–57) to late afternoon (the conversation
between Krause and Georg, *BA* 54–58, EJ 57–61) to evening (the
tryst between the young girl and her older lover, *BA* 58–59, EJ 61–
63). By the end, the reader has the impression of having spent a day in
the vicinity of the Rosenthaler Platz. This "day in the life of the city" is
also the structure of the film "Berlin, the Symphony of a Great City."[27]
Second, the chapter is spatially focused on the Rosenthaler Platz in the
East End of Berlin. The stops on the trolley line 68 are listed, from
north to east, with the Rosenthaler Platz in the middle and ending, significantly, with the Herzberge Insane Asylum (*BA* 52, EJ 53). The cen-
trality of the square is reemphasized at the end of the chapter when the
trolley-line device is repeated, this time listing the stops on line 99 (*BA*
58, EJ 61).[28] The chapter's focus on the square[29] is balanced by the
attention paid to four main streets radiating from it, which are not
simply enumerated, but rather give rise to digressions which document
the diverse activity in this one urban space. Mention of the Brunnenstrasse leads to a lengthy list of the various offices of the AEG, the giant
General Electric Company, located in that street. The Invalidenstrasse
leads toward the Stettiner Station and so to a flurry of fragments of
train-station dialogue, and so on. That the mention of each street is
centrifugal and digressive explains an otherwise inexplicable lack of
grammatic agreement: at the beginning of the list, the narrator uses a
plural verb, anticipating all the streets as compound subject, but gets
led afield by his first street which remains the only formal subject:
"From this square run the wide Brunnenstrasse toward the north, the
A.E.G. runs along its left side in front of the Humboldthain. The A.E.G.
is an immense enterprise, which embraces, according to the 1928 telephone directory. . . ." (*BA* 52–53, EJ 54).[30] This centrifugal tendency,
whose effect is to imply that everything in this space has an equal claim
on our attention and interest, is however kept in check by the space
itself, to which the narrative again and again returns and which is the
space of the whole chapter. The rhythm imitates that of the constantly
arriving and departing streetcars.

The spatial organization of the first chapter of book 2 around a
focal point is matched by the intimation that this moment in 1928 is
also a temporal focal point, with extensions both into the past ("Al-
bert Pangel, master furrier, who may look back upon an activity of

almost thirty years as honorary official"; *BA* 51, *EJ* 52) and into the future. The narrator, become suddenly prescient, switches to the future tense to inform us that the boy Max Rüst, just now boarding the Number 4 streetcar, will later become a sheetmetal worker, have seven children, become a partner in the roofing firm of Hallis and Co., win a quarter jackpot in the Prussian lottery at 52, retire, and die at 55 during a settlement suit against his former employer. The narrator then goes on to quote the texts of Rüst's obituary and the letter of thanks sent out by his survivors (*BA* 54, *EJ* 56).

The most important organizing principle of the chapter, however, is variation in the role of the narrator-monteur himself, for here, as in the entire novel, the narrative voice is itself montagelike: not a constant preterite presence with a firmly established vantage point, but a compound voice, a series of contrasting attitudes, a prismatically broken point of view in keeping with Döblin's injunction in "The Structure of the Epic Work" to be "decisively lyrical, dramatic, even reflective." Looked at in this light, the chapter falls naturally into three sections which we shall examine one by one.

Probably the most aggressively avant-garde pages of the novel are those which open this chapter (*BA* 49–50, *EJ* 50–51). Döblin has found the simplest possible way to eliminate the narrator altogether— he has abandoned linguistic for graphic representation; here, the reader encounters a series of eleven emblems reproduced on the page. To be precise, only the first emblem, the bear and chevron of Berlin's coat of arms, eliminates language completely. With this one image Döblin evokes the city in its entirety, lending heraldic ornament to the mock solemnity of the alliteration in "Franz Biberkopf betritt Berlin" and anticipating in abstract the chapter and the novel to come.

The ten emblems which follow are akin to the emblemata of the Renaissance. That is, the pictures themselves, signifying various municipal departments,[31] are accompanied by explanatory mottos: next to the Red Cross flag are the words "Health Department" and so on. As in the emblemata, the relationship of picture to motto is completely univalent, while the text of the chapter that follows is a sort of *explicatio* adding complexity to the straightforward graphic representation. The immediate effect of this column of pictographs is to introduce the functional complexity of the metropolis as an orderly whole.[32] This complexity and the logos which suggest it have a high degree of independence from the novel defined as "The Story of Franz Biberkopf."

There are clearly connections between some of the emblems and Biberkopf's story, not so much with its plot as with some of its leit-motivic imagery: "Underground Construction" (picture of a construction ditch), "Traffic" (picture of a streetcar). Others, however, like "Gas Works" or "Finance and Tax Office," have little or no connection and, most interestingly, a municipal department which might immediately suggest itself, the police, is absent. The city is here represented as a set of parts functioning for the most part independently of Franz Biberkopf, although some touch his life.[33]

Following immediately upon the emblems are the texts of three public announcements: a proposal for a change in a house façade, the granting of a hunting license, and the retirement of a welfare commissioner. They resemble the emblems in possessing intrinsic interest and a high degree of independence within the novel.[34] Whereas the list of municipal departments at least pretends to comprehensiveness, these announcements seem to be a fortuitous collection. The reader may supply them with a conjectural context if he chooses—say, physical proximity on a Litfass pillar or in a newspaper[35]—but it is their essence not to need one, and thus not to need a narrator. We are all familiar with the language and tone of such announcements. We need no more information to interpret them and Döblin supplies none. He writes of his fascination for such self-explanatory data in "The Structure of the Epic Work": "In the course of writing one historical book or another, it has happened that I could hardly restrain myself from simply copying entire documents. Indeed, I sometimes sank down among the documents and said to myself, I can't improve on these" (*AzL* 114). In the passage under consideration, the announcement of the granting of a hunting license is just such an authentic "document," extracted from the official gazette of Berlin-Weissensee of January 1928 and pasted into the manuscript of the novel with only the names changed and a few dates crossed out in pencil.[36] This first section is in the strictest sense documentary.

Following this objective, narratorless introduction to the city, the second section displays a narrator actively involved in the text in several ways. This central section is more narrowly organized by the space of the Rosenthaler Platz and begins with the reflexive, impersonal construction, *Der Rosenthaler Platz unterhält sich* (*BA* 51, *EJ* 53). Eugene Jolas translates this as "The Rosenthaler Platz is busily active," but a more literal translation is "The Rosenthaler Platz amuses itself." The city itself now joins Biberkopf as an important "character" in the novel, and the sentence encompasses all activity on the square: human, mechanical, and meteorologic. It is not dehumanizing, but simply impersonal, and the verb itself is undeniably positive, suggesting both enjoyment and self-sufficiency.

At first, the narrator restricts himself to simple, declarative sentences. We have already mentioned an example: "Car No. 68 runs across Rosenthaler Platz, Wittenau, Nordbahnhof, Heilanstalt, Weddingplatz, Stettiner Station, Rosenthaler Platz, Alexanderplatz, Straussberger Platz, Frankfurter Allee Station, Lichtenberg, Herzberge Insane Asylum" (*BA* 52, EJ 53). Primarily, he lets the elements of his montage create the ambience for him: a weather forecast for Berlin and surroundings, a list of streetcar stops, instructions to streetcar passengers, the list of telephone extensions for the AEG, fragments of advertising copy. As the section proceeds, we encounter for the first time an actual narrative in very simple form, precipitated by an element in the montage:

> . . . getting off or on while the car is in motion may lead to fatal accidents.
> In the middle of the Rosenthaler Platz a man with two yellow packages jumps off from the 41, an empty taxi glides just past him, the copper looks at him, a streetcar inspector appears, cop and inspector shake hands: damned lucky, that fellow with his packages.
>
> (*BA* 52, EJ 54)

This narrative, in its objectivity and simple grammatical parallelism, is a good example of the *Kinostil*. In the midst of the flow of the montage, the tracking camera halts briefly to record a small scene, and then moves on. It will be seen that throughout this chapter the narrator strictly refrains from the kind of analysis of thought and motive in which the traditional narrator indulges and of which film is incapable. While the narrator can be prescient, as in his knowledge of Max Rüst's future, he is by no means omniscient. Even in his virtuoso flight into Rüst's future, he confines himself to the external, documentable facts of the life: profession, number of children, text of obituary, and so on.[37] With more justification than Isherwood's Herr Issyvoo he could say of himself, "I am a camera."[38]

In the Berlin Program of 1913, as we have seen, Döblin spurns the psychologizing manner and calls for a *Kinostil*. It is important, however, to be clear about what the *Kinostil* entails. Fritz Martini repeatedly speaks of Döblin's debt to film, but has a very one-sided conception of film's influence on the novel, identifying it as "that hypnotizing flow of images and scenes, the breathless activity, the shifting interpenetration of outer and inner action, which in its most compact unity allows no division into layers."[39] Yet in the same essay, Martini himself quotes Döblin's dictum, "In the novel one must layer, pile up, turn over, shove." And in the next sentence Döblin says, "Forward is never the watchword of the novel" (*AzL* 20). Martini overlooks the fact that film can be analytic as well as hypnotic, calm as well as *à bout de souffle,* and that "the shifting interpenetration of outer and inner action" is a specifically literary technique impossible, for the most part, in film, unless a film adopt a literary device like the off-camera narrative voice in Truffaut's *Jules et Jim* or Rainer Werner Fassbinder's *Berlin Alexanderplatz.* The *Kinostil* is in the end only a metaphor useful to describe the peculiarities of Döblin's style.[40]

The middle section of the chapter, a sort of sustained tracking shot around the Rosenthaler Platz, ends with Max Rüst and three other personages boarding the Number 4 streetcar. The brief glimpse into these lives forms the transition to the third and final section of the chapter, a more intense look at two sets of individual figures. Even in these two longer scenes—the first a conversation between an old morphine addict and a younger man who has just lost his job, the second between a young girl and her older lover[41]—the reader does not gain any privileged insight into the characters. In fact, the narrator is here less a narrator than a playwright, for these scenes are dramatic dialogues, with the narrative voice restricted to stage direction:[42] "Small café on Rosenthaler Platz. In front they are playing billiards, in the back, in a corner, two men sit puffing and smoking and drinking tea. One of them has a flabby face and gray hair, he is sitting with his raglan on: 'Well, shoot. But keep still, don't fidget around like that'" (*BA* 54–55, EJ 57).

We have seen that the urban montage which opens book 2 of *Berlin Alexanderplatz* has three sections, the first characterized by documentary style and absence of narrator, the second by cinematographic style and narrator as monteur, and the third by dramatic style with narration restricted to stage directions.[43] In none of these sections do we get the guidance and reassurance of a traditional novelistic narrator introducing the setting for his story. Döblin has consciously excluded such a narrator in the conviction that the experience of a city must be presented in a more dynamic and objective way. There are nevertheless some guiding principles at work here by means of which Döblin indirectly suggests his point of view toward the metropolis. Most significantly, there is a movement from the impersonal to the personal. We have noted, for instance, that the middle section begins with the impersonal construction *Der Rosenthaler Platz unterhält sich*. Next comes a weather forecast placed here precisely because there is nothing so irrespective of person as the weather. Next comes the list of stops for the 68 streetcar—again valid for everyone—then the first actual mention of people in the fare schedule for the streetcar: "Fares for adults are 20 pfennigs, for schoolchildren 10 pfennigs, reduced fares allowed for children up to the age of 14, apprentices and pupils, poor students, war cripples, persons physically unfit for walking as certified by the district charity offices" (*BA* 52, *EJ* 53). Here people are classified purely with respect to the means of transportation, by the external categories of age, profession, and physical condition. Not until the brief narration of the near-accident quoted above do we arrive at an individual case and hear an individual voice. This contrast between the impersonal language of information, regulation, and advertisement on the one hand, and individual human voices and narratives about individuals on the other continues throughout the montage, moving gradually toward the closing focus and hold on Max Rüst.

Like the central montage, the chapter as a whole obviously moves from the impersonal to the personal. It begins with the narratorless emblems of municipal departments and public announcements, both of which portray the city as a functional collective. The central montage, as we have seen, gives us several glimpses of anonymous individuals—the man with the yellow packages, the waiter from Dresden, travelers at the Stettiner Bahnhof, five workers paving the sidewalk in front of the bank in the Elsasser Strasse—before naming the four people boarding the Number 4 car. The final section presents individual, differentiated lives with the immediacy of drama.

This movement from impersonal to personal implicitly conveys a certain attitude toward the phenomenon of the city, an attitude as complex as the chapter itself. We have already noted that the view of Berlin at the beginning of book 1 is a view of chaos from the subjective perspective of the newly free Biberkopf. The chapter under discussion serves to correct that view. The city is presented initially, in its own officially promulgated terms, as an orderly and well functioning set of departments, although the casual omission of precisely the police department, whose function is ostensibly to protect the community against disorder, and which plays an important role at the end of the novel, looks suspiciously like an attempt to make things appear more orderly than they really are. The three announcements which follow particularize the sense of order; they illustrate the city functioning according to established laws and customs. There are elements in the central montage which have the same effect: the list of streetcar stops, of AEG departments, of regulations for the public transportation system.[44] On the whole, it seems a well ordered complexity. Yet as the chapter begins to focus on individuals, the impression of lawfulness and order is undercut. The individuals appearing in the chapter counterpose a negative to the positive image of the city presented in the emblems, comprising a spectrum ranging from banal disorder to death. We are shown a near-accident, a double suicide, a woman with an umbilical hernia, the petty exploitation of a coachman by his boss, and a fourteen-year-old stutterer on his way to the "clinic for the defective in speech, the hard of hearing, the weak-visioned, the weak-minded, the incorrigible" (*Beratungsstelle für Sprachkranke, Schwerhörige, Sehschwache, Schwachbegabte, Schwererziehbare; BA* 54, EJ 57). The institutional name, with its insistent repetition of the syllables *schwach* (weak) and *schwer* (difficult) and its mixture of physical, mental, and social complaints is a kind of litany of human affliction.

This impression of unhappiness and suffering within the city is then carried forward and elaborated by the two dramatic dialogues of the chapter's final section. The clerk Georg recounts his firing to the unsympathetic addict Krause, anticipating similar barroom discussions of politics and unemployment later in the novel. Then we see a "young girl" (*BA* 58, EJ 61), a piano student, secretly meeting her leering older lover. This tryst also has anticipatory force. It is characteristic of the relation between the sexes throughout the novel—and specifically in the case of Biberkopf—that women are exploited by men: as prostitutes earning money for their boyfriends, as sexual objects to be used and discarded, as convenient outlets for physical violence. Here the exploitation is more subtle and must be read between the lines. It is visible in the difference in their ages, her naiveté and his cynical hypocrisy, and the second-person forms they respectively employ: he uses the familiar *du* while she addresses him with the formal *Sie*. The mood is reminiscent of Arthur Schnitzler's "Liebelei," a *fin-de-siècle* drama of dalliance that ends in tragedy.

The city, then, so bravely marshalled under the various insignia of the first section, is shown by the end of the chapter to be a place of disorder, danger, suffering, and even death. The narrator does not state this directly, but merely suggests it by his arrangement of the montage elements and the human situations he chooses to show us. Yet in spite of this gloomy summary there is a seemingly paradoxical yet undeniable celebration of the multiplicity of the city in the sheer exuberance of presentation.

Although the narrator refrains from explicit judgment of the city, there is evidence that Krause, the morphine addict in the third section of the chapter, speaks for the narrator on both the city and man's place in it.[45] In his physical appearance ("flabby face"), his cynicism, *Schadenfreude,* and unrepentant degradation, Krause is undoubtedly an unattractive figure. But as a former secondary school teacher, he is one of the few well-educated characters anywhere in the novel. Döblin, who like Thomas Mann hated the harsh discipline of the Gymnasium as a schoolboy, no doubt took wicked delight in this portrait of the *Oberlehrer* as junky.[46] Nevertheless, Krause's education does allow him to be more articulate about his feelings than, say, a Biberkopf. Moreover, he possesses that quintessential Berlin virtue, wit in the face of life's misery:

> When I didn't find my wife and child at home and there was only a letter, gone to mother in West Prussia and so on, life a failure, a man like me, and the scandal and so on and so forth, I slit myself here, here on the left arm, looks like attempted suicide, eh? We should never neglect the opportunity to learn something, Georg, I knew Provençal all right but anatomy—I mistook the tendon for the pulse. I don't know much more about it today, but that doesn't matter now, that's all over. In a word: pain and regrets were nonsense, I went on living, the woman also went on living, the child, too. In fact, more kids came on the scene in West Prussia, a brace I think, seems I operated at a distance; we're all alive and healthy.
>
> (*BA* 57, EJ 60–61)

Finally, although this and the following section are formally dramatic, consisting of dialogue with the narrator's contribution limited to stage directions, there is one exception: "The man in the raglan swallows some hot tea, it's good to drink hot tea with sugar and rum, and listen to somebody else yapping. It's cozy here in this place.

'You're not going home today, Georg?'" (*BA* 56 EJ 59). Since here the present is the tense of narration, one can interpret this passage either as narrative comment, *style indirect libre,* or as stream of consciousness. All three techniques are used in the novel, and in the end it makes little difference how one labels this passage. Either the narrator speaks his own opinion or he allows us a direct or indirect peek behind Krause's spoken words into his thoughts, which he does not do in the case of Georg or any other figure in the chapter. In either case, the passage serves, along with Krause's intelligence and wit, to heighten his importance and identify him with the narrator.

But how can anyone, least of all a broken-down morphine addict, be a spokesman for a positive view of a city that seems so inexorably to grind down its inhabitants? At issue in this conversation is not whether injustice, disorder, and unhappiness exist in the world, but how one meets the disorder that is undoubtedly there. The young clerk Georg expresses indignation at his unjust firing: "I'm used to order, and that damned business is rotten from top to bottom" (*BA* 56, EJ 58). His rebellion against disorder has led to his sacking, and now he despairs and can't find the courage to go home and face his pregnant wife with the news. He considers his fate unique: "What do you know about it? . . . Just put yourself in my place" (*BA* 56, EJ 59) and scoffs at the idea that the "wreck" (*BA* 58, EJ 61) Krause could understand.

Krause responds not only with evidence that he has had his share of trouble, but with the suggestion that on the basis of his experience he has adopted a new attitude toward the world's disorder: "Just stay here and keep quiet, Georg. Drink a bit, then play some billiards. At any rate, don't let disorder get the upper hand. That's the beginning of the end" (*BA* 57, EJ 60). In rebelling against disorder, Krause implies, Georg is fighting a losing battle. But that does not mean that one must fatalistically surrender to it. On the contrary, one must not "let it get the upper hand." Heroic struggle and fatalistic surrender, exemplified by Georg, emerge again, as they did in *Wadzek's Battle with the Steam Turbine,* as two sides of the same coin, both outmoded posturings. The position reached only at the end of *Wadzek* is thus clearly stated at the beginning of *Berlin Alexanderplatz,* although it will cost Franz Biberkopf an arm, his beloved Mieze, and almost his life to arrive at it.

About his own life Krause says, "I have no regrets. I don't feel any guilt about it, we have to take facts, like ourselves, the way they come. You shouldn't be a big shot about your fate. I'm an enemy of Destiny, I'm not a Greek, I'm a Berliner" (*BA* 57, EJ 60). Not just a German, but specifically a Berliner, for the metropolis with its millions of parallel lives is especially conducive to this attitude which accepts the facts about the world and the self while at the same time rejecting the idea of an inevitable and unique fate. The passage anticipates the extensive comparison of Biberkopf and Orestes at the end of book 2 (*BA* 103– 108, EJ 121–128).[47]

The delicate balance between individuality and the collective, which has given rise to much critical debate about the end of the novel, is already clearly struck in this scene. At the end of the novel, Biberkopf, veteran of the First World War, refuses to be drawn into any future war. He rejects with the last words he utters both what Hans-Peter Bayerdörfer, following Döblin himself, calls the "false collective"[48] of war and the idea of individual fate: "It's no use revering it merely as Fate, we must look at it, grasp it, down it, and not hesitate" (*BA* 501, EJ 634). It is Georg's *Dicketun,* his showing off with his personal fate, that arouses Krause's scorn, and at the end of the conversation, he attacks exactly this pretension in a metaphor that again identifies him with the narrator: "The fly, let's see, it's all in the point of view. A fly stands under the microscope and thinks it's a horse. Just let the fly get in front of my telescope some time!" (*BA* 58, EJ 61).

It is in the context of the city, with its multiplicity of individual lives, that the narrator can develop his own telescopic perspective. At the end of another urban montage, in the first chapter of book 4, the narrator describes floor by floor the lives—some squalid and some merely ordinary—of the inhabitants of a building in the Linienstrasse where Biberkopf has holed up after being betrayed by Lüders. At the very end of the chapter, the narrator forestalls objections to the supposed dreariness and monotony of these lives (and by extension, to his choice of a Biberkopf as hero):

> Wonder what those two get out of life? Well, first of all, they get each other, then last Sunday a vaudeville and a film, then this or that club meeting and a visit to his parents. Nothing else? Well now, don't drop dead, sir. Add to that nice weather, bad weather, country picnics, standing in front of the stove, eating breakfast and so on. And what more do you get, you, captain, general, jockey, whoever you are? Don't fool yourself.
>
> (*BA* 136, EJ 160–61)

With the social leveler Death as his alter ego, the narrator of *Berlin Alexanderplatz* is emphatically egalitarian. It is a summary of the celebration of the city amid its undeniable disadvantages, a peroration to the preceding montage, when Krause declares: "I enjoy the Rosenthaler Platz, I enjoy the cop at the Elsasser corner, I like my game of billiards, I'd like anyone to come and tell me that his life is better than mine" (*BA* 57–58, EJ 61).

□

We have already seen how Döblin's reinterpretation of the city as the "coral colony for man, the collective being" in "The Spirit of the Naturalistic Age" set the stage for the acceptance and celebration of the city. A more personal and self-ironic version of the same message is contained in the autobiographical sketch "First Glance Back," published just a year before *Berlin Alexanderplatz*. It begins with a section entitled "Dialogue in the Münzstrasse" in which Döblin introduces himself in the present, as a public health system doctor in Berlin's East End. At the time Döblin wrote this sketch, he was hard at work on the novel, and so it is not surprising that he presents himself sitting "in a small café on the Alexanderplatz" (*SLW* 108). What he has to say here illuminates the significance of this environment for the novel.

It occurs to him that he would sometimes like to get over to the western part of the city, where there are amenities such as trees, the zoo, the aquarium, and the botanical gardens. This idle thought generates an anonymous figure, a temptation externalized as a Jewish gadfly who immediately begins to needle Döblin with the suggestion that he's out of place here in the proletarian East End, that he really belongs in the West "among people," and that the reason he doesn't leave is simply self-degradation, "Sadism! Towards yourself!" (*SLW* 109). Döblin finds this hysterically funny, but once he has recovered his composure, he rejects decisively the suggestion of his interlocutor. He refers him first to the passing throngs of workers, "nothing but gray, simple people," and asserts that he is one of them: "We are the working folk, the proletariat[49] . . . that is my heart and that is my blood" (*SLW* 109). Döblin in his medical persona, like Krause the addict, rejects the idea of fate—here the psychological fate of his alleged masochism—and asserts the integrity, the logic of the urban life he has chosen, without denying an occasional longing for more pleasant surroundings: "Defects—I've got them like any other decent person. But for the rest, my motto is: this is my home, and I'm doing fine, I'm doing excellently. (Although I'd like to get out to the country, see a tree or a little lake once in a while.) I'm a frog and hop around here quite contentedly. Without sadism and without masochism. I only supply them in novels. I'm a working man and a proletarian" (*SLW* 110).

It is a confirmation of the positive character of the city in the novel when, towards its end, Döblin returns his resurrected hero to the neighborhood of the Alexanderplatz and recapitulates the thematic material related to the interaction of man and city. It is Biberkopf who has changed, not Berlin: "First the Alex. It's still there. . . . And the streetcars are chock-full of people, all of them have something to do, the tickets still cost 20 pfennigs" (*BA* 494–95, *EJ* 626–27). In his afterword to a new printing of the work in 1955, Döblin emphasizes this basic relation between the novel's two main components: "Since Berlin remained what it was, it fell to the punished man to change himself" (*BA* 508). He has changed specifically in his relation to the city. Freshly released from the Buch Asylum, he does not feel the panic that gripped him upon his release from Tegel at the beginning of the novel: "As he gets out at Stettin Station, at the suburban section, and the great Baltikum Hotel greets his eyes, nothing moves—nothing at all. The houses keep still, the roofs lie quiet, he can move securely below them, he need not creep into any dark courtyards" (*BA* 493, *EJ* 624). Biberkopf has been transformed in Buch, and his reentry into the city is, the narrator declares, "a re-encounter, more than a re-encounter" (*BA* 493, *EJ* 624). It is not just that Biberkopf can now encounter the city calmly and without panic. There is something more which contradicts those interpretations that see in the city a demonic chaos against which Biberkopf struggles fruitlessly. The question of whether Döblin intends to present the city as a chaos or as a complexly ordered fabric with both positive and negative aspects—essentially as a metaphor for human life itself—is intimately related to the critical controversy regarding the interpretation of the last chapter and the significance of fate in the novel. In general, those scholars who interpret the city as chaotic also see Biberkopf as a victim of fate and interpret the moral of the last chapter as the obliteration of his individuality and acceptance of his fate.[50] On the other hand, those critics who regard the presentation of the city as a complex fabric with clearly positive aspects also argue for an ending which balances and harmonizes Biberkopf's indi-

viduality ("Reason is the gift of man, jackasses replace it with a clan";
BA 500, EJ 634) and his solidarity with his fellows ("Much unhappiness comes from walking alone"; BA 500, EJ 633).[51]

In the penultimate chapter, the city itself, unchanged throughout
the novel, stands in a new, positive relation to the hero who *has*
changed. Döblin clearly locates the responsibility for progress in the
individual: "He walks around the town. There are many things there
to make a man well, if only his heart keeps well" (BA 494, EJ 626).
There follows a collage of such "things" on the Alexanderplatz, including some of the leitmotivic images that earlier in the novel con-
noted the threat of dark, subterranean powers: the steam pile driver,
the foundations of the demolished Hahn Department Store, the warning against stepping off a moving streetcar, and then the repeated assertion, "All these are nice things that can help a man get on his feet, even
if he is a bit weak, provided his heart is in good condition" (BA 495,
EJ 627). This assertion is neither paradoxical, nor a sign that Biberkopf is as feebleminded as ever, but rather a declaration of the fruitful
and positive relation possible between man and metropolis, evidence
that Biberkopf has reached the level of consciousness toward his urban
milieu that the narrator has had from the beginning.[52] The key to this
fruitful relation is Biberkopf's "sound heart," his acceptance of his
own past (including Ida, Mieze, and even Reinhold) coupled with his
rejection of the uniqueness of his individual fate.[53] The "heart" image,
rejected in favor of "ideas" by Wadzek, is now presented as the key to
a sound relation between individual and collective. The final image of
modern metropolitan life is a composite of many parallel lives, a confirmation of their interrelatedness which the narrator has shown all
along:

> He is no longer alone on Alexanderplatz. There are people to the right,
> and people to the left of him, some walk in front of him, others behind
> him.
>   Much unhappiness comes from walking alone. When there are sev-
> eral, it's somewhat different. I must get the habit of listening to others,
> for what the others say concerns me, too.
>   (BA 499–500, EJ 632–33)

The montage technique has its origins partly in the experience of
the metropolis and the conviction that the traditional bourgeois novel,
with its focus on the individual psyche, cannot do justice to that experience. At the same time, this does not mean that montage automatically portrays the metropolis as fragmented, chaotic, and dehuman-

ized. Döblin's urban montage in *Berlin Alexanderplatz* presents reality in all its complexity. For Döblin, the multitudinousness of the city is clearly a positive aspect, and one for which montage is particularly suited. The city in montage is able to relativize even such an apparently unique paragon of evil as Reinhold, by showing that his stutter does not constitute a "fate," is not an "explanation" of his malice. From its multitude of parallel lives, the city provides a counterexample in the person of Max Rüst: "At present this Max Rüst is 14 years old, has just finished public school, it supposed to call by on his way home at the clinic for the defective in speech, the hard of hearing, the weak-visioned, the weak-minded, the incorrigible, he has been there at frequent intervals, because he stutters, but he is getting better now" (*BA* 54, EJ 56–57).

The city montage at the beginning of book 2 thus serves multiple functions that make it far more than a mere presentation of setting. The brief interpolated narratives in particular have an anticipatory, parallelizing and relativizing function in relation to the main narrative, the "Story of Franz Biberkopf." Max Rüst the stutterer anticipates Reinhold the stutterer. Georg, the railer against an unjust fate, presages Biberkopf.[54] Each of the multitudinous interpolated figures is in principle the *richtiger Nebenmann*, the "proper comrade" who represents, according to the original dust jacket copy of 1929,[55] the end point of Biberkopf's odyssey and the starting point of his new life. It is, in the end, not possible to separate Biberkopf from the Berlin in which he lives. Only taken together do they constitute the novel.

The problem posed by the story of Franz Biberkopf, its ethical theme if one will, is almost simplistic. Biberkopf's failing is basically hubris. At the beginning of the novel, he is determined to live decently, independent of others, on the strength of his own character. The three disasters which befall him with increasing severity are brought about by his own boastful pride in his strength and good fortune. After the third, he suffers a final fall, gains insight, and is redeemed at the last hour. The script of the radio play "Berlin Alexanderplatz," on which Döblin collaborated in 1930, articulates Biberkopf's failing more clearly even than the novel, when Death calls him "You little demon of pride!" (*Du Hochmutsdeibel; DHF* 316).[56]

Translated into the Berlin dialect that permeates the novel, this hubris is the *Dicketun* that the Oberlehrer Krause criticizes in his young friend Georg. Just before he murders Mieze, Reinhold uses precisely this expression to describe what it is in Biberkopf that attracts his malevolence: "I don't know what to do with the bozo, he always did have a big mouth, but wait a minute, there's a car back of us, and I thinks to myself, now watch out, m'boy, you with your highfalutin' airs [*Dicketun*], boasting to us about being decent. And out of the car he flies. Now you know where he left his arm" (*BA* 386, EJ 487–88). At bottom, Biberkopf's sense of himself as an individual dependent on his own resources, an isolated hero against the world ("The first man who comes along gets one in the jaw"; *BA* 31, EJ 27), is the same as the exaggerated sense of heroism that leads Wadzek to barricade himself in his villa in Reinickendorf. Wadzek's behavior is from the beginning so grotesque, however, that he cannot achieve Biberkopf's status of exemplary Everyman, or *deutscher Michel*, as he has been called by Robert Minder.[57]

Biberkopf's initial attitude is more or less characteristic of novelistic heroes, from the beginnings of the genre in the Spanish picaresque to the present. The novel must, after all, have a hero and that hero must be an individual, living in the world but clearly differentiated from and standing out against it. But Döblin rejected this pattern from the beginning of his career. Although he proposes the criterion of exemplariness for Biberkopf, he does not return to the format of the traditional novel in *Berlin Alexanderplatz*. The point of Biberkopf's agony is precisely the destruction of the idea of unique fate, the idea that prompts him to complain to Death, "I don't know nobody else who had things happen to 'im like I did, such wretched, miserable things" (*BA* 477, EJ 603–604), echoing Georg's complaint to Krause, "What do you know about it?" (*BA* 56, EJ 59). In this sense, what happens to Biberkopf is the opposite of tragedy, while preserving the outer form of tragedy.[58] He is not destroyed by an inevitable fate, but is redeemed through his final realization of guilt, responsibility for his own life, and dependence on others:

> Franz weeps and weeps. I'm guilty, I'm not a human being, I'm just a beast, a monster.
> Thus died, in that evening hour, Franz Biberkopf, erstwhile transport worker, burglar, pimp, murderer.
>
> (*BA* 488, EJ 617)

This passage, with its echoes of biblical diction, suggests that Biberkopf's end is modelled on a Christian rather than a Greek worldview.

The particular metaphors Döblin uses to suggest the process are those of refining ore (*BA* 480, EJ 607) and baking bread (*BA* 481, EJ 609), both processes of purification by fire, from which objects emerge transformed.[59]

The specific process by which Franz's redemption is accomplished is that of a review and acceptance of his past, under the repeated admonition "So let it come" (*BA* 480ff., EJ 607ff.). So pass before his mind's eye Lüders, Reinhold (who reminds him explicitly that he, too, has murdered), Ida, and Mieze. In keeping with the universal significance of Biberkopf's story and with his integration into the city, however, it is not just these figures who pass review. The narrator interpolates a montage of anonymous masses moving from the provinces toward Berlin, thus anticipating within Biberkopf's agony the larger social context into which he will be released. Biberkopf's acceptance of responsibility for his past thus merges into his need to live with others:

> So let it come—the night, however black and nothing-like it be! So let them come, the black night, those frost-covered acres, the hard frozen roads. So let them come: the lonely, tile-roofed houses whence gleams a reddish light; so let them come: the shivering wanderers, the drivers on the farm wagons traveling to town with vegetables and the little horses in front. The great, flat, silent plains crossed by suburban trains and expresses which throw white light into the darkness on either side of them. So let them come—the men in the station, the little girl's farewell to her parents, she's traveling with two older acquaintances, going across the big water, we've got our tickets, but good Lord, what a little girl, eh, but she'll get used to it over there, if she's a good little girl it'll be all right. So let them come and be absorbed: the cities which lie along the same line, Breslau, Liegnitz, Sommerfeld, Guben, Frankfort on the Oder, Berlin, the train passes through them from station to station, from the stations emerge the cities, the cities with their big and little streets. Berlin with Schweidnitzer Strasse, with the Grosse Ring of the Kaiser-Wilhelm Strasse, Kurfürstendamm, and everywhere are homes in which people are warming themselves, looking at each other with loving eyes, or sitting coldly next to each other; dirty dumps and dives where a man is playing the piano. Say, kiddo, that's old stuff, you'd think there was nothing new in 1928, how about "I kiss your hand, Madame," or "Ramona."
> So let them come: the autos, the taxis, you know how many you have sat in, how they rattled, you were alone, or else somebody sat next to you, or maybe two. License Number 20147.
> (*BA* 480–81, EJ 607–608)

The tone of this montage is strikingly similar to Molly Bloom's great affirmative peroration at the end of Joyce's *Ulysses*. But there the streaming, conscious thoughts of a single figure focus the reader on the individual, whereas the montage here is not Franz Biberkopf's but rather the narrator's, who by this point in the novel has merged almost completely with the figure of Death.[60] The streaming movement of the passage is embodied in the trains which are its central image. Like the streetcars of book 2, they are dynamic and serve here to articulate "the black night." And in the midst of this montage, the figure of the little girl bound for America relates not only to Döblin's personal experience as a young child torn from his home and removed to Berlin, but also to Biberkopf: we see her parents giving her the same empty rules for behavior which Biberkopf has vainly tried to follow: "If she's a good little girl it'll be all right."

□

For many readers, Franz Biberkopf's redemption and illumination at the end of the novel have seemed altogether too abrupt, and moreover curiously ambivalent. The final chapter of the novel in particular, with its title echoing the march motif that accompanies Biberkopf's aggressively individualistic battle against life, has given rise to controversy: "Forward March and get in Step and Right and Left and Right and Left" (*BA* 497, *EJ* 629). The chapter is divided into two parts. The first half reports Reinhold's trial for the murder of Mieze. Biberkopf, in the witness stand, still feels "a curious devotion" to Reinhold (*BA* 498, *EJ* 630) and eschews "shooting off his mouth before the judge" (*sich vor dem Richter dicktun; BA* 498, *EJ* 631) as Reinhold expects him to. His confrontation with Death and with his own hubris has finally taught him that "The world is made of sugar and dirt" (*BA* 479, 498, *EJ* 606, 630–31), not just of sugar, and that Reinhold is no unique paragon of evil: "I know who you are. I now find you here, m'boy, in the prisoner's box, outside I'll meet you a thousand times more, but my heart will not turn to stone on account of that" (*BA* 498, *EJ* 631). Reinhold gets ten years for the murder; Biberkopf is offered a job. The novel threatens to end in breathtaking triviality: "Immediately after the trial Biberkopf is offered a job as assistant gatekeeper in a medium-sized factory. He accepts. I have nothing further to report about his life" (*BA* 499, *EJ* 632).

But then comes the second half of the final chapter, the half that poses problems for interpreters of the novel. It does not in fact report anything further about Biberkopf's life, but rather turns to his frame of mind in his post in the "medium-sized factory." The narrator declares his story to have been "a process of revelation of a special kind" with Biberkopf now standing at the end of the "dark road," beneath a street-lamp, "able to read the sign" (*BA* 499, EJ 632). Now that his personal problems of hubris and guilt have been illuminated and understood, Biberkopf is directly confronted with the social context in which he must resume his life. As we have seen, the social is linked to the personal at the point where Biberkopf realizes he cannot stand alone, but must live among and depend upon his fellow men in the city and in life in general.

Indeed, expressions of a generalized solidarity abound, both on the part of the narrator and of Biberkopf, who now share the same insight and speak the same language:

> He is no longer alone on Alexanderplatz. There are people to the right, and people to the left of him, some walk in front of him, others behind him.
>
> Much unhappiness comes from walking alone. When there are several, it's somewhat different. I must get the habit of listening to others, for what the others say concerns me, too. Then I learn who I am, and what I can undertake. Everywhere about me my battle is being fought, and I must beware, before I know it, I'm in the thick of it.
>
> He is assistant gatekeeper in a factory. What is fate anyway? One is stronger than I. If there are two of us, it grows harder to be stronger than I. If there are ten of us, it's harder still. And if there are a thousand of us and a million, then it's very hard, indeed.[61]
>
> (*BA* 499–500, EJ 632–33)

What has particularly disturbed many readers is the fact that the call for solidarity is mingled with the drum rolls and trumpet calls of marching masses who pass Franz's window, masses whose political allegiance is unclear; they could be communist, anarchist, socialist, or fascist. Are these the fellow men with whom Franz ought to ally himself? And if so, then why is it any more likely for him to join the Left than the fascist Right?

The latter, in fact, would seem the more likely possibility. Throughout the novel Biberkopf, who thinks of himself as apolitical (*BA* 294, EJ 367), has evinced the kind of yearning for security and order that makes him susceptible to Nazi propaganda. After his release from Tegel, he peddles racist newspapers ("He is not against the Jews, but he is for law and order"; *BA* 85, EJ 97), and does so again after recovering from Lüders's betrayal (*BA* 184, EJ 223). He nearly gets into a fight with his old army friend Georg Dreske and other Communists when they see him with his swastika armband. While selling Nazi papers conforms to his idea of "decency," he shuns the Communists just as he shuns Herbert and Eva. In his rage at their baiting, he screams: "We've gotta have order, order, I'm telling you, order—and put that in your pipes and smoke it, order and nothing else . . . and if anybody comes and starts a revolution now and don't leave us in peace, they ought to be strung up all along the street . . . then they'll get theirs, when they swing, yes, sir. You might remember that whatever you do, you criminals" (*BA* 99, EJ 116). After he has lost his arm and given up trying to be decent, he is drawn to the antisocial, radical solipsism of the pickpocket Willi ("a reasonable man believes only in Nietzsche and Stirner, and does what he pleases; all the rest is bunk"; *BA* 306, EJ 384), with whom he attends anarchist meetings in order to bait the participants (*BA* 291–99, EJ 363–74).

James H. Reid has drawn attention to the space the novel devotes to this encounter with the anarchists,[62] and infers that the old anarchist worker with whom Franz talks is "Döblin's mouthpiece in *Berlin Alexanderplatz.*" Franz, who has resumed his old life as a pimp and petty criminal, articulates his stubborn doctrine of individuality: "A man's got only himself, just himself. I look after myself. I'm a self-provider, I am!" The anarchist counters with the need for solidarity: "And I've told you that three dozen times already: you can't do anything alone. We need a fighting organization" (*BA* 298, EJ 373). Yet if this worker articulates the message that makes *Berlin Alexanderplatz,* according to Reid, a political novel, then one would expect his message to be much more clearly repeated in the final chapter.

The solidarity proclaimed in the final chapter, however, seems thrown into question and almost contradicted by two other elements. First, there is Biberkopf's own caution:

> Often they march past his window with flags and music and singing. Biberkopf watches coolly from his door, he'll not join the parade any more. Shut your trap, in step, old cuss, march along with the rest of us. But if I march along, I shall have to pay for it later on with my head, pay for the schemes of others. That's why I first figure out everything, and only if everything's quite O.K., and suits me, I'll take action. Reason is the gift of man, jackasses replace it with a clan.
>
> (*BA* 500, EJ 633–34)

Then there is the apparent reason for his caution: these masses are marching in solidarity, to be sure, but it is the mindless solidarity of an army marching into war and death. The drum rolls of the Dance of Death chapter (*BA* 488−90, EJ 618−20), in which the imperialist armies of Napoleon and Kaiser Wilhelm II and the revolutionary armies of the French and Russian Revolutions, the Peasants' Wars, and the Anabaptists all fall, without differentiation, under Death's sway, are repeated at the very end of the novel, in a paragraph printed in italics in the German edition and bold face in the English translation:

> The way leads to freedom, to freedom it goes. The old world must crumble. Awake, wind of dawn!
> And get in step, and right and left and right and left, marching: marching on, we tramp to war, a hundred minstrels march before, with fife and drum, drrum, brrum, for one the road goes straight, for another it goes to the side, one stands fast, another's killed, one rushes past, another's voice is stilled, drrum, brrumm, drrumm! THE END
> (*BA* 501, EJ 635)

Hans-Peter Bayerdörfer has gone further than anyone else in trying to explain the apparent contradictions of this chapter. He carefully differentiates between the positive solidarity, based on the insight Biberkopf has achieved, and the false, mindless solidarity created by force and legitimized by the idea of fate. The latter, according to Bayerdörfer, is embodied in the figure of the Whore of Babylon and leads to war. If death becomes ideologized as a sacrificial, heroic death in war, then its meaning, in Bayerdörfer's reading of Döblin, is perverted in the service of the Whore of Babylon.[63] The last paragraph is set off typographically not because it contains the moral of the novel, which would then be that Biberkopf ought to sacrifice his new-found wisdom and submit to war as the inescapable fate of mankind. Rather, it shows that the power of the false collective of war continues to exist in the world in which Biberkopf must live. "True to his role as a street-ballad singer, however, [the narrator] cranks out one more verse of the Song of the World on his organ. To be sure, there is an ambiguous twinkle in his eye in the sentence that introduces the song quote [i.e., "The way leads to freedom, to freedom it goes. The old world must crumble"], and that ambiguity has led to misunderstanding. Formally, the epilogue forms the last refrain of the street ballad. As for its content, it also has the character of a refrain that reproduces the unending reprise

of the battle songs of the world."[64] Bayerdörfer's point is that Biberkopf has in the end achieved the political insight of the narrator into
the dangers of the crumbling and violent Weimar Republic, but that
the narrator refuses to suggest any easy answer to the question of what
is to be done with that insight; he admits that "he is unable to spin out
his story beyond this point. He eschews the possibility of presenting a
utopian New World, and instead points to the potential for politiciz-
ing the level of consciousness that has been achieved."[65]

Döblin himself was well aware of the dilemma in which the final
chapter leaves both Biberkopf and the reader. In a 1931 letter to the
Germanist Julius Petersen he wrote,

> This book was conceived as the first volume of a two-volume work. The
> second was supposed to (or will?) present the active man, although per-
> haps not the same person; the conclusion is a sort of bridge—but the
> other bank is missing. And then, my basic spiritual "naturalism" co-
> alesced in a particular phase. A more passive-receptive element with
> tragic overtones is opposed to an active element that is more opti-
> mistic. . . . In *Berlin Alexanderplatz,* I definitely wanted to bring Fr.
> Biberkopf to the second phase—I didn't succeed. Against my own inten-
> tion, simply from the logic of the action and the plan, the book ended as
> it does; it was beyond rescue, my hopes were dashed. The conclusion
> really ought to play—in heaven: one more soul saved—well, that wasn't
> possible, but I couldn't resist playing fanfares at the end, whether they
> were psychologically plausible or not. Up to now I see no resolution to
> the dualism.
>
> (*Briefe* 165–66)

In spite of its moving call for solidarity, the final chapter leaves
Franz Biberkopf alone at his gatekeeper's window. By Döblin's own
admission, his hero has not reached the "second phase" of positive action. On the other hand, neither has he been "saved" through sublima-
tion from the real situation of a "humble workman" (*BA* 501, *EJ* 634)
in the Berlin of 1928 to "heaven"—the timeless metaphysical-religious
plane of the biblical parables of Job and Isaac, parables of sacrifice and
humility that accompany his story but, in the end, do not absorb it.
Döblin never wrote the projected second volume, and even if the Nazi
accession to power had not occurred and he had not been forced into
exile, it is doubtful that he ever would have. In his next Berlin novel,
however—written in exile—he would readdress the dilemma of a hero
left hovering on the brink of action and push it a step further. Before
we turn to this novel, *Men without Mercy,* we need to take a brief look

at an aspect of *Berlin Alexanderplatz* that is intimately related to Biberkopf's isolation at the end of the novel: the role of women.

☐

Although the structure of Franz Biberkopf's three-tiered fall and redemption has been thoroughly discussed in the secondary literature, it is curious that almost no attention has been paid to the common element in all three "blows" against the hero: in each case, it is Franz's relation to women that is involved. He brags to Lüders about his conquest of a widow; he first participates in and then tries to cure Reinhold of his "traffic in girls"; he parades his good fortune with Mieze in front of Reinhold. In addition, of course, he has served four years for the unpremeditated murder of his girlfriend Ida. Upon his release at the beginning of the novel, he regains his equilibrium in Berlin primarily by raping Minna, Ida's sister.

The category in which Biberkopf habitually thinks about women is that of business—precisely what one would expect of a pimp. He excuses his infidelity with the widow by emphasizing its monetary aspect: "Pshaw, it's business, business is business" (*BA* 118, EJ 139). His arrangement with Reinhold is explicitly "traffic in girls" (or "white slavery" in the Jolas translation; *BA* 193, EJ 235). And even before Franz has met Mieze, his friend Herbert suggests her commercial possibilities: "If you're a man who knows what's what, Franz, then maybe you kin make something out of the gal. I've seen her. She's got class" (*BA* 281, EJ 350). Eva persuades him with relative ease to accept Mieze's voluntary prostitution, and he gets murderously angry only when she falls in love with one of her customers (*BA* 367–69, EJ 461–64). Franz's boastful exploitation of women is the main component of the hubris of which he must be cured.

It is all the more astonishing that Robert Minder, the French Germanist who met and worked with Döblin during the war, could call *Berlin Alexanderplatz*—and indeed, most of Döblin's works—"books without women."[66] Minder continues, "The writer himself was not unaware that in the middle [of his novels] there is almost always a grimly intense struggle of love between two male partners. A struggle of love that plays itself out on levels other than the purely sexual, and which are therefore all the more threatening. This struggle has a fundamental influence on the total behavior of the characters. Its most hidden cause lies in the exaggerated paternal authority that has astonished foreign observers of German culture for centuries." It is true that the metaphysical battle in *Berlin Alexanderplatz* is waged between Franz, the exemplary Everyman, and Reinhold, the epitome of malice, of "the cold force" (*BA* 456, EJ 576). Similarly, Wadzek battles against Rommel and Schneemann. The furious battle of the sexes in the early novel *The Black Curtain* was left behind when the Berlin Program rejected the "erotic" as a primary novelistic theme and Döblin had developed the solution of sacred prostitution in *The Three Leaps of Wang-lun.*

Yet to call *Berlin Alexanderplatz* a "book without women" is to miss the fact that beneath the sublimated homoeroticism of the metaphysical battle between Biberkopf and Reinhold, the battle of the sexes in fact continues, although Döblin has tried to resolve it in the idea of sacrificial prostitution. We have seen that in *Wadzek,* the image of woman is split between the poles of the devouring, solipsistic Pauline and the self-sacrificing, masochistic Gaby. That novel, however, failed to achieve a satisfying resolution of the polarity. In *Berlin Alexanderplatz,* women have been rendered unproblematic through the elimination of Pauline's side of the polarity. The sacred prostitution of *Wang-lun* has been secularized and universalized. In the Berlin underworld that is Biberkopf's universe, *all* women are prostitutes.

On the surface of the novel, Franz's exploitative, self-serving relations with women are the major component of his hubris. From the beginning, he makes women subservient to him, takes out his anger, aggression, and frustration on them. When he finds himself impotent after his release, he blames his victim, Ida, the "beast" or "bitch" (*BA* 37, EJ 37; Jolas translates *Biest* as "tart" and then "wench"). His instinctive response is to return to her and regain his potency by force. The violence of his feeling cancels time and allows her sister Minna to replace the dead Ida: "Prison had never existed, nor the conversation with the Jews in the Dragonerstrasse. Where's the slut, it's her fault" (*BA* 38, EJ 37). Part of the chapter's title is a military metaphor, "Victory all along the Line!" (*BA* 37, EJ 36), and his rape of Minna is introduced by the march rhythms so prominent at the end of the novel: "A little twitching of the face, a little twitching in the fingers, then we'll go there, bumbledy, bumbledy, bumbledy, bee, tumbledy, rumbledy, tumbledy, bee, rumbledy, bumbledy. . . . He walks along left wheel into the room. Rumbledy, bumbledy" (*BA* 38, EJ 37).

The military motif is continued in the picture decorating Minna's living room: "So that's the room, the stiff-backed sofa, the Kaiser hanging on the wall, a Frenchman in red trousers giving him his sword. I have surrendered." But rather than swelling with pride at the sight of this icon of German nationalism, Biberkopf reveals the fear which motivates him by reversing the significance of the picture: "'What do you want here, Franz? Are you crazy, or what?' 'I'll sit down.' I have surrendered. The Kaiser presents his sword, the Kaiser must return the sword to him, that's the way the world runs" (*BA* 38, EJ 37). It is this fear of utter defeat and impotence that motivates the rape which follows. When it is over, the metaphor of victory returns. The world has been set right: "He clambered up, laughed, and spun around with joy, delight, beatitude. The trumpets are blowing, hussars ride forth, hallelujah. Franz Biberkopf is back again! Franz is discharged! Franz Biberkopf is free!" (*BA* 40, EJ 40). The rape has been brutal enough, leaving Minna with a black eye and scratches on her neck. But Minna is also shown in the end acquiescing to the inevitable:

> And she, the sister, what strange thing is happening to her? She feels from his face, from his lying still on her, that she has to give in, she defends herself, but a sort of transformation comes over her, her face loses its tension, her arms can no longer push him off, her mouth grows helpless. The man says nothing, she lets lets lets him have her mouth, she grows soft as in a bath, do with me whatever you please, she dissolves like water, it's all right, just come, I know it all, I love you, too.
>
> (*BA* 40, EJ 39–40)

After the rape, Franz can afford to be magnanimous: "She was lying on the floor, tossing herself about. He laughed and stretched himself: 'Well, go ahead and choke me. I'll keep still, if you can do it'" (*BA* 40, EJ 40). Later, he replaces her torn apron, stops by to see how her black eye is healing, and buys her two veal cutlets. They embrace before she sends him away for good (*BA* 42–43, EJ 43).

Otto Keller has suggested that this denouement prefigures Franz's ultimate salvation by showing that he "would also be capable of genuine devotion . . . as Minna obviously also seems to sense."[67] This is probably an accurate assessment of Döblin's conscious intention. Biberkopf's affection for Minna—once he has raped her—prefigures

his love for Mieze, and conversely, Minna's melting surrender anticipates Mieze's selfless devotion to him. For all his ugliness and brutality, he is consistently attractive to the women in the novel. But the
rape of Minna anticipates Franz's relation to Mieze in another sense
that was perhaps less conscious on Döblin's part. Both Minna and
Mieze conform to a pattern that demands that the woman be conquered and humiliated before she can be allowed to love or, in Mieze's
case, to be the salvation of Franz. Only when she is prostituted can she
be transfigured.

If there is unanimity among Döblin's interpreters about anything, it
is about the figure of Mieze. For Roland Links, she is "a person . . .
who really sticks by [Franz], on whom he can count"; for Klaus
Müller-Salget, "the only person who accepts him completely, who
gives herself to him without reservation"; Otto Keller universalizes,
calling her "the truly loving person, who sacrifices herself for others"
and "the most beautiful figure of the novel on the realistic level of
plot."[68] Theodore Ziolkowski adopts Biberkopf's perspective when he
calls Mieze "his most prized possession."[69] Indeed, the novel leaves no
doubt that Mieze, always dressed in white, is the embodiment of purity
and selfless love. She is from the beginning the "proper comrade" for
Franz, and his great guilt is that he fails to realize that until it is
too late.

But it seems also to be true that just as Minna must be raped in
anger, amid military metaphors of conquest, before she can give in and
love, so Mieze must be murdered before she can be Franz's salvation.
She is the most sacred of all Döblin's sacred prostitutes, submitting to
literal martyrdom in order to become canonized.[70] It is not accidental
that Mieze receives a past, a biography, a *vita sancta,* only after she is
dead. It seems, in fact, to rise like a miasma from the trunk into which
her body has been stuffed:

> They open the trunk in which Mieze lay. She was the daughter of a
> streetcar conductor from Bernau. There were three children in the fam-
> ily, the mother deserted her husband and left the home, why, nobody
> knows. Mieze was alone in the house and had to do everything herself.
> Sometimes at night she rode in to Berlin and went to dance-halls or to
> Lestmann and other places nearby, occasionally she was taken by this
> one or the other to a hotel; then it was too late and she didn't dare come
> home, so she stayed on in Berlin and met Eva; that's how it started. They
> were at the police station near the Stettin Depot. A cheerful life began
> then for Mieze, who at first called herself Sonia, she had many acquain-

tances and friends, but later on she always lived with one man, a strong fellow with one arm whom Mieze loved at first sight and to whom she remained true till the end. A bad end, a sad end, was the last end of Mieze. And why, why, why? What crime had she committed? She came from Bernau into the whirl of Berlin, she was not an innocent girl, certainly not, but her love for him was pure and steadfast; he was her man and she took care of him like a child. She was struck down because she happened by chance to encounter this man; such is life, it's really inconceivable. She rode out to Freienwalde to protect her friend, and there she was strangled, strangled, killed, extinguished; such is life.

$$(BA\ 416-17,\ EJ\ 526)$$

It is particularly interesting that in *Berlin Alexanderplatz,* this kind of capsule biography is usually provided only for nonrecurring, secondary characters—the people, for instance, inhabiting the building where Franz is hiding at the beginning of the fourth book (*BA* 132–36, EJ 156–61). We learn next to nothing about the family history or social background of Franz Biberkopf or Reinhold.[71] Their lack of past means both that they are caught up in the dynamism of the present moment that dominates the novel's unidirectional plot, and that their struggle can all the more easily be raised to the metaphysical level of the biblical and classical allusions that the narrator increasingly mounts into the text. Mieze's biography, almost more than her murder, marks her exit from the novel. She has become a case among other cases.

On the level of plot, she is the apotheosis of all the women in the book. But while the monstrous, devouring side of woman—in *Wadzek* embodied in the figure of Pauline—has been banished from *Berlin Alexanderplatz* on the realistic level, the many-tiered structure of this novel allows its introduction on the metaphysical, apocalyptic level:

> And now come here, you, come, and I will show you something. The great whore, the Whore of Babylon, that sits there beside the water. And you see a woman sitting on a scarlet colored beast. The woman is full of names of blasphemy, and has 7 heads and 10 horns. She is arrayed in purple and scarlet and decked with gold and precious stones and pearls, having a golden cup in her hand. And upon her forehead is written a name, a mystery: the great Babylon, the mother of all abomination on the earth. The woman has drunk of the blood of all the saints. The woman is drunken with the blood of the saints.
>
> (*BA* 260, EJ 322)[72]

Is it any accident that this apocalyptic adversary of the illuminating, purifying, preserving figure of death ("it is my duty to preserve"; *BA* 474, EJ 599) is female, and furthermore a whore and a vampire? The symbol of violence and self-centered evil in the novel, she makes her first appearance in book 6, just before Biberkopf launches his "Third Conquest of Berlin" by giving up his attempt to live decently and resuming his life of crime. She then accompanies his downward course until the Dance of Death chapter, when she is driven off by a triumphant Death after Biberkopf's redemption (*BA* 488, *EJ* 618).

But her entrance into the novel also happens to precede by only twenty pages the introduction of Mieze. Indeed, the first repetition of the Whore of Babylon motif, inserted in the middle of an unequivocal narrative warning that Franz Biberkopf has become a criminal, "and the worst is yet to come" (*BA* 277, *EJ* 345), is followed only two pages later by the first appearance of Mieze (*BA* 280, *EJ* 349). Throughout the remainder of the novel, the image of the monstrous, apocalyptic Whore recurs in close proximity to the stages of Mieze's tragedy: just after Franz, in the depths of pain, loneliness and self-pity, calls out "Where is Mieze, anyway, leaving me lie here like that. Ow, ouch, ow, ow, oooooooh" (*BA* 319, *EJ* 401); after Mieze's body has been found by the police and the narrator has related her biography (*BA* 419, *EJ* 529); after Franz has discovered that she is dead (*BA* 425, *EJ* 537); and then finally, during his catatonia (*BA* 467, 474, 488; *EJ* 589–90, 599, 618).

The Berlin prostitute Mieze and the Whore of Babylon, both introduced more than half way through the novel, are complementary. They repeat the polarity in Döblin's image of women embodied in *Wadzek* by the figures of Gaby and Pauline. We have seen how Wadzek's escape with Gaby fails to resolve the polarity: he persists in his domineering approach to her and intends to resume the capitalist battle in America. In *Berlin Alexanderplatz,* the polarity is complicated and obscured by the fact that Mieze appears on the plot level, whereas the Whore of Babylon belongs to the mythological imagery that the narrator mounts into the story of Franz Biberkopf, thereby raising it to the level of the exemplary. Nevertheless, each woman must be done away with before Biberkopf can reach his ultimate illumination. The Whore, in whom Pauline's solipsism has been raised to the absolute level, is finally driven away by Death, the great equalizer, who thus triumphs in their battle for Biberkopf's soul. At the archetypal level, Mieze is the sacrificial lamb through whom Franz is redeemed. In his personal life, as in his political consciousness, he has achieved illumination at great cost. The final chapter holds out the hope that in both spheres of his life, he is now prepared to recognize and cherish the "proper comrade," but it is no more than a hope. The anonymous masses of the city who surround him are as yet only potential comrades. The narrator, at the end of his wisdom, leaves the ending open and the hero alone.

4

Men without Mercy

By the time Döblin came to write his next Berlin novel, the urgency of the need to resolve Franz Biberkopf's dilemma at the end of *Berlin Alexanderplatz* had become only too evident. Events had overtaken Döblin. The marching masses had become unambiguous reality. *Men without Mercy* is the first novel that Döblin wrote entirely during his exile.[1] At the end of February 1933, a month after Hitler's appointment as chancellor, Döblin fled Berlin for Switzerland, and later in the same year moved on to Paris. It was the beginning of a bitter exile that would last until 1945. The novel was written in Paris in 1934 and published by the Querido Verlag in Amsterdam in 1935.

Men without Mercy is formally Döblin's most conventional novel and in its content his most autobiographical. Its images and motifs hark back to *Wadzek* rather than to *Berlin Alexanderplatz* and it seems in many ways to be the diametrical opposite of the great novel of 1929. It totally eschews the narrative daring of *Berlin Alexanderplatz* in favor of a conventional, omniscient third-person narrator, a relatively economical plot, and a severely restricted cast of characters.[2] Döblin later characterized the book as a "groping in the novel form" (*Tasten in Romanform; AzL* 392), expressly choosing the designation *Roman* he had so vehemently rejected during the teens and twenties in favor of *Epos* or *episches Werk*. It is unclear whether this phrase means that he was groping formally, or using the novel form to explore a murky theme.

In contrast to the geographical and temporal precision of *Berlin Alexanderplatz*, *Men without Mercy* is set in an unnamed modern metropolis at an unspecified time. The geography of the city and the events narrated, however, suggest Berlin during the 1870s—the booming *Gründerjahre* when many major German companies were founded—through the depression of the twenties and early thirties, with the First World War excluded. In the retrospective essay "Epilog" of 1948, Döblin calls the novel "a family history with a dash of autobiography" (*AzL* 392). The titles of the three books in which the novel is divided suggest the primacy of economic and social forces: Poverty, Boom, Crisis.

In its linking of psychological history and social and political circumstances, *Men without Mercy* has close ties to two of Döblin's earlier works: the 1927 autobiographical essay "First Glance Back" and the 1931 political tract *Wissen und Verändern!* (Know and Change!). Such clear links between fiction and nonfiction were rare in Döblin's earlier works. As we have seen, in his imaginative writing he relied heavily on subconscious inspiration and almost automatic composition, which led in many cases to sprawling and amorphous novels rescued by the intensity and power of their language. In *Berlin Alexanderplatz* the density of cross-reference within the montage and the straightforward, unidirectional plot make for a unity lacking in its predecessors.

Men without Mercy achieves a different kind of unity much more akin to that of the realistic novel Döblin had always scorned. One reason for this change in style is that unlike Döblin's other novels, *Men without Mercy* has a central theme straight out of bourgeois realism: marriage and the family: "It's a very real big-city novel, about marriage. I'm writing very simply (or so I believe), telling what I know" (*Briefe* 197). Since the "Open Letter to Marinetti," Döblin had explicitly spurned "eroticism" in the epic novel, yet as we have seen, the sexual problematic lies just below the surface of his works, and in a novel like *Wadzek*, it subverts Döblin's original intention. In *Men without Mercy*, the theme of marriage and the family is consciously at the center. While the grotesque caricature of a bourgeois family in *Wadzek* has no apparent dimension of social criticism, Döblin's realistic treatment of the theme in *Men without Mercy* has clear political and social implications. Indeed, the novel is realistic in order to be political.[3]

Men without Mercy is Döblin's only *roman à thèse*, and the overriding didactic intention dictates the clarity and schematization that make the novel unusual. Why did he choose to write such a novel? It has been suggested that its relatively short length and tight composition betray the new influence of French literature on the exiled writer.[4] Walter Muschg is surely right that the novel's naturalistic style also reflects a temporary loss of faith in the independence of the imagination.[5] It is likely, moreover, that the exile Döblin wanted to produce a work that would reach as many readers as possible, although the nov-

els immediately preceding and following *Men without Mercy—Baby-
lonische Wanderung* (Babylonian Journey) and the trilogy *Amazonas,*
respectively—make no such concessions to the reading public. What is
certain is that Döblin saw his previous existence as a politically engaged writer radically called into question by the triumph of the Nazis,
a triumph all the more devastating because he had not anticipated it.
In 1935, he declined an invitation to speak on the anniversary of the
Nazi bookburning and wrote to Thomas Mann, "My books, at any
rate, deserved to be burned" (*Briefe* 207). *Men without Mercy* is an
indictment of both himself and German society for failing to realize
the ideals of the aborted revolution of 1918 before it was too late—for
failing, in effect, to resolve Biberkopf's dilemma.

□

Let us first see how the family theme is anticipated in the 1927 essay
"First Glance Back." This was Döblin's first lengthy venture in an
autobiographical mode, and it took the formal milestone of his fiftieth
birthday to prod him into undertaking it. We have already noted
Döblin's declared aversion to autobiography. In order to maintain
ironic distance to himself, he composed this essay in the form of an
imaginary examination of his person and psyche (including graphol-
ogy and palm reading). In the beginning, it resembles a psychoanalytic session,[6] but takes on more and more the character of a legal
interrogation. In spite of—or rather, because of—this elaborate distancing structure, it becomes evident that Döblin has achieved no calm
objectivity toward his own past. The pain caused by the two great injustices of his youth, his father's abandonment and the persecution he
suffered in school, persists (totally suppressed, by the way, is Döblin's
own repetition of his father's pattern in his relationship with Frieda
Kunke, a fact that would certainly have had to emerge in genuine
psychoanalysis).

Döblin at first tells the story of his father with jocular sarcasm; but
at the insistent urging of an anonymous psychoanalytic interlocutor,
he tells it twice more, moving from absolute condemnation ("He was
a scoundrel, when all is said and done"; *SLW* 119) to understanding
and conditional forgiveness: "They should have let him go as a young
man or given him a shrewish wife or a very shrewd one: the curb or
completely free rein" (*SLW* 125).

Having inherited his talent for writing from his father, Döblin possessed suppressed sympathy for him and equally suppressed resentment of his mother, who treated her son's writing with the same contempt as she had Max Döblin's artistic talents: "When I was already a
doctor, I published a book and my mother asked, 'Why do you do
that? You have a business, don't you?' She meant my medical practice." But with a characteristic guilty conscience, he adds, "Now that
she's dead, by the way, I find that the woman was not so wrong. Actually, I should have given it up. . . . Writing seemed to her a frivolity, a
waste of time, unworthy of a serious person" (SLW 123).

   Döblin and his siblings suffered the difficult adjustment to their new
family circumstances and to life in Berlin. His oldest brother, Ludwig,
the most obvious model for Karl in Men without Mercy, went to work
for his uncle when the shattered family moved to the capital in 1888:
"On him fell the main burden that the absconded family founder had
thrown off, and he bore it brilliantly" (SLW 127). But in 1929, a year
after Döblin wrote this essay, Ludwig committed suicide; his business
had suffered in the crash of 1929 and he had had an unhappy extra-
marital affair (SLW 352–53). Döblin's sister Meta was pressured into
marriage by the petit-bourgeois proprieties of the family: "Although
we possessed nothing, every effort was made to avoid placing her in a
job. No idea was more foreign to the family than that a daughter
would simply earn money like everyone else and stand on her own two
feet" (SLW 129). After a divorce and a second, happier, marriage to a
simple artisan, she was accidentally killed by a grenade fragment during the general strike and workers' uprising in the eastern quarter of
Berlin in March 1919.

   Döblin himself was an eyewitness to this strike and its bloody suppression (1,200 dead) by government troops under Gustav Noske, and
wrote a brilliant reportage about it, "Kannibalisches" (Cannibalism),
which appeared in Die Neue Rundschau in June 1919 (WV 10–25).
The strike's goal was to rescue the workers' and soldiers' councils,
which had been formed at the end of the war, from the attempts of
the Social-Democratic government under Friedrich Ebert to dismantle
them.[7] Döblin's eyewitness report describes the government's use of air
power, artillery, and then—after the strike was already crushed—its
summary executions of civilians under martial law. He abandons his
objective, reportorial stance to condemn this killing "arranged and le-
gally carried out by the authorities, as if dictated by wisdom" (WV 22).

After a bitter attack on the intellectuals for allowing this to happen without protest, however, he makes it clear that his quarrel is basically with the means, but not the end of the government action: "A death or two is not what bothers me; we all must die. It is the infinitely disgusting senselessness of it I cannot stand. And you can't placate me with some proverb like 'You've got to break some eggs to make an omelette.'[8] The law of the state must not be reestablished by means of an impudent violation of the natural right to justice" (*WV* 23). In spite of Döblin's theoretical sympathy for the antiauthoritarian organization of the workers' councils, a sympathy he was expressing at the same time he wrote this reportage,[9] he seems unable to agree with their defense in practice. His inability to take the side of the strikers seems all the more strange in light of his sister's death, which was due precisely to the fury of Noske's attack. He does not even mention her death in "Cannibalism," because to do so would have ruined the carefully calculated effect of the reportage, which depends on an impartial first-person observer gradually realizing that the government really is resorting to aerial bombs and summary executions. His sister's death was a merely personal tragedy, a senseless accident.

"Cannibalism" was a warning to the infant German republic that a revolution that resorted to brutality in order to curb its radicals was in danger of losing its soul. By the time Döblin came to write "First Glance Back" nine years later, he had apparently lost all hope that the ideals of the revolution would ever be realized by the Weimar state. His attitude toward the March 1919 general strike had undergone a radical change; his isolation between the fronts had become exacerbated. To be sure, he still mentions the victims of the mass executions: "You had to have seen the corpses lying there in front of the school— the men with their caps covering their faces—to know the meaning of class hatred and the spirit of revenge" (*SLW* 128). But in the wake of the failed revolution, the senselessness of his sister's death gains symptomatic importance. He no longer blames the intellectuals for that failure, but the other workers of Berlin:

> All was quiet while this was happening in Lichtenberg, and all the many tens of thousands of workers in Berlin remained still. It was then that I saw how necessary it was that this so-called revolution be suppressed. I am against incompetence. I hate incompetence. These people were incapable of action. You can't beat around the bush with tail-draggers, idiots, and big mouths. That's how it was then, and I'm on the side of whoever doesn't beat around the bush, whether he's on the Left or the

Right. . . . As foreign and hostile as the White troops seemed to me, I stepped back and concluded: this is good; they're better than those fellows over there. They're getting their just deserts. Either they know what revolution is and carry it out, or they deserve a beating for playing at it.

(*SLW* 128–129)

This is Döblin's most bitter condemnation of the failed German revolution, couched in language that comes close to sounding fascist in its diction.[10] In the familial context of "First Glance Back," the vehemence of his scorn for the failed revolution is related to his scorn for his father. In both cases, bitter disappointment leads him to emotionally charged overstatement. He modifies his condemnation of his father in the course of "First Glance Back," and Helmut Kiesel has pointed out that even in *November 1918*, he never again sides with the reactionary "White" troops of Noske.[11]

If Döblin is in the end ambiguous about the role of his father in his life, his judgment of the *Gymnasium* he attended is clear: the school was a repressive, authoritarian institution whose aim was to instill industriousness, obedience, and devotion to duty and the Prussian state. Döblin was an outsider from the first, because he was three years older than his classmates (having lost time in the move from Stettin to Berlin) and a Jew. Yet it was not his fellow pupils who persecuted him, but the teachers, and in "First Glance Back" he calls them back from the grave to account for their crimes. In the course of this "Ghost Sonata" (*SLW* 142), he recalls various humiliations, including the time when, at the age of nineteen, he was slapped in the face for talking: "And I—the fury is still inside me today—I didn't hit back. Such were the methods of objectivity" (*Sachlichkeit; SLW* 157).

The concept of *Sachlichkeit* is at the heart of the debate between the teachers and their former pupil.[12] We have seen how Döblin used the word positively to describe the ideal of objectivity, the "style of stone" of the Berlin Program. Now *Sachlichkeit* undergoes a revaluation as an ideological category. It becomes the chief component of the Prussian mentality, an internalized oppression. The teachers claim it as one of the virtues taught at the school: "To be *sachlich* is to be Prussian" (*SLW* 149). Döblin, making use of the root of the word (*Sache*), gives it the connotation of "reification," reducing a human being to a thing: "You wanted to make me, this 'I,' utterly into your object. Into an object. That was it. Into a vessel of your objectivity" (*SLW* 150). And Döblin declares that this supposed objectivity is not really objective at all, but rather serves the purposes of the state: "You didn't want to hear the word 'I.' I don't give a damn for the 'I' either, but in your case, someone did say 'I.' It came from a single source: the state!" (*SLW* 150). The common thread running through both the trauma of the family and the school is the struggle between authority and freedom. Döblin's attitude toward this struggle, like his attitude toward the revolution, is perforce ambiguous. He must condemn his father's flight to freedom as irresponsible and destructive. Yet he cannot wholly take his mother's side either, for there are clear parallels between the authority of propriety and convention she exercised over her family (clearest in the case of Döblin's sister), and the authority—exercised by the *Gymnasium* teachers—of the state over the individual. Döblin passionately rejects the latter: "I have not served [the state]. Not I! Even today I serve no state. No one can ever persuade me to" (*SLW* 150–151). One suspects that his rejection of state authority is the more vehement because such rejection was impossible in the case of his mother.

To see how and why Döblin combines such autobiographical elements with a political vision in *Men without Mercy,* we must look more closely at Döblin's political position in the final years of the Republic, already anticipated by his attack on the revolution in "First Glance Back." We have seen that the novelist himself was acutely aware of the dilemma in which he left Franz Biberkopf at the end of *Berlin Alexanderplatz,* the limbo between insight into a violent and coercive social order and concrete action to change that order. In the final years of the Weimar Republic, this was anything but a purely aesthetic question. *Berlin Alexanderplatz* was immediately attacked in the journal *Linkskurve,* the organ of the League of Proletarian Revolutionary Writers, whose reviewer Klaus Neukrantz discovered concealed in the novel "a reactionary and counterrevolutionary attack against the thesis of organized class struggle." About the central character, Neukrantz wrote that the "artificial, mystical, unenlightened Franz Biberkopf, the 'good person'" had been "intentionally isolated . . . from the proletariat's mission of class struggle."[13] Although Döblin responded with a brilliant and stinging counterattack ("Katastrophe in einer Linkskurve"; *SPG* 247–53), the charges of the orthodox Marxists had a grain of truth to them.[14] Of course, he had never intended Biberkopf to be a typical proletarian. He does not become a "humble working man" until the end of the novel, but even then there is no answer for him as straightforward as joining the "organized class struggle." As we have seen, he is at the end theoretically ready for some sort of solidarity, but still alone.

The question of proper action and of activist literature was much on Döblin's mind in the increasingly polarized and violent atmosphere of the early thirties in Germany. Certainly the language and style of *Berlin Alexanderplatz* represent among other things an attempt to speak to a wider audience than Döblin had in his previous novels, and its popularity attests to the partial success of the attempt. At the end of 1929, in a speech on the naturalist poet and playwright Arno Holz, Döblin demanded the "elimination of the monopoly on education" and "lowering the general level of literature" and urged his fellow writers to "turn towards the great mass of the people" (*AzL* 145). He also said that the naturalist movement, stifled early in the century by the dominant bourgeois culture, was now being continued" in the form of political theater and committed art" (*AzL* 144).

Döblin here aligns himself implicitly with Bertolt Brecht and Erwin Piscator, his fellow members of the Gruppe 1925, an informal gathering of left-liberal and Communist writers that discussed politics and art between 1925 and 1928.[15] In fact, at the time he gave his speech on Arno Holz, Döblin himself was already at work on "Die Ehe" (Marriage; *DHF* 172–261), a piece of "political theater" whose theme anticipates *Men without Mercy*. The idea for a play critical of the bourgeois institution of marriage originated in the Gruppe 1925, and Erich Kleinschmidt has suggested that the project was also a response to the criticism *Berlin Alexanderplatz* had received from the Left.[16] Of course, Döblin's hatred of the institution of bourgeois marriage goes all the way back to "Modern." The play is a piece of agitprop theater heavily influenced by Brecht's techniques of alienation: it makes use of a "Speaker" who directs the action and addresses the audience, of texts and pictures projected on a screen, and of songs and recitatives used to comment upon and alienate the action. It consists of three unrelated "scenes" devoted, respectively, to a young proletarian wife who dies during an illegal abortion forced upon her by poverty and unemployment; the family of an unemployed gardener, unable to find housing and torn apart by an inhumane welfare system; and a cynical marriage of convenience among the *haute bourgeoisie*.

Although "Marriage" was banned as Communist propaganda two weeks after its premiere in Munich in November 1930, there is more Marxism in Döblin's first story "Modern" than in the entire play. Its message is simply that money rules the world, and that the institutions of marriage and the family are callously undermined (among the proletariat) or cynically exploited (among the bourgeoisie) by capitalist society. The play is a curious mix of pathos in the first two scenes and heavy-handed satire in the third. In spite of all the techniques of Brechtian distancing and alienation, the Speaker unnecessarily belabors the villains of the piece (*DHF* 191) or falls into the pathos of righteous indignation (*DHF* 225), without in the end making clear what the point of the play is. The programmatic slogan "Know and Change!" is projected onto the screen at the beginning of the first scene (*DHF* 182), yet when the widower of the woman who dies having an abortion asks the pertinent question, "What should I do?", the Speaker's only answer is the doggerel "You've got to march along with the rest, my boy, nobody gets anything for free, first you've got to clench your fists, then slap the pavement with your shoes" (*DHF* 200), sung to the tune of a "saucy march." Klaus Müller-Salget has pointed out the superficial similarity to the march rhythms at the end of *Berlin Alexanderplatz*, but calls the verses in "Marriage" "nothing but a rhymed soap bubble." [17] Whether or not "Marriage" succeeds as a piece of political theater, it is an indication of Döblin's increasing interest in activist art, in an art able to reach a broad audience and to have some effect upon society. It is also important that the theme he chose for his only political play was the seemingly private one of marriage. Especially the last scene suggests that the power struggle within marriage is for him a reflection of a similar struggle in society as a whole. The play's programmatic call to "Know and Change!" became the title of Döblin's next book, a tract in which he tried to define his own political position.

Begun as a response to an open letter to Döblin from the university student Gustav René Hocke, *Know and Change!* grew into Döblin's most extensive political statement. Both the book and the controversy it ignited are a testimony to the fragmentation of the German Left in the last years of the Weimar Republic. [18] Hocke's question to Döblin was at once naive and straightforward, an intellectual's version of the husband's question from "Marriage": where is an intellectual to stand in the increasingly sharp conflict of parties and opinions? What can one, as an intellectual, do? [19] Döblin's answer is a critique of Marxism and a call for true socialism, which he defines as "Freedom, spontaneous alliance among people, rejection of all compulsion, rebellion against injustice and compulsion, humaneness, tolerance, dedication to peace" (*WV* 141). This, says Döblin, is the heart of the socialist idea, the ideal that must inform any concrete action. The Communists, he writes, make the mistake of reducing socialism to the doctrines of historical materialism and economic determinism. Döblin rejects the central Marxist concept of class struggle as the means to a socialist future, since it simply perpetuates militarism and violence: "From a thing comes nothing that wasn't already in it" (*WV* 141). Döblin defines the place of the bourgeois intellectual as "beside the workers," but not among them (*WV* 170). The intellectual must declare his solidarity with their goals, but insist on the values of true socialism not just in the ends, but also in the means.

Döblin's socialism is in essence an ethical ideal, uninformed by any sense of how it could or should be practically organized. But it is at any rate self-evident that the modern capitalist state does not meet the criteria of true socialism and must be done away with. Döblin has returned to a critique of industrial capitalism, thus coming full circle from his position in "The Spirit of the Naturalistic Age." The 1924 essay, as we have seen, glorified "Man the collective being" and suggested that the present phase of the naturalistic impulse inevitably involves imperialism and the "gigantic wars" it produces. Döblin now inveighs "Against Collectivism, the Ideal of the Anthill and the Machine" (*WV* 173) and demands "elevation of the person, the individual" (*WV* 175). In the philosophical work *Unser Dasein* (Our Existence), written about the same time but not published until 1933, Döblin even retracts the image of the coral colony central to "The Spirit of the Naturalistic Age": "Although there is no 'absolute' Person, we humans certainly do not exist on the level of the coral animals" (*UD* 421).

This new shift in position results from a new interpretation of history. Like "The Spirit of the Naturalistic Age," the tract *Know and Change!* contains a historical overview. But whereas in the earlier essay, Döblin was interested in the international development of the scientific method and technology, he now outlines the course of German social and political history. He essentially follows the lines of the standard liberal analysis of the failure of the German bourgeoisie to reach political maturity. Martin Luther's revolution only went half way, because while securing freedom of thought and conscience for the individual—in theory, at any rate—it left him politically the subject of the absolutist German princes. The individual was thus split, even more than during the Middle Ages, into a spiritual and a temporal half. According to Döblin, Luther began the intellectual flowering which ended in naturalism, that is, in a world no longer split between the here and the hereafter, but a unity in which spirit inhabits everything and man unfolds his being in the present moment. This is essentially the world view Döblin had already expounded in *The I over Nature* and would repeat and expand upon in *Our Existence.*

In Germany, however, the social liberation that should have accompanied this spiritual liberation was frustrated and blocked. After the suppression of the Revolution of 1848, the bourgeoisie made a pact with the feudal ruling class, the nobility and the military, to eschew political power in favor of economic and industrial power. In this situation, the torch of naturalism and its social and political correlative, socialism, passed to the working class. This is why in Döblin's logic the intellectual, who necessarily desires the realization of the socialist ideal, must ally himself with the workers. Throughout his analysis, he is uncomfortable with the terms "bourgeoisie" and "proletariat" because he regards them as ideological, Marxist categories: "'Proletariat' is a program; we don't accept it" (*WV* 190). He divides German society into the feudal ruling class and the exploited majority, the "citizenry" (*Bürgerschaft*). Thus bourgeois and worker in Döblin's view actually belong to the same class, and it is the bourgeois who after 1848 betrays his class and the socialist ideal by cooperating with the oppressors. This analysis allows the bourgeois intellectual to ally himself with the workers and yet still remain within his class (*WV* 216–228).

Yet in spite of its declaration of solidarity with the working class (a declaration Döblin also makes in "First Glance Back"), *Know and Change!* in the end is caught in a dilemma which leftist critics of the work immediately pounced upon with glee, as Döblin himself noted: "It enticed them to the wildest dances of joy that a book should begin with the question of what we should do, and end with the sentence, 'And so you will soon know what is to be done'" (*SPG* 271). Since Döblin explicitly rejects class struggle and scorns political parties in general, it is indeed unclear what the intellectual is to do aside from advocating the ideals of socialism and declaring his sympathy for the workers. Leo Kreutzer writes that Döblin achieves the "pretense of a solution" by simply equating insight and action, "knowing" and "changing."[20] Biberkopf's position at the end of *Berlin Alexanderplatz* has still not been overcome.

What prevents Döblin from articulating concrete measures is his basic anarchism, consistent throughout his career but increasingly articulated in his later years. As early as 1924, the answer to the terrible, hypertrophic technocratic state in *Mountains Seas and Giants* were the small bands of "settlers." And the motto to Döblin's 1926 work *Reise in Polen* (Journey in Poland) is a rebellious quote from Schiller's *Wilhelm Tell:* "There is a limit to the tyrant's power," followed by Döblin's commentary: "Let all states—and the state in general—take note" (*RP* 5). In 1928, Döblin resigned from the German Social Democratic Party "out of protest against bureaucracy and bossism,"[21] and it is with an anarchist, not a Communist, that Franz Biberkopf conducts the only real, extensive political discussion in *Berlin Alexanderplatz*. It is not surprising, then, that Döblin ends *Know and Change!* with a call for a return to "the normal and natural grouping of people in small associations," for a "dismantling of the public sphere" and a "reordering of private life" (*WV* 263). Döblin's idea seems to be that the state will gradually disintegrate as the society reorganizes itself into small bands and interest groups: "It can only be a question of the powerful increase of real, i.e., small social groups and their 'private' life, which will then lead to a weakening of the state" (*WV* 266).[22] The helplessness that speaks from this sentence is palpable, especially when one remembers that the Nazis had already become the second strongest party in the Reichstag by 1930.

The intellectual still ends up between the classes, where Döblin had always thought of himself as being—both as a writer and a doctor: "[Health Service doctors] get their ideas and their ethical categories from the class from which they come, the bourgeoisie, and as a rule, they keep to them their whole life long. . . . Economically, the Health Service doctor stands somewhere between a free professional, a government official, and an employee, but—without being any of the three, and his spiritual situation is just as indecisive" (*SPG* 244). Döblin, predisposed to isolation by his profession and temperament, experienced increasing political isolation in the divided Left of the late Weimar Republic, a condition that became almost absolute in his exile after 1933.

☐

Döblin wrote *Men without Mercy* in 1934, in exile outside Paris, and his loneliness no doubt encouraged the inward turn of the novel toward self-reflection about his family and their fate. We have seen that later in his life, Döblin characterized *Men without Mercy* as a "family history with a dash of autobiography," and there can be no doubt that the family and its internal struggles lie at its center.[23]

Karl, the central character, arrives in the city at the age of sixteen along with his mother and two younger siblings. Their father has squandered his wife's dowry on irresponsible business ventures and then died. The mother (who receives no other name throughout the novel) brings her children to Berlin, where she has a brother, a furniture manufacturer, who can help them. She is hounded by her husband's creditors, and uses for the first time the leitmotif of the novel's title to describe them: "They give no quarter—they'll have their pound of flesh" (*P* 18–19, *MWM* 19). In despair, she tries to commit suicide, but Karl saves her. From then on, he is in her psychological debt.

He is at first a naive country bumpkin, easily impressed by the imposing palaces and museums of the royal quarter on a hill overlooking the city. But in looking for work, he meets an older boy named Paul, a charismatic proletarian leader who opens Karl's eyes to the injustices perpetrated against the working classes. Paul draws the younger boy into his revolutionary activity, and repeats the leitmotif: "You'll come with me into battle, and I tell you straight, no quarter will be given" (*P* 85, *MWM* 99). The mother, on the other hand, wants to succeed within the system by becoming more ruthless than the oppressors. The struggle of the vampirelike mother with the revolutionary Paul for Karl's soul culminates in book 1, "Poverty." The mother prevents her son from fleeing with Paul, whom the police are seeking, by locking him in their apartment.

Book 2, "Boom," is the shortest of the novel but covers the most narrated time. It begins with the marriage of the thirty-year-old Karl, now a successful young business partner of his uncle, to Julie, a girl from an upper-class family. Karl's mother has won, and he has left his youthful idealism behind. In a flashback, we learn that his conformity to the capitalist ideal has been bought at the price of his spiritual death. His hatred for his mother has been suppressed and converted into self-loathing. In the business world he uses his power ruthlessly, while at home he is overprotective of his wife and rigidly ritualistic in their sexual relations. Only the fact that he insists on living in the old proletarian neighborhood where he grew up intimates the hold that the supposedly buried past continues to have on him.

In book 3, "Crisis," both his public and private worlds begin to crumble. Julie rebels against the rigid constraints of their marriage and begins a love affair with the attaché of a foreign embassy. At the same time, an economic crash begins abroad and threatens to engulf Karl's country. Karl profits from the distress of the lower classes, and when they become restive, he begins to finance right-wing paramilitary formations. His wife leaves him for her lover, taking their two children with her. Karl swindles a business partner and becomes increasingly isolated from both the middle-class industrialists and the upper-class investors. He begins to lead a double life, patronizing prostitutes at night in shabby, working-class clothes while he continues his business during the day. Amid rising social unrest, the revolutionary Paul turns up again after years in exile. Karl's love for him comes flooding back, but Paul tells him it is now too late to switch sides.

In the armed struggle that now ensues, Karl is determined to fight on the side of the workers. Hoping to reach the revolutionaries by pretending to march with a civil defense squad, he is caught in the fire between the fronts and killed. The rebelling workers are overcome and the revolution is suppressed. Karl's mother returns to the provinces, while his passive younger brother Erich, a pharmacist, remains in the city.

□

The Manichean dualism in Döblin's image of women, embodied in the figures of Gaby and Pauline in *Wadzek* and Mieze and the Whore of Babylon in *Berlin Alexanderplatz,* recurs in *Men without Mercy* in the figures of the mother and Julie. In the course of the novel, the focus shifts from the relationship between mother and son in books 1 and 2 to that between husband and wife in book 3, where the mother disappears for long stretches of the narrative. In the first half of the novel, however, she dominates and determines the action.

The figure of the mother is one of the most powerful in the novel, a late and complex variation on the figure of Pauline Wadzek. Karl's mother is the ultimate battleground for Döblin's conflicting feelings about women because she is closest to the source of those feelings, his own mother. In *Wadzek* the style of stone, by limiting itself strictly to externals, made of Pauline a repellant monster. The realistic narrative to which Döblin has reverted in *Men without Mercy* allows the emergence of a much more differentiated and subtly drawn character. The narrator of *Men without Mercy*, like the narrator in *Berlin Alexanderplatz*, moves freely from dialogue to unvoiced thoughts, from third to first person:

> "I've no one else now, Karl. Sit down a moment, you're a big boy, you understand things now. I must unburden myself to someone; you saw all that went on at home, all that trouble with your father, and the auction (I wasn't able to say a word to him, either, but I can't stand it any longer, even if I have no one but the wall to talk to, I shall scream it out). Someone will have to help me, I can't go on like this." (She glanced at her clenched fist, he has left me in the lurch, he used me, he never considered me, never, never, and now he's landed me in this mess as well).
>
> (*P* 19, *MWM* 19–20)

The narrator is at pains to present the mother fairly, showing the reasons for her bitterness and calculating ambition. He sketches the history of her family of provincial artisans and petty officials, something Döblin has previously done only for the positive female figures Gaby and Mieze. The mother's marriage was a love match, an attempt to "shake off the lethargy of her dying class. It had been her longing for warmth, candour, love, for frank speech and laughter, that had drawn her towards her husband" (*P* 156, *MWM* 187). Her misfortune is to have chosen the wrong man, and the disaster of her marriage has deformed her longing for love into guilt and a need for security. The father's exploitation and oppression of the mother is paradigmatic for all familial relationships in the novel:[24] "The Family Grinds You Down" (*Die Familie mahlt Menschen*), as one of the chapter titles has it. The images used to describe the family are primarily of battle. The father was the "common enemy" (*P* 15, *MWM* 14) of Karl and his mother; mother and son in their turn are locked for years in "a wearing war of position" (*P* 125, *MWM* 148). The mother's victory over Karl, her crushing of his spirit and idealism, is thus not an isolated event, but repeats and perpetuates her husband's crushing of her own need for love. Karl will carry the same oppression into his relationship with Julie. Döblin uses Karl's family history to suggest that middle-class families are by nature oppressive and love-denying.

When one looks at families from other classes in the novel, a shift of focus is evident. In describing Julie's upper-class family, Döblin is consistently satiric. The focus shifts again when the working class is under observation. When Karl and Paul come upon a working-class tragedy in which an angry mother kicks her daughter and accidentally kills her, Paul makes Karl understand that the origins of lower-class callousness and brutality lie in oppression and exploitation (*P* 58–61, *MWM* 67–70). This difference in treatment is an echo of the contrast in "Modern" between sarcasm concerning the "ladies' question" and pathos toward the "women's question." It is also present in the difference between the first two acts of the agitprop drama "Marriage," dealing with the working class, and the satire of an industrialist's family in the third act. Throughout his career, Döblin savagely satirizes the upper-class family while treating the working-class family with sympathetic naturalism and often with pathos, as a product of the repressions and dislocations of industrial capitalism.[25]

Karl's little family—neither proletarian nor upper class—are presented as timelessly archetypical. The mother is mythologized into "a kind of modern Hecuba" (*P* 131, *MWM* 157), just as Karl toward the end of the novel is raised to the level of mythic hero by the old school principal whom Julie consults: "Karl is a fighter, a brave man who has forced his way up to his present position. And now the demons whom the gods send to plague mankind are assailing him. . . . He's not made of the stuff of the weaklings of today" (*P* 330–31, *MWM* 398).[26] In *Berlin Alexanderplatz*, Döblin uses mythological parallels in montage to lend resonance and depth to the story of his Everyman Franz Biberkopf. In *Men without Mercy*, the central characters themselves—especially the mother, Karl and Paul—have an archetypal aspect that is heightened by the schematization of their names and of the setting.

When Julie enters this constellation by marrying Karl, she is gradually transformed from the "spoiled only daughter of a prominent architect" (*P* 148, *MWM* 178)—still an object of satire in the wedding scene that opens book 2—into an increasingly complex and sympathetic character. Early in their marriage Karl systematically molds and defines her as the perfect wife, and the narrator makes it plain that he is repeating what his mother has done to him. But after ten years of marriage, Julie begins to grow restive under the yoke of this all-too-perfect union. When Karl praises their home as a "fortress" in which they can take shelter from the storms of society, she realizes, "I must be the prisoner, Herr Commandant" (*P* 197, *MWM* 234). This conversation is the beginning of her realization that she has been cheated of love and fulfillment by this marriage, and it is not long before she begins her affair with the attaché José. For Julie the affair begins as a desperate escape from the emotional straitjacket of her marriage, for José as an amusing erotic diversion, but they gradually realize that they have fallen in love. Julie abducts the two children from Karl's apartment and they eventually settle in a suburban cottage, an idyll where they revel "in the joys of living together for the first time amid the beauties of early summer" (*P* 303, *MWM* 365). In a parenthetical aside in the last paragraph of the novel, we learn that "Julie and the children left the country shortly afterwards and broke away from [the family's] destiny" (*P* 370, *MWM* 446). This "happy end" for Julie and the children suggests the possibility of attaining real happiness in marriage, of escaping the family that "grinds you down," of breaking the chain of inherited oppression.

But Julie's escape from Karl's "destiny" is only a subplot, almost an afterthought. Its significance is to some extent reduced by the cliché nature of her love affair,[27] and even more by Julie's reaction to Karl when they meet to discuss the divorce. He has begun his double life, living in a cheap hotel and patronizing streetwalkers, and he tells her about it. The prostitutes signify for Karl both libidinal liberation and a chance to punish Julie: "You had the woman, whatever her name was, in your arms, you triumphed, she hadn't gone away, you embraced her and flung yourself on her. She had at once to suffer and to give love and punishment, humiliation and degradation" (*P* 307, *MWM* 370). Suddenly Julie is attracted to Karl precisely because of his new life. Just as the prostitutes symbolize her for Karl, she now offers to become one of them:

> "Shall I come to you, Karl?" What was she saying? "Would you like to, Julie? Where? To my room in the suburbs?" "I'll think it over. I must have a word with you tomorrow or the day after, d'you hear?" "I shall be here." As they got up, she gave him her hand. Suddenly she had a desire to lay her head on his breast, but at the sight of his uncanny, fixed stare she retreated (what's he doing to me?).
> (*P* 313–14, *MWM* 378)

Julie's offer fits the pattern of relationships we have already seen in Döblin's works, especially in *Berlin Alexanderplatz*. As soon as she sees Karl's inner torment, she is ready to sacrifice herself to him; but more than this, she is clearly attracted to the idea of playing the role of a prostitute. Similarly, the young intellectual with whom Karl briefly flirts thinks, "Who was this who was embracing her? And she was allowing such a thing to happen? He could kiss me as though I were a silly little goose, or rape me as though I were a streetwalker" (*P* 246, *MWM* 293). Once the self-effacing, masochistic relationship has been established, Julie is of no more importance in the novel. She has not really liberated herself from Karl's oppression, only managed to escape it into a cliché of conventional happiness. Karl's "destiny" involves not her but Paul, the only person Karl has really loved.

☐

Again we find a relationship with homoerotic overtones at the center of a Döblin novel. In the disguises he wears to hide from the police, the young revolutionary Paul favors female clothing. Dressed as a street-walker, he meets Karl:

> With a wheedling glance Paul offered him his arm, whispered: "If any-one comes, we'll pretend to be a loving couple." And just then two men came out of the house, smoking and talking loudly, walked unheeding past the pair, who were locked in a tender embrace. Karl had never yet held a woman in his arms. Now from close to he inhaled the fragrance of the dress, felt the soft stuff and embraced—Paul.
> (*P* 99–100, *MWM* 116)

After Paul has left the city, the young Karl is "in a state of positively physical longing" for him (*P* 125, *MWM* 148), and when Paul returns after years away, this yearning returns and automatically displaces the "bestiality" of his double life among the streetwalkers of the pro-letarian districts (*P* 340, *MWM* 409).[28]

In a more radical way than Julie in her relationship to José, Paul represents an alternative to the oppression of Karl's petit-bourgeois family. Paul is unencumbered by any family ties: "[The mother] was unable to discover anything about Paul's family; he told her that he had come here alone from a provincial town at the age of fourteen, there had been too many of them at home, he had soon managed to get on" (*P* 77, *MWM* 89). He scornfully calls Karl "you mother's darling" (*P* 58, *MWM* 67), and it is clear to both Paul and the mother that they are adversaries in the battle for Karl. They both use the leitmotif "no quarter given" to refer to the heartlessness of the social struggle, and they begin from the same premise: that society is controlled by a rich minority who exploit the poor majority. But whereas Paul is com-mitted to changing the society, the mother has chosen for Karl the path of conformity to society's expectations and individual achievement. Rather than rebel, she will beat the exploiters at their own game. She regards her poverty as a purely personal misfortune which she must overcome, just as the ex-convict Biberkopf vows to live a decent life and rely only on himself. When Karl tries to explain to his mother the lessons of social justice and solidarity he is learning from Paul, it is clear both how close and how far apart are the two adversaries for Karl's soul:

> Had anyone, before the night she attempted suicide, when she had still been wandering about like a hunted animal, used such expressions, she would have vehemently agreed with him. To give vent to her despair she would herself have brought forward very much the same denunciations. She too would have gone forth with a torch against those others, those cruel, hard oppressors. Terribly true words, true yesterday, today, true for ever. How well Paul knew how to get at her Karl! But she would not let him get at him. What concern of this fellow Paul's was her poverty? It was her personal misfortune, she'd find a way out all right.
>
> (*P* 87, *MWM* 102)

In the first book of the novel, Paul's analysis of society is the same as the mother's, although their conclusions about what should be done differ radically. In the third book, it becomes clear that the analysis and program of the mature revolutionary Paul, laid out during a conversation with the pampered intellectual Erich toward the end of the novel, is identical to Döblin's own analysis and program in *Know and Change!*[29]

The old noble ruling class is still in power, deriving its legitimacy from empty tradition and outworn principles: "They live on falsehood, are utterly hollow, but there they are, in control, bathed in the glories of the past, heirs of the bygone ages, resting on the laurels and ideas of others" (*P* 336, *MWM* 404). The bourgeoisie (or the "earners"—*die Verdiener*—as Döblin calls them both here and in *Know and Change!*) have the economic power but have sold out to the old ruling class, whom they emulate: "The men at the top have given these money-grubbers—the stupidest, most wretched crowd the earth has ever produced—have given these robbers, criminals and their toadies, the clerks, a free hand, and in return they are kept by them. And that (he raised his voice) is their inexpiable crime, a crime for which they'll one day have to pay dearly" (*P* 336–337, *MWM* 405).

The only hope for change lies in the working class, but it has been led astray by its political leaders. Paul scorns the proletarian parties who preach gradualism:

And what are these masses doing, who are supposed to be everything, they and their leaders and parties? Are they rising up in revolt because the selfishness, incapacity and wretchedness of the governing class cry out to heaven? No, they're carrying on their old quarrels, whining and protesting about unemployment, about low wages, while fundamentally they only want things to be as they were. The slave feels happy in his chains. And yet how much force and courage there is in some of them!
(*P* 338, *MWM* 406)

The legitimate and gradualist party in the novel corresponds to the German Social-Democratic Party. These are the men whom Karl meets when he begins his apprenticeship in his uncle's factory:

They were workers, a quiet, steady type of men such as the countryside produced and the workshops needed. They talked in the same way as Paul and Gustav, had the same views on a number of things, but they were docile. For, according to them, if the capitalist had nothing to do, they themselves would have no work, and moreover, without the capitalists the workers would be mere ciphers; still they must not put up with everything, they had to protect their interests against wage cuts; had to have accident and health insurance, provision had to be made for the welfare of the women in the workshops and factories, and the insurance societies must be made to grant maternity benefit.
(*P* 126–27, *MWM* 151)

The economic crisis that begins in the third book causes a schism and the formation of a more radical, revolutionary proletarian party, corresponding to the German Communist Party: "Those who were well fed and were merely a little anxious stood by the old gang, those who were gnashing their teeth in despair joined the new faction. . . . They were no longer isolated individuals, directing their attacks against particular individuals in the camp of the enemy, but were a definite group, their ranks as closed as the ranks of their adversaries. Soon semi-military formations grew up among them" (*P* 232, *MWM* 276).

In opposition to both of these organized parties, Paul's philosophy is clearly anarchist and favors spontaneous action. He issues proclamations "against the discipline of these . . . organizations" (*P* 351, *MWM* 423). Moreover, Döblin's polemics against the Marxist doctrine of class struggle in *Know and Change!* are echoed in Paul's handbills: "Who is it that has let things go so far that the fight for justice, reason and the dignity of man has been turned into a class war? Shame on the rulers and possessing classes of this country, who have laid the burden of this fight on the poor and the very poorest in the land!" Paul attempts to appeal across class lines, and this distinguishes him from the radical workers' party: "An appeal was made to the enslaved bourgeois, the duped shopkeeper, to all who worked and laboured" (*P* 352, *MWM* 424).[30] But while Döblin's solution in *Know and Change!* had been nonviolent, Paul issues a straightforward call to the oppressed to arm themselves and overthrow their exploiters (*P* 340, 352, *MWM* 408–409, 424). This is a significant change, and may reflect Döblin's realization, in hindsight, that only direct, armed action of some kind could have prevented the Nazi accession to power. Paul forms his followers into fighting battalions: "The only organisation that was worth anything on the other side, he said, was the Army, and hence the country needed this other army, for, he said with a laugh, one must always hear both sides of a question" (*P* 334, *MWM* 402). But the novel leaves his ultimate goal unclear: "he hoped here—not to win a victory, but to drive the enemy into a corner" (*P* 333, *MWM* 401).

In fact, the only concrete force in the novel that unifies the revolutionaries is the charismatic personality of Paul, "his old power of gathering people around him and impressing his will on them" (*P* 333, *MWM* 401), the same power and charm that had attracted the young Karl. This charisma suggests that Döblin still regards history as primarily created by great leaders like Wang-lun and Wallenstein, whom the masses need to give them direction.[31] Perhaps because Paul has no historical model but originates in the abstract idea of an ideal revolutionary, he is a rather pale character, not without touches of kitsch:[32] "What a deep, penetrating look came from those wide, hard, glittering blue eyes! Had he always had such bright eyes?" (*P* 324, *MWM* 390–91).

But there is a much more problematic aspect to him and his program. We have seen that Karl finally loses his soul to the capitalist system when he learns to enjoy "the atmosphere of power, of contempt for mankind" (*P* 144, *MWM* 173). In this novel, power is always the power of the exploiters, and always engenders contempt for the weak. Paul, the ideal revolutionary, must therefore be powerless by choice, must hope "not to win a victory." The uprising he directs from his secret headquarters is thus from the beginning certain to be crushed by the forces of the state. The figure of Paul, caught between the need for action and the rejection of the power necessary for success, is ultimately contradictory. It is no surprise that Döblin allows him to disappear from the novel even more thoroughly than Julie: we don't learn what happens to him during the uprising. He too is ultimately only important as the embodiment of revolutionary ideals impinging on Karl's life.

□

Karl is himself a vehicle of political ideas. Walter Muschg calls him a "representative of the German bourgeoisie" (*P* 378), but more than that, his life is a telescoped version of the history of the German middle class as Döblin outlines it in *Know and Change!* His youthful idealism corresponds to the ideals of 1848; his rise as an industrialist, to the depoliticizing of the bourgeoisie after 1848. His final attempt to join the revolutionaries reflects the attempts of left-liberal intellectuals (Döblin among them) to find a common ground with the proletarian parties during the Weimar Republic. What makes Karl more than the abstract vehicle for this parallelism, and a more convincing character than Paul, is the way the novel interweaves his personal and his political life.[33]

Wadzek's life begins to unravel when he realizes that he can no longer separate business and family life. This pattern is repeated in *Men without Mercy*, but expanded by the sociopolitical dimension. The family is here presented as the embryo of the whole society: "things are so arranged in this world that people need one another; that man cannot live without woman, woman without man, children without parents, and these little groups cannot live without larger groups, larger groups, again, without still larger groups" (*P* 173, *MWM* 207). The ship metaphor of human interdependence, so foreign to the spirit of most of *Wadzek*, and the solidarity called for at the end of *Berlin Alexanderplatz* are in *Men without Mercy* the presupposition of the novel. Döblin now states explicitly that humans are the products of both a familial and a social past.

The life of Karl's archetypical, mythologized family is, like political life, dominated by a struggle for power. The symbolic power of a battle painting Karl first sees in the Pantheon on the hill above the city derives from its simultaneous reflection of political and psychic reality. In *Berlin Alexanderplatz*, the painting on Ida's wall that celebrates Germany's victory over France in the Franco-Prussian war serves as an ironic comment on Biberkopf's impotence; Biberkopf, reversing the meaning of the picture, sees the Kaiser handing back the sword to the

Frenchman (*BA* 38, *EJ* 37). In *Men without Mercy,* a similar depiction of military victory entails a similar reversal, but this time the reversal is carried out by society rather than the individual. Now an entire population revels in its own exploitation: "[The King's] obedient people, to whom he had in due time conceded certain liberties in gratitude for their bravery in the war, had, loyal to the past, made the best possible use of them; they laboured and laboured and—one might almost say, from the lowest to the highest—did their utmost to increase the power and wealth of the state, in order in their turn to show their gratitude and to be in every respect a truly royal people" (*P* 78–79, *MWM* 91).

In relation to Karl, the painting has additional ironies. Consciously, he interprets it as a straightforward emblem of victory and success. At the crest of his business career and as head of an apparently exemplary family, Karl is "the king on the hill after the victory" (*P* 200–201, *MWM* 238). When his business is threatened and his marriage begins to collapse, he thinks, "Soon I shall be the vanquished king carrying his sword to the other king on his horse at the top of the hill" (*P* 270, *MWM* 325). In both passages, the personal sphere is figuratively connected to business and politics, and both are subsumed in the painting, a symbol both Karl and the population as a whole have thoroughly internalized. Karl has accepted his mother's interpretation of society. Like Wadzek and Biberkopf he heroicizes himself, he must stand or fall on his own.

It is manifest that Karl's marriage is merely an adjunct to his rise in society: "He knew that he owed it to society, to his family and to his rising fortunes to marry" (*P* 146, *MWM* 175). The fate of this marriage is intimately connected to the fate of the economy. The happiness and perfection Karl believes he has achieved in marriage are merely a reflection of the optimism and prosperity of the *Gründerjahre:* "The boom bore them along with it and watched over them" (*P* 151, *MWM* 181). When Julie for the first time expresses her unhappiness at his authoritarian household regime, he immediately perceives her as a traitor, a "revolutionary" (*P* 197, *MWM* 234). The connection between the two spheres of his life is of course invisible to Karl, whose watchword is "My house is my castle" (*P* 150, *MWM* 180).[34] To even mention business to his wife "would be tantamount to a declaration of bankruptcy" (*P* 193, *MWM* 229).

What Karl does to Julie only perpetuates what his mother has done to him. The parallels and the interconnectedness between the repressive family and the repressive society are most clearly stated in the first book, "Poverty," where the mother makes the decision to use Paul as her tool of both survival in society and revenge against her dead husband. It is Karl's mother, not Paul, who first opens his eyes to the rapaciousness of the economic system. It is she who deflates his image of the grandeur of the imperial quarter: "'Didn't they charge admission?' 'No,' he answered. She laughed, 'I bet they didn't. They let you in free so that you can admire them. If we're here long enough, they'll let us pay taxes for the privilege'" (*P* 29, *MWM* 31).[35] Unlike Karl, the mother has no illusions about the nature of society. Yet her response is emulation of the worst in her exploiters: "They won't get anything from me. I hate them. I don't care if they know that I'm cheating them. They think they're the only ones who can play that game. I can do it, too" (*P* 47, *MWM* 54). She accepts the world the ruling class has defined as unchangeable, and determines to use her son to triumph over that world.

The narrator speaks at one point of a "threefold crime": "the crime of the mother against her son, his crime against himself . . . his betrayal of society" (*P* 153, *MWM* 183). They are all aspects of the same crime. The psychic turning points in Karl's life are, first, the point at which he is reconciled with his mother and internalizes his hate for her as self-loathing, and second, his internalization of the values of the ruling class. His transformation is complete when he tastes and enjoys "the atmosphere of power, of contempt for mankind" (*P* 144, *MWM* 173). This is the negative *Sachlichkeit* that Döblin attacks as the repressive Prussian heritage in both "First Glance Back" and *Know and Change!*: "He now belonged to that type of man who not only constructs machines, but has learned from them" (*P* 144, *MWM* 173).[36] That Karl can now rationalize away the poverty he sees in the streets and finance right-wing paramilitary groups is only the logical consequence of his development. His thinking is ruled by a kind of perverted Marxism, a cynical economic determinism. Through the introduction of cheap mass-produced furniture, Karl attracts the money of the rising working class: "The whole question of consumers' purchasing power was carefully investigated, and the public was induced to buy— one might even say to set up house and enter into matrimony—by means of a clever installment system" (*P* 180, *MWM* 215).

Yet this cynical calculation only masks the fact that Karl himself

feels determined by the objects that surround him, the totems of bourgeois existence. He lectures his wife: "Clothes make the man, that
is certain, but furniture makes the family. One is almost powerless
against a sideboard, a leather-upholstered suite, when they stand
round one on a carpet specially selected for them. They prescribe one's
gait, one's expression, even one's thoughts" (P 195, MWM 231–32).
After Julie leaves him he wanders through the house and must subdue
these objects once more, must prove that he is their master. He finally
destroys his "museum," the grand salon in which hangs his copy of the
battle painting, and this destruction seems the symbolic precondition
for the reappearance of Paul. The demonic power of similar physical objects in *Wadzek's Battle with the Steam Turbine* has been de-
mythologized in *Men without Mercy*. Now they clearly refer to the
economic and social structure which Karl has allowed to determine
his life.

☐

On the level of both the family and society, *Men without Mercy* is
a novel of betrayal and the possibility of redemption. It begins as a
chain of betrayals: the father betrays the mother, the mother Karl, and
Karl his own ideals and his wife. As a representative of the middle
class, he betrays society by exploiting the workers and making common cause with the ruling aristocracy. It is less clear that either private
or social redemption is possible. The problematic question of solidarity and action so emphatically posed by both the end of *Berlin
Alexanderplatz* and *Know and Change!* does seem to be advanced a
step further when Karl tries to join the rebelling strikers. The narrator
assures us, moreover, that as a result of the uprising, "the yearning for
human dignity had emerged from its old hiding-place . . . and had
taken hold of the masses" (P 369, MWM 444). Marxist and leftist
critics of Döblin admire *Men without Mercy* for the lucidity of its image of bourgeois society and the intensity of its sympathy for the oppressed, and always adduce this passage as evidence.[37] But as we have
seen, the revolutionary Paul is not allowed to wield the kind of power
he would need in order to carry out a real revolution of this society. He
may make a heroic sacrifice, serve as an example for those who come
after, but no more.

The final images of the novel, in contrast, are deeply pessimistic. The unrepentant mother returns to her native province to live out her life, and on the societal level, there is an impending war:

> This countryside that surrounded the cities of an unregenerate race of men was already preparing to receive the tens of thousands of warriors, who, innocent or guilty or only partly guilty, had allowed this age to grow up until the time came for them themselves to lie their length beneath the soil. No matter how luxurious the harvests that this soil bore in summer, the fields were weary of bringing forth ears of corn, soon they were to bear nothing but wooden crosses.
>
> (*P* 370, *MWM* 445)

This grandiloquent passage, uncharacteristic of the novel and significantly located just before its end, has not at all been anticipated in the preceding text and can only refer outside the novel, to the war that Döblin saw approaching in Europe. The hope placed in the yearning for human dignity and freedom is dashed on the rocks of this ending.

For Döblin, the partisan of the open-ended novel, the formal recapitulation of lines from the beginning of the novel at the end of *Men without Mercy* is an especially powerful expression of that pessimism:[38] "They were waiting in their black clothes on the little uncovered station, the mother motionless in the hot sun between two peasant women" (*P* 11, *MWM* 9); "They were waiting in their black clothes on the platform of the vast railway station, the old bowed mother beneath her veil, and Erich" (*P* 369, *MWM* 444). The schematization of the whole novel—the anonymity of the city and the land—militates against the kind of specificity of detail that gives *Berlin Alexanderplatz* so much life. The montage that lends the latter novel its substance and depth is to a great degree dependent on the contemporaneity and authenticity of that detail, qualities that make the novel as fresh today as it was in 1929. The city of *Men without Mercy*, with its government quarter on a hill dominating the surrounding proletarian neighborhoods, is merely a spatial representation of the novel's social message. The schematization of *Men without Mercy* is certainly a result of Döblin's desire to show clearly the interlocking psychic, social, and political mechanisms of oppression. In his last Berlin novel, the tetralogy *November 1918*, he unites the documentary detail of *Berlin Alexanderplatz* with the political pessimism and didactic intention of *Men without Mercy*.

5

November 1918: A German Revolution

Begun in France in 1937 and finished in California in 1943, the immense tetralogy *November 1918: A German Revolution* is Döblin's last Berlin novel and the longest of his works.[1] With a heightened sense of urgency born of the war and the writer's tenuous existence in exile, *November 1918* takes up yet again the question of individual action or passivity in an unjust social order. This question is now connected directly to the watershed of twentieth-century German history, the failed revolution of 1918–19. Even before the outbreak of the Second World War, Döblin saw clearly, "With Hitler, the army defeated in 1918 returns to Germany . . . and the war that was only interrupted in 1918 is continued" (*Briefe* 185). *November 1918* is thus a historical novel different in kind from the earlier novels *Wang-lun* and *Wallenstein;* its history impinges directly on the time of its writing.

Döblin's Berlin novels, beginning with *Wadzek,* are a progression in which the relation of the individual to society becomes increasingly real and urgent. *November 1918* is the culmination of that progression. In the essays that provide the theoretical underpinning for his novels, we can trace the course of Döblin's thinking about the social role of fiction. In the "Berlin Program" of 1913, he declared imaginative writing to be a "public affair" but promoted, in the "style of stone," a stark confrontation between the reader and a "reality liberated from soul." The author's hegemony was broken; he became nothing but a medium through which "reality" flowed. By 1929, in "The Structure of the Epic Work," Döblin had modified his position to allow the authorial narrator to take an active role, as in *Berlin Alexanderplatz,* where he explores along with his hero his own place in society. Finally, in the essay "Der historische Roman und wir" (The Historical Novel and Us), written the year before he began *November 1918,* Döblin formulated the conjunction of the personal and the political we have already seen in *Men without Mercy,* calling the modern novel a "special report of personal and social reality" (*AzL* 176). He concedes even more authority to his narrator, who is now "not motivated by an impulse of illusory objectivity, but rather by the only authenticity that exists for individuals in this world: *by the partisanship of the active person*" (*AzL* 182, emphasis in original).

More clearly than ever before, Döblin had a social and political purpose in mind with *November 1918,* and that purpose was nothing less than to examine the origin of the German disaster in the twentieth century, and to ask what the individual could have done to prevent it. At one point, the subtitle of the tetralogy was to have been "Berlin November 1918,—In Warning and In Memoriam" (*Zur Warnung und Erinnerung*) (*Briefe* 269). Moreover, Döblin's "partisanship of the active person" meant something more than just his life-long sympathy for the poor and the exploited. In the midst of writing *November 1918,* Döblin experienced a personal and religious crisis that led to his formal conversion to Roman Catholicism in 1941, just before beginning *Karl and Rosa,* the final volume of the tetralogy. Even the first three volumes reflect his impending turn to Christianity.

November 1918 is substantially different from both *Berlin Alexanderplatz* and *Men without Mercy* in the way it frames its fiction in a social and political context. While it resembles the latter novel in its conjunction of the personal and the political and in a central hero who is representative of the middle class, it has abandoned the abstract anonymity of time and place that weakens *Men without Mercy.* The structure and narrative method of *November 1918* at least superficially hearken back to Döblin's masterpiece *Berlin Alexanderplatz.* In addition, a connection between the two novels is suggested by the identical initials of their heroes (Franz Biberkopf and Friedrich Becker) and by Döblin's own remarks in the late essay "Epilog": "My intention was to lay out the old landscape and to have a man move through it, a sort of Manas and Franz Biberkopf (the probe), in order to experience and test himself (me)" (*AzL* 394). This sentence also points to the unusually close identification of Döblin himself with Friedrich Becker. Like *Berlin Alexanderplatz, November 1918* features a montage-like multiplicity of characters and documentary details that surround the narrative of the central character.

But the superficial similarity between the two novels is misleading. Rather than to *Berlin Alexanderplatz, November 1918* bears resemblance to the multiple and mutually independent narrative strands of Hermann Broch's *Huguenau oder die Sachlichkeit* (Huguenau or Objectivity) and Anna Seghers's *Die Toten bleiben jung* (The Dead Stay Young), two other German novels that try to come to grips with the legacy of world war and revolution. Friedrich Becker, the wounded veteran and high school teacher, is less constantly the center of his novel than is Franz Biberkopf. The suggestive referentiality of the montage in *Berlin Alexanderplatz* raises Biberkopf's life to exemplary and tragic significance. Becker's life, although also meant to be exemplary, is lived out in counterpoint to a great historic tragedy. The Becker narrative is interwoven with numerous parallel narratives of both historical and fictional figures who in one way or another invite comparison to him: Rosa Luxemburg, Karl Liebknecht, Erwin Stauffer, Hans Maus. The parallel lives only fleetingly hinted at in *Berlin Alexanderplatz* are treated *in extenso* in *November 1918;* there is no clearer example of the concatenation of the personal, the sexual, and the political than the novel's portrayal of Rosa Luxemburg.

The structure of *Berlin Alexanderplatz* is determined by three increasingly severe blows of fate against Franz Biberkopf; its time frame is 1927–28, a year chosen at random by the narrator. By contrast, the structure of *November 1918* is provided by the political crises of the German revolution, and its chronology adheres closely to the historical record. The first novel of the tetralogy, *Soldiers and Citizens,* begins on November 10, 1918, the day after Kaiser Wilhelm II abdicated and fled to Holland, the first day of the first German Republic. The second novel, *Verratenes Volk* (A People Betrayed), ends with the aborted right-wing putsch of December 6, 1918, and its attendant killing of left-wing demonstrators by government troops. The third novel, *Heimkehr der Fronttruppen* (The Troops Return), springs forward in time to end with the Versailles peace conference and the death of Woodrow Wilson. The fourth, *Karl und Rosa,* reaches its climax in the murders of Karl Liebknecht and Rosa Luxemburg on January 15, 1919.[2] The narration of Friedrich Becker's final years, which follows these murders, is a kind of postlude whose legendary tone and hazy chronology burst the bounds of the tightly controlled and detailed treatment of time in the bulk of the tetralogy. We will examine this postlude below, when we take up the religious aspect of the novel. For the vast majority of the tetralogy, as in the fictional revolution of *Men without Mercy,* Döblin lets the public, historical dimension of his theme provide the framework for the individual life of the hero. Becker's fate is important as it relates to the fate of the revolution.

Although the German revolution began with a sailors' mutiny in the Baltic and North Sea ports, its fate was to be decided in the capital, Berlin, and it is there that most of *November 1918* takes place. We need to ask how the image of the city is transformed by this explicit historical dimension.

□

Most of *Soldiers and Citizens,* the first volume of the "Berlin novel" *November 1918,* is in fact set far from Berlin. The tetralogy begins in a small, unnamed Alsatian town on the periphery of the German Revolution. This beginning has partly autobiographical origins: Döblin himself was stationed in the Alsatian town of Haguenau at the end of World War I and experienced the end of the war and the beginning of the revolution from this vantage point. He wrote about it in a 1919 feuilleton entitled "Revolutionstage im Elsass" (Days of Revolution in Alsace; *SPG* 59–71). This essay contains many scenes and figures later incorporated into the fiction of *Soldiers and Citizens.*

More important, it also shows that the officer Alfred Döblin was initially just as nonplussed by and contemptuous of the revolution as his hero Friedrich Becker at the beginning of *November 1918.* What he reported in Haguenau was primarily the petty greed and hypocrisy of the local population and the naiveté of the German soldiers who are simply glad that the war is over: "They don't intend to be chewed out by the officers anymore, that's over and done with. And if somebody is late returning from leave, he won't be locked up anymore. That was all" (*SPG* 60). "Early in the morning my orderly has disappeared with twenty marks; that's how they're celebrating the revolution" (*SPG* 63).

Döblin sets the first volume of the tetralogy in Alsace not only because of these memories, but because this microcosmic setting gives him the opportunity to focus on miniature "revolutions" of naiveté, greed, and self-interest without having his story overwhelmed by the immensity of Berlin.[3] But this means that Döblin's hero Friedrich Becker reaches the same provisional conclusion about the revolution that Döblin himself did in his 1919 essay. A marching group of Socialist voters struck the writer as participants in "a small-scale club affair" (*SPG* 70); Becker calls a similar group "churchgoers" (*November* 1 : 194).[4] The revolution is examined skeptically in its smallest constituents before it has even got properly underway.

In the first volume, the metropolis toward which the soldiers and civilians of the small town look is not Berlin, "the gigantic, gray and dreary city" (*November* 3:17; Woods 1:315), but Strasbourg, repeatedly apostrophized as lovely and charming (*November* 1:118, 129, 176; *November* 2:39; Woods 1:30). Although this formulaic characterization is challenged by the arrival of a delegation of sailors from Kiel to form an Alsatian Soldiers' Soviet, Strasbourg remains too bourgeois and Francophile to succumb to the German revolutionary fever: "This Alsace, their dear homeland, proved to be a hard nut for the revolutionaries to crack. . . . The city rejected what it didn't want with cold determination" (*November* 1:218, 221). The characterization of Strasbourg as "lovely," however, is not primarily a political and social designation but rather serves to identify the city with a particular character, the nurse Hilde from the military hospital where Becker lies wounded. She is a native of Strasbourg, and when she returns to the city after the chaotic evacuation of the small town, she feels both an inner peace and unity of mind and body. Through the fluid imagery of the narrator, Hilde is joined to the city itself and becomes its *genius loci:*

> For an unimaginably long time, since her childhood, she had not felt so in possession of her limbs, such a reconciliation between her body and her feelings. She strolled pensively along the little gray-green river.
> And as she walked along and moved her body, she became wedded to the slow, opaque current, to the old Church of St. Nicolas. At the Kaufhausgasse, she turned in toward the center of the city and was drawn along the Küfergasse. . . .
> She had lived four years on the edge of death.
> Now her former life rushed back upon her, with a vague sense of well-being she flowed toward her former life.
>
> (*November* 1:129)

The center around which this city stands—both the actual center and the metaphorical center for the believing Catholic Hilde—is the medieval cathedral, where she goes to pray even before going home. Her religion is one of pure devotion and surrender:

> What did she feel as she left the Kammerzellhaus and ventured out onto the square, the huge building above her, beside her? She approached a gigantic, protective, overshadowing being. Nothing in her but thankfulness, happiness and rapture. . . . the cathedral took her to itself, the dark, gigantic hall seized her and enclosed her. Out of her overflowing heart she . . . wished to pour out and surrender the excess of strength and happiness that she felt.
>
> (*November* 1:131)

As is to be expected in light of Döblin's treatment of women, Hilde's pure surrender has connotations other than the purely religious. Indeed, there is a great deal of unresolved ambiguity in this character, as we shall see. Here it suffices to say that the correlate of Hilde's religious devotion is her sexual surrender. In the final days of the garrison town, she has loved a dying pilot, bestowed sexual favors on Friedrich Becker, and been raped by his friend Lieutenant Maus. In Strasbourg she will soon be confronted with her prewar lover Bernhard; she had become an army nurse to escape from her sadomasochistic relationship with him. Behind this affair looms the figure of Frau Anny Scharrel (*November* 1:328ff.), Bernhard's aunt and an embarrassingly conventional *femme fatale:* "Frau Scharrel was still beautiful, exotic. . . . It was evident that southern blood flowed in the veins of Frau Scharrel" (*November* 1:329).

Thus Döblin's fictional Strasbourg, through its identification with the character Hilde, becomes a two-sided image: charming and naively devout, but also bourgeois and treacherously sensual. We will take up the theme of sensuality below. For the theme of revolution, however, Strasbourg is a dead end, because it would soon be occupied and annexed by the victorious French, an event that the socialist mayor Peirotes accepts with resignation while the bourgeoisie looks forward to it with unconcealed delight. The true revolutionaries leave in disgust for Berlin (*November* 1:292).

The shift in Döblin's conception of his task as a novelist that is suggested by the phrase "partisanship of the active person" is clearly evident in the way he treats Berlin in *November 1918*. We have already seen how the geography of the city in *Men without Mercy* is ideologically organized. *November 1918* continues this process, but now in a much more convincing way. From small details of technique to programmatic statements about the city, the novel places the fictional city in the service of its view of the revolution and, ultimately, of its Christian faith.

Let us first compare the montage of *Berlin Alexanderplatz* with the use of documentary material in the tetralogy. Like the earlier novel, *November 1918* makes extensive use of such documents as speeches, newspaper articles, handbills, and popular songs.[5] In *Berlin Alexanderplatz* such material is mounted into the text without narrative mediation. It is the direct representation of urban multiplicity that the narrator as well as the reader must confront and come to terms with in the course of the novel. The montage elements are in principle anonymous and thus available to everyone rather than being simply the private experience of one particular character.

November 1918 is much more conventional in the way it incorporates such material into the text. Here, documentary texts are almost always tied to a specific character, situation, and narrative intention.[6] In *Soldiers and Citizens*, for instance, a long list of copper and brass household articles to be impounded for use in wartime production is perused with profound *Schadenfreude* by an old man whose wife is simultaneously looting the abandoned barracks (*November* 1:92–95). Similarly, a young hatmaker reads through a pile of old newspapers. The narrator cuts back and forth in the style of *Berlin Alexanderplatz* among reports from the front, classified advertisements, and a serialized romantic novel (*November* 1:102–5). But the entire passage, like the list of impounded articles, serves the narrative intention of underlining the irony of the German defeat: "A German lady who was paying up her account had left her a pile of newspapers. The lady had collected them as souvenirs of victory, but now there was no victory, only the newspapers" (*November* 1:102). The narrator of *Berlin Alexanderplatz* never gives us this kind of explicit interpretation of his documents.

Newspapers, the quintessentially urban sources of information that Döblin had often praised in the 1920s as "the daily bread of all people" (*AzL* 288) and had used extensively in *Berlin Alexanderplatz,* are regarded with much more skepticism in the tetralogy. To be sure, much of the narrative of *November 1918* is based on contemporary newspaper reports. Manfred Auer has spoken of the "omnipresence of sources" to characterize Döblin's use of documentary material to chronicle the course of the German revolution.[7] He emphasizes that while Döblin bases his narrative of events on the reports of large-circulation, liberal newspapers like the *Berliner Tageblatt,* his evaluation of those events is much more indebted to the newspapers of the radical left, especially to *Die Rote Fahne,* the organ of the Spartacists.[8] Within the fiction, and especially in *Soldiers and Citizens,* newspapers become a motif of misdirection, of the abuse of public credulity, a screen of unreality between an event and its significance.[9] The German press had consistently misled the people about the progress of the war. After the cease-fire, the druggist of the Alsatian town flatters his vanity by publicly reading the latest newspapers from Strasbourg that exult in the German defeat (*November* 1 : 35 – 37). One of Becker's first acts after he is introduced into the novel is to order an "auto-da-fé" (*November* 1 : 111), the burning of the newspapers from which his friend Maus reads him the shameful conditions of the ceasefire. Maus, clinging desperately to his newspapers, cannot see beyond his outrage at Germany's shame, while Becker categorically rejects these immediate "truths" (*November* 1 : 110) for the greater truth that the war is over, thereby becoming, paradoxically, "the victor" (*November* 1 : 111).

November 1918 contains none of the large-scale city montages that articulate the structure of *Berlin Alexanderplatz* and make Berlin itself a character in the novel. We have seen how the city montage at the beginning of book 2 of *Berlin Alexanderplatz* allows the city to speak for itself in a multitude of voices. It is up to the reader, in the course of the novel, to construct the significance of the city from such data. In the tetralogy, Berlin is initially an emblem of uncertainty, seen first through the eyes of the returning soldier Hans Maus and wrapped in a symbolic fog (*November* 1 : 235, 236). When the narrator at last gives us an overview of the city, it is in the context of a particular historical event, the funeral of the proletarian victims of the first few days of revolutionary street fighting. It is the bird's eye view of an omniscient and controlling narrator with a specific agenda in mind:

Thousands of people crowded the sidewalks and hung from the windows. The black, solemn, threatening procession trundled past them like a giant bowl of food, and they sniffed at it. For this was a mighty city, stretching for miles in all directions, with long streets, poor ones and rich ones, lined with decaying and new buildings, innumerable gray apartment blocks, flanked by dark courtyards, added wings, and connecting buildings. Here factories and workshops, shops, warehouses, slaughterhouses, dairies had developed. Gas lines, electric lines had been laid, water lines, sewers connected the buildings. Subways, streetcars, buses traveled incessantly back and forth in the city, telephone lines stretched between people in different parts of the city, they could talk to each other from their rooms. They had gradually created something called a metropolis, with hard work, with stubborn effort, it had come into being by the work of their hands, through their indefatigable diligence. For they worked, worked beyond all bounds, knew only work, desired only work, thirsted and hungered for work alone. If they felt natural hunger and thirst, they considered them a nuisance, disposed of them, and devoted themselves again to their urge to work. They hung around gloomily when they couldn't find work. They schemed at making money. Many desired honor, luxury, and those too were motives to work. To whip themselves up and because they didn't know what was

happening to them, they became absorbed in the clamor of the newspapers, that gave them feelings of irritation, hate, rancor, occasionally
enjoyment, malicious joy. They went to the movies and the screen
showed them love, beauty and adventure. In the streets they were confronted with prostitution. They went to the circus and watched boxers
knock each other down.

They lined the sidewalks by the thousands and gaped. Led by a band,
the majestic, gigantic beast of public life, the open-mouthed dragon,
crawled past them. They had experienced the howling, flag-waving
giants of the war; skeptically they watched the new monster—the revolution that looked so much like war.

(*November* 1 : 258–59)

Here the event of the funeral gives rise not to a montage, but to a
narrative critique of the modern capitalist metropolis whose inhabitants are enslaved by their need to work and narcotized into acceptance
of their lot by the newspapers and cheap entertainments that supply
them with second-hand emotions. Although the description of the city
is generalized (it could apply to any large industrial city), its intent is to
provide an explanation for the outbreak of revolution.

Collectively, the inhabitants have built the city in its innumerable
parts, but they have lost control of their lives. Their communality is a
false one, the "gigantic beast of public life" that Döblin had attacked
as a "Moloch" even before his exile (*UD* 418–21). At the end of
Berlin Alexanderplatz, Franz Biberkopf watches anonymous masses,
of indeterminate political persuasion, march past his gatekeeper's window. He seems determined to avoid being absorbed by them, to seek
his own kind of solidarity with the "proper comrades" apart from any
particular party. The metropolis is a microcosm, ceaselessly generating
the raw material out of which Biberkopf must construct his new life.
How he will accomplish this is left tantalizingly open. In the tetralogy,
the marching masses have acquired specific political identity but Berlin
has in a sense become anonymous, a somewhat abstract backdrop before which the tragedy of revolutionary failure will be played out.

Volume 2 of the tetralogy, *A People Betrayed,* opens with a somewhat more specific panoramic description of the city that again clearly
serves a specific historical, explanatory intention on the part of the
narrator.

Berlin was a proliferation of buildings sprawling low and somber across
the sand of Mark Brandenburg. A shabby excuse for a stream, the
Spree, flowed between them. The little river took on an iridescent black
from the sewage emptied into it, buildings turned their backs on it,

sheds and coalyards lined its banks. In the Hansa district near the zoo the world surrounding its murky, proletarian waters opened up somewhat, and it caught a glimpse of trees and boats and was glad to leave behind the heaps of stone that were the source of the refuse. But for some distance out onto the plain the poor river was hemmed in again by industry, by complexes as big as cities, where still more men and women toiled inside.

The city of Berlin spread out across sand that long ages before had lain at the bottom of the sea. Where fish once swam, men lived now, and in such numbers and on such poor soil that the majority of them were in want, barely eking out their lives by drudgery. To the north, south and east of the city, in a great circumferential band, stood factories erected to supply distant cities and countries. Many of them had been built during the war—the one that had lasted from 1914 to 1918 and now was lost—and many others had been converted to war production. But the war was over. What was to be done with the factories? Neither their owners nor the city[10] had the money to convert them to peacetime production. There were eager buyers, but none who could pay while trade with the outside world was closed off.

So strikes broke out. The hatred of the workers for their employers exploded. There was an immediate danger that they would occupy the factories.

(*November* 2:9; Woods 1:5)

Again, the narrator views the city from above, as it were, enabling him to summarize it as a polluted, industrial city filled with impoverished workers on the brink of radical political action. This overview is especially important here at the beginning of the middle two volumes, in which the narrative of the failed revolution is most prominent. The growth of the city is characterized by the use of the words *Häuserwucherung* and *wucherte* ("proliferation of buildings" and "spread out"). The verb *wuchern* denotes wild, rank growth; the nominalized form *Wucherung* also has the meaning of "tumor," "cancerous growth." Cities in *November 1918* are not heterogeneous microcosms like the Berlin of *Berlin Alexanderplatz*. The tendency is rather to reduce them to unambiguous significance. When the narrative imagery identifies Hilde with the peaceful flow of Strasbourg's "gray-green river," the city becomes an emblem of inner peace and unity between the works of man and nature. This significance finds its natural expression in Hilde's devotions in the Strasbourg cathedral, the center of the city. In the Berlin panorama quoted above, the "murky proletarian waters" of the Spree are the polluted emblem of the shattering of the unity of man and nature (a unity proclaimed as an article of faith in *Unser Dasein*) by modern industry and technology. Berlin "spreads out" like a cancer over its buried and forgotten geologic past. Later in

A People Betrayed, the personified Spree has a monologue in which its waves yearn to leave the city and reach the open country. A woman's suicide in the river is its only connection with the city's inhabitants:

> "How right she is not to want to join in all that commotion up there. We couldn't bear it either. Why do they all come to us looking so serious? They lose their minds up there.
> "And now we will swim peacefully on out to the tall pines and the gentle hills. We will receive morning, noon and evening, when the sun brings them out to us, and we will enjoy the clouds and all the many stars that the night plays with."
>
> (*November* 2:205; Woods 1:166)

This passage harks back to the metaphor of the river of death in "On Heavenly Mercy" and to other early stories like "Die Segelfahrt" (The Sailboat Ride), in which drowning is a means of reunification with nature. It also anticipates the end of the tetralogy, in which the bodies of the two main protagonists, Rosa Luxemburg and Friedrich Becker, are both cast into the water.[11]

The emblematic intent of Döblin's portrayals of Berlin in *November 1918* reaches its culmination in the third volume of the tetralogy, *The Troops Return.* The return of the mass of frontline troops to the capital city, beginning on December 10, 1918, appropriately provides the title for the entire volume, for the event brings to a head the struggle for control of the new German Republic. The Ebert regime, in collaboration with the officers of the General Staff, hopes to use these troops to crush the left-wing Spartacist radicals once and for all, while the leftists plan to agitate among the returning soldiers and convert them to the revolutionary cause.

Döblin presents the entry of the troops into Berlin in a magnificent set piece in which the geography of the city becomes charged with political meaning (*November* 3:152–58; Woods 1:409–14). The divisions begin their march, bands in the vanguard, in the West End, the well-to-do section of Berlin. There they are greeted with wild enthusiasm, showered with flowers by the cheering, singing populace. Both soldiers and onlookers wave the black, white, and red flag of the defunct Empire. When they reach the Brandenburg Gate, they have penetrated to the heart of the imperial city, but it is now metaphorically empty, inadequately filled by the presence of Friedrich Ebert, the new head of state, "a small rotund man in a heavy coat" (*November* 3:154; Woods 1:411). Immediately upon his appearance, the satiric tone takes over the narrative, apparent in the increasingly mordant substitutes Döblin invents to replace the phrase "he said":

"Welcome to the German Republic," Ebert shouted. "Welcome home." And as he saw fit, he gave them a mixture of words of welcome, political commentary and admonition.

He flattered the troops. "You could march home with your heads held high. Never have men achieved greater things."

He wooed the soldiers spiritedly, but they, to the extent they heard anything at all, did not think much of the whole affair.

"Your sacrifices have been unparalleled," the brand-new head of state disclosed to them. "No enemy has conquered you. Only when the superiority of the opponent's numbers and materiel became too crushing did you cease to struggle."

Then he rubbed their noses in what had occurred in the meantime. "The old rulers, who lay like a curse upon our noble deeds, have been shaken off by the German people. The hope of German freedom lies now with you. Our unfortunate nation has grown poor. Our task is to rebuild for the future."

Toward the end he let a few words fall about a "socialist republic" that would be a "homeland of hard work." He then called for a cheer for "the German fatherland, for a free and democratic Germany"; the cheers, however, were restricted to the immediate area around the platform.

(*November* 3 : 155–56; Woods 1 : 412)

As the immense crowd gradually dissipates, the troops march off to their barracks. But now they march through the proletarian neighborhoods in the east and north of the city. Here the flags are red—not black, white, and red—and the onlookers regard the soldiers with silent distrust and even mockery. They are suddenly seen stripped of their military glory, "like some fetish from the jungle, with spears and rattles" (*November* 3 : 157; Woods 1 : 413).

The satirical deflation of military glory achieved by ideologizing the geography of the city is continued through the simple narrative device of repetition: twice more in the following days, contingents of front-line troops enter the city, and each time is an occasion for the narrator to repeat the symbolic march through the city in increasingly abbreviated form. By the second repetition, the satiric scene disintegrates into horribly vivid flashes of combat memories. Döblin still has the sudden shift of narrative tense and tone and the film-like cuts of *Berlin Alexanderplatz* at his command, but now the psychological truth they convey is simultaneously a political truth about the sources of both the revolution and of the counterrevolution which would crush it.

They rattled into town, marched in, trumpets blowing: the 4th Guard Infantry Division, the 1st Guard Regiment, the 5th Guard Infantry Regiment and the Reserve Infantry Regiment No. 93. The tread was sharp as they passed through the Zoological Garden in the winter rain. The war had left its mark on these men. Their bodies were emaciated, their faces stern and morose. They could still hear the cracking of rifle shots, the barking of machine guns, the boom of the heavy shells. Every man of them was armed with hand grenades. The muzzles of their machine guns glow, the steam hisses from drain pipes, bring water tanks, bring water.

Heavy artillery is stationed over in that village, the red cloud of smoke, a man is screaming, why doesn't he stop? Someone get over there fast, he's gone crazy. Direct hit.

"Home again you'll start anew, live again as you once did, find a wife so fair and true, and Santa Claus will bring a kid." . . .

Brandenburg Gate. The speaker's platform. And some guy is standing up there in a top hat beside a high-ranking officer, and he mumbles, "You have returned undefeated."

(*November* 3 : 231–32; Woods
1 : 460–61)

As the religious core of the tetralogy emerges more and more clearly in the figure of Friedrich Becker, Berlin as a presence within the novel fades in importance. Döblin's project in *Berlin Alexanderplatz* was to reach the universal by way of the most careful attention to particulars; he needed the metropolis as the most intense and concentrated possible collection of details of modern life. It is precisely these details surrounding Biberkopf that make him a vibrant and plausible figure. The first volume of *November 1918*, written before Döblin's conversion (although already anticipating it in the visionary figure of Johannes Tauler), is the richest in both parallel narratives of relatively equal importance and in its loving attention to minute detail. As Döblin's Christian faith begins to manifest itself more strongly in the subsequent volumes, it provides the universal framework, ready-made, that *Berlin Alexanderplatz* can only suggest at its conclusion. Döblin explained the process in retrospect: "The clarification was complete. My standpoint was a given. A different world view, a different way of thought had begun" (*AzL* 395). In these circumstances, the particulars of metropolitan life are less important, because they are no longer at issue. The partisan narrator now has no need for them except as they reflect and underline his two major and interlocking concerns: "Two things ran along beside each other: the tragic petering out of the German revolution of 1918 and the dark distress of [Friedrich Becker]. He faces the question of how in the world he is to reach the point of action" (*AzL* 394), especially as a believing Christian. The personalized "author," in one of his periodic programmatic narrative deliberations, states unequivocally that as far as the religious theme is concerned, all settings are of equal value:

> We will try to hold our peace while [the characters from the Alsatian town of volume 1] do battle with their consciences and ultimately, whether we want to or not, we will be swept along in their wrestlings with Satan, in their strivings after God.
> It is all the same whether in trying to reassure ourselves we use the mirror of a large city or a small town.
> (*November* 2 : 306; Woods 1 : 228)

The drama of Becker's conversion occurs in Berlin but is played out almost exclusively in the seclusion of his room, his "laboratory" (*November* 3 : 219; Woods 1 : 454). When his friend Maus persuades him to venture out to a political meeting, Becker calls him "my Mephisto" (*November* 3 : 29; Woods 1 : 325). We will discuss the Faust parallel below. Here it suffices to say that he is a recluse who leaves his room with the utmost reluctance. The outward reason for Becker's reclusion is that he is still convalescing from a serious wound, but the deeper reason is that he cannot confront both the political turmoil of the city and his own personal "demon" (*November* 3 : 18; Woods 1 : 316) simultaneously. Only after his private struggle with the devil and his conversion in *The Troops Return* is he ready to test his new faith among others.

He does, however, make occasional sorties out of the apartment, and one of these shows clearly the change in the role of the city from *Berlin Alexanderplatz* to *November 1918*. Toward the end of the second volume, Becker goes to a military hospital for a checkup and carries away with him what the narrative explicitly calls a "cheerful image" (*November* 2 : 360; Woods 1 : 259). In the wounded soldiers lying forty to a ward and swathed in bandages, attended by doctors and nurses, Becker discerns the old, positive image of the colony of social insects: "It was an ant colony. The teeming masses of little creatures took care of their larva [*sic*] inside parchment wrappings, fussed over them, set them out in the warm sun" (*November* 2 : 360; Woods 1 : 259).

As Becker walks home from the hospital, he observes the everyday life of the streets. It is "touching and pleasant" and seems to "fit" the image of the ant colony:[12]

Women were washing windows. An old woman walked past with a pram. Two men were taking a rest on a bench. The tram rang its bell merrily as it passed.
People had built all of this by working together. They had sat down together and drawn up a plan and tried it out, and now it works and they live in these houses and ride in these cars along tracks.
(*November* 2: 360–61; Woods
1: 259–60)

It is the image of the good city, the city whose inhabitants live together in peaceful interdependence, like ants in their colony. This image seems to be confirmed in the next moment, when Becker is accidentally knocked down by a bicyclist and a Polish Jew helps him to his feet and stays with him until he has recovered. The image of ant larvae being cared for is now connected to this particular helper figure, "one example of the many forms of help people offer to one another when they live peaceably together. For they form circles, rings and chains, great rounds of dancers, as if listening to music" (*November* 2: 362; Woods 1: 261). This passage seems to push the utopianism of the "good city" too far: it is almost immediately shattered when the Jew tells Becker of a recent pogrom in Lvov from which he has fled to Berlin.

Otto Keller has shown how the story of Stefan Zannowich, told to Franz Biberkopf by a similar *Ostjude* in *Berlin Alexanderplatz*, is meant to serve as an exemplum for Biberkopf, a prefiguration of his own fall through hubris, but one that he misunderstands and ignores.[13] Becker's encounter with the Jews lacks this kind of global significance in the tetralogy. In fact, it seems at best a sort of half-hearted self-quotation on Döblin's part, especially when one compares the sparse dialogue in this scene with the sense of vibrant Hasidic oral tradition in the story of Stefan Zannowich.

In *November 1918,* the image of the good city filled with helpers does not really come alive in the figure of the Jew, because it is only a transition from the negative, polluted, capitalist metropolis to something else. It is significant that within the anthill metaphor, Becker identifies himself with the larvae, the inchoate forms ready to metamorphose. His tutelary saint Johannes Tauler speaks to him in a dream: "The pupa in its cocoon, the thin skin rips open. How long still, until the skin rips open and you must leave the cocoon" (*November* 2: 370; Woods 1: 267).

The inadequacy of the anthill metaphor and the good city it represents becomes clear when one considers another passage reminiscent of *Berlin Alexanderplatz*. Close to the end of *Karl and Rosa*, the last volume of the tetralogy, Friedrich Becker has been wounded in the fighting around the police headquarters, and lies under arrest in a prison hospital among other captured Spartacists. The nurse Hilde helps him to escape, and they stroll together in the center of Berlin. In its situation and position within the novel, the passage is very like Biberkopf's reunion with the Alexanderplatz after his release from the psychiatric ward. The narrator of *Berlin Alexanderplatz* assures us that the teeming life of the city can "help a man get on his feet, even if he is a bit weak, provided his heart is in good condition" (*BA* 495, EJ 627). Becker is similarly elated to be free in the city: "What bliss just to be alive. There was the square with its teeming humanity. The trolleys and cars drove merrily up and down" (*November* 4:567; Woods 2:468). Yet the everyday life of the city does not help Becker "get on his feet," nor does he any longer use the metaphor of the ant colony. Now the men in hospital beds are Spartacists, waiting helplessly for the club to fall.

Since his vision of the good city in volume 2, he has both been converted to Christianity and made a spontaneous decision to fight on the side of the revolutionaries in police headquarters. Now the everyday life of the city is perceived as a veneer of normalcy and insouciance that allows the populace to ignore the murder of the Spartacist prisoners, the death of the revolution, and the imminent murders of Karl Liebknecht and Rosa Luxemburg: "They held their newspapers before their noses, and what terrible things were printed there, all of it happening a quarter hour away from them. They'll read about me this evening. The wounded were lying in Moabit Hospital and in the barracks the prisoners were waiting for the blow of the club" (*November* 4:568; Woods 2:468). The possibility of a good city filled with helpers proves too insubstantial in the face of the tragic historical situation. The city is reproached and its destruction foretold by a long quote from the prophet Jeremiah: "The whole city shall flee for the noise of the horsemen and bowmen; they shall go into thickets, and climb up upon the rocks" (*November* 4:568; Woods 2:468).[14]

It is appropriate that Jeremiah is evoked here, in Becker's final appearance in book 8 of *Karl and Rosa*. Its last three chapters are devoted to the murders of Liebknecht and Luxemburg, and then in book 9, the last of the novel and the tetralogy, Becker reappears, after

a hiatus of three years, as himself a latter-day Jeremiah. We will treat
this legendary epilogue below. Here suffice it to say that at the end, the
city Becker attains, the city toward which the whole tetralogy has
moved, is the heavenly Jerusalem, promised him by the angel Antoniel:

> "The holy city, it lies afar, no man can take it by force.
> "The holy city beyond the mountains, beyond the snowy peaks. It
> lies there, showered in flower petals. All the blood of the martyrs and
> saints rains down upon it. The city lies afar, the hovel of God."
> (*November* 4: 661; Woods 2: 547)

□

The difference between the treatment of the city theme in *Berlin Alexanderplatz* and in *November 1918* is related to differences in the character of the narrative voice that speaks within each novel. By turns
satirical, historical-documentary, naturalistic, realistic, grotesque, and
explicitly religious, *November 1918* is in its narrative style a much
more heterogeneous work than *Berlin Alexanderplatz*. We have seen
that although the earlier novel makes an initial impression of a babel
of narrative voices, upon closer reading a consistent narrative stance
emerges. The narrator of *Berlin Alexanderplatz* is a *monteur* who
carefully arranges the multitudinous fragments of urban reality, carries
on a dialogue with his hero Franz Biberkopf, and gradually becomes
identified with the figure of Death. Moreover, the end of the novel
makes clear that the narrative standpoint coalesces with that of Biberkopf, that the narrator is in the end no more foresightful than his hero.

The narrator of *November 1918* is both more and less traditional
than the narrator of *Berlin Alexanderplatz*.[15] On the one hand, he has
the mannerisms and attitude of the traditional omniscient narrator.
Typical of such mannerisms is his frequent use of the first person plural, whose effect is to create a conspiracy between the narrator and the
reader at the expense of the independence of the fictional characters.
Here, for instance, is the old porter's wife, Mother Hegen, as she participates in the looting of the abandoned German barracks in the small
Alsatian town that is the setting for *Citizens and Soldiers:* "Our quiet
old woman, the wife of the pastor's porter, where do we find her? The
woman who punctually looked after the blind Captain for a decade
and carefully collected horse manure from the street, annoyed at any

disturbance in her routine—what had gotten into her? What a transformation at her age, a revolution in miniature" (*November* 1 : 140).
As we shall see, the satire of such a personal "revolution in miniature"
becomes a leitmotif. The narrator's "we," intended ironically, ends up
sounding patronizing.

In another remarkable passage in the first volume, the narrator
positively rubs his character's nose in her dependence on his whims,
and in the process reveals much about his own stance.[16] He directly
addresses Hanna, the daughter of respectable middle-class parents, as
she weeps over the departure of her lover, a junior officer in the fleeing
German garrison:

> Why so nervous, dear child? Why make things so difficult for your-
> self? You've got too much imagination. And on the other hand, you don't
> have enough imagination, or you would know, for example, that you will
> soon stand up, look through the house in desperation for someone who
> can help you, with whom you can talk, and maybe even cry. . . .
> And then an envious and indignant creature within you will raise its
> head, and at its behest and urging you will put on your best coat, get
> your pretty boots, powder yourself, put on lipstick, don your hat and go
> to town. There you will drink hot chocolate, not look at the clock, and
> without noticing it, you will become more and more mellow until you're
> quite mellow indeed . . . The poet knows all this. It is nothing new for
> him, he almost always wanders about quietly like this, and within him,
> figures are forming, still vaguely, they move within him as if in a pleas-
> ant, moist garden, a hothouse, but after a while he opens the door—he
> has to, to make room for new ones—and they move out, he follows
> them, embraces them with a loving look, they disappear.
> I predict, and I take my watch in my hand and can say to the second
> when you will stand up, tortured and confused, when you will go to the
> closet, open it, which coat you will choose. And I must admit, Fräulein
> Hanna, although I have taken part in your conversations and assigna-
> tions in the most decent possible way, with the discretion proper to a
> narrator, that I am now delighted to see you get up, and commanding
> your body that is so delicate yet shapely, I will help to dress it—for I do
> help you to pull on your fur boots, I tug your hat into place in front of
> the mirror, I look into the mirror with you and dab your pert little nose
> with powder and accompany you along the street to carry you off from
> your grief.
>
> (November 1 : 114–15)

In his theoretical statements about prose composition, and most
notably in the essay "The Structure of the Epic Work," Döblin always
stressed the inaccessibly subconscious origins of the work of art. In
this passage, however, where the narrator characterizes himself as a

protean "poet" and preens himself on the fertility of the "pleasant, moist garden," the "hothouse" of his imagination, he puts Hanna, the product of that imagination, into her place with patronizing superiority. Unlike the narrator of *Berlin Alexanderplatz*, who only played with the idea of omniscient foresight in the passage on Max Rüst, this narrator can indeed foresee what is to come. This foresight is both his pride and his curse: in the fiction, his foresight is a function of his imaginative control over the narrative, as he makes abundantly clear in this passage, but in the context of the whole tetralogy, the privileged foresight of the narrator is his despairing knowledge of the revolution's failure, a fact he is powerless to change.

His pleasure in his power over the private lives of his fictional characters is all the more keen. The passage is an indication of a narrator whose primary pose, at least here at the beginning of the tetralogy, is that of the puppet-master disposing over the fates of his marionettes.[17] In addition, it is not merely fortuitous that he chooses to make this statement apropos a female character. For all his protestations of decency and sympathy with the products of his imagination (he "embraces them with a loving look"), there is an element of indecency in his enjoyment of "commanding your body that is so delicate yet shapely." The verb in German is *gebieten*, which suggests only command and domination. But the omniscience that the narrator flaunts here is seldom so explicitly expressed (the passage is unique in the tetralogy for its use of the first person singular, thus drawing all the more attention to itself as a programmatic statement of narrative control). In fact, as the tetralogy progresses, many of the secondary narrative strands begun in the first volume, among them Hanna's, are simply dropped without being brought to a conclusion. The narrator concentrates more and more on his central character, Friedrich Becker, and on the historical figures for whom he has the most sympathy, Karl Liebknecht and Rosa Luxemburg. In the process, the pose of omniscience is gradually abandoned, so that among other things, the tetralogy is the record of a changing narrative stance.

Although the narrator of *November 1918* is more omniscient and controlling than the narrator of *Berlin Alexanderplatz*, he is also more heterogeneous in his modes. His characterization of the world at the beginning of volume 3 also describes his method for encompassing that world in his fiction: "The world, howling with realities, sweating facts in a thousand places at once, would not have been the world had it not produced a jumble of figures—mock-heroic ones, tragic ones, unsullied ones" (*November* 3:9; Woods 1:309). As we shall see, the narrator assigns his figures to such categories and then treats them in the appropriate mode: satire, tragedy, burlesque.[18] Some historical figures like the Social-Democratic politicians Friedrich Ebert, Philipp Scheidemann, and Gustav Noske are presented only in fierce satire. Others, like Kurt Eisner, are treated with sympathy. Rosa Luxemburg, as we shall see, is made into a religious mystic and martyr. Curiously enough, Wilhelm Groener, Paul von Hindenburg, and the other officers of the General Staff are treated with restrained, objective realism.[19] There are wonderfully funny grotesqueries and brutally straightforward descriptions of political assassinations. The metaphysical struggles of Friedrich Becker with the Devil alternate with the banal ladies'-magazine prose of the narrative of Erwin Stauffer.

Thus *November 1918* is very different from *Berlin Alexanderplatz* or from a novel like Anna Seghers's *Die Toten bleiben jung*, in which all the characters, whatever their politics, are treated in the same realistic fashion by a narrator who refrains from any explicit declaration of sympathy. Döblin's tetralogy stands or falls with its technique of disjunct narrative. This technique is in one sense radically modern: it blocks any possibility of reading *November 1918* as a chronicle of historical movement, like Seghers's novel, or as history in the process of becoming myth, like Thomas Mann's biblical tetralogy *Joseph und seine Brüder*, two novels also written in exile during the Third Reich. In *November 1918* the chronicle of the German revolution is constantly shattered and thrown into question by the shifts in style.

But although the technique is modern, its problematic aspect is related to the traditional omniscient narrative stance so prominent in the first volume of the tetralogy. By treating different characters in different narrative modes, Döblin stacks the deck from the beginning, making clear his own sympathies and antipathies.[20] His narrator, exercising the "partisanship" promoted in the essay "The Historical Novel and Us," controls the reader's response to a historical character like Ebert in the same overbearing way that he controls a fictional character like Hanna. Fully realized and complex characters like Becker and Rosa Luxemburg stand next to one-dimensional straw men like Ebert, Noske, and—on the positive side—Woodrow Wilson. To a certain extent the one-dimensionality of these latter figures compromises the credibility of the former. Let us look in more detail at the major groups of characters in the tetralogy and how our response to them is controlled by the narrative mode in which they are presented.

□

Döblin, like many other Weimar intellectuals, had been initially enthusiastic about the changes promised by the revolution: "If what is happening now, socialism, is carried to completion, if the disease is eradicated, then for the first time in history one can speak of real progress" (*SPG* 79). His disappointment was all the more bitter when the revolution failed to bring about a new society.[21] The essays he wrote from 1919 to 1921 under the pseudonym Linke Poot were a caustic commentary on the failure of the political leadership to effect a real change in the militaristic German state that had plunged the country into the disastrous war. In fact, by 1927 his bitterness had reached the point where he declared himself glad that the revolution had been suppressed.

Döblin's condemnation of the political leadership, especially of the German Social-Democratic Party (SPD) had lost none of its bitterness by the time he wrote *November 1918*. The mode in which the narrator treats the official caretakers of what Sebastian Haffner has called the "betrayed revolution"[22] is savage satire. Friedrich Ebert in particular, as chairman of the SPD and leader of the provisional revolutionary government, comes in for Döblin's unmitigated scorn. Ebert's first major appearance in the tetralogy—at the beginning of the second novel, *A People Betrayed*—sets the tone for his treatment throughout. He is an unimaginative party functionary with petit-bourgeois aspirations, overwhelmed by the surroundings of the Imperial Chancellory in which he suddenly finds himself wielding power. His primary concern is to emulate what he considers the proper, statesmanlike behavior of his imperial predecessors:

> The entrance and the removal of the coat still had not gone smoothly. They still handed him the portfolios instead of having the footman follow him in with them. These wretched comradely habits. As if they were still dealing with a meeting of the Party's executive committee on Lindenstrasse.
> He sat down in the immense president's chair, where Prince Bismarck, the Iron Chancellor, had once sat. Our people can't learn any-

thing. But it's my fault, too. I have to learn not to hold my arms like that when they take off my coat. And then there's the way I walk and hold my head. . . . But suddenly he stood up, taken by a new and more pleasant thought, and began slowly, slowly to stride back and forth across the carpet, his head laid back, the smoking cigar in his mouth. He said to himself, always one step after the other, left—right, left—right, and never change your expression. When you're thinking, never change your expression. He cast his eyes around the room. Naturally, no mirror to check the effect in.

(*November* 2 : 28–29; Woods 1 : 21)

The scene is strongly reminiscent of Brecht's comic Hitler figure, Arturo Ui, who takes elocution lessons from a broken-down Shakespearean actor. For Ebert, the revolution has already been accomplished by bringing him and the SPD to power. His concern is not to carry out a real reform of the old order, which would mean breaking up and reorganizing the officers corps and the entrenched bureaucracy, but rather to stabilize and legitimize the status quo, to live up to the dignity of the office he has so abruptly been thrust into, to leave his party past behind him. This means that he perceives his enemies to be not the reactionary officers of the General Staff, but rather the socialists to his left, both the Independents with whom he shares power in the Council of People's Representatives, and the Spartacists under Karl Liebknecht and Rosa Luxemburg who have refused to participate in the government. That is why he feels the need to ally himself via a secret telephone line with Groener, Hindenburg, and the General Staff. He believes he needs their military might to keep the radicals of the Left in check. But at the same time, he knows he is caught in a dilemma. The generals are cooperating with him only as a matter of temporary convenience. They plan to gobble him up at the first opportunity: "I see and hear and know what Kassel is plotting against you, against us all, myself included, because they will no more spare me than the others—and we can do absolutely nothing to stop them, they'll scatter us all like a brood of hens" (*November* 2 : 154; Woods 1 : 124).

Although they appear throughout the tetralogy, Ebert and his colleagues never change, never grow[23] (it should be kept in mind, of course, that the whole work lasts only two months). Their historical significance, like that of the generals with whom they are joined in a league of mutual distrust, fixes them into permanence. The narrator's ferocity, as we have noted, is directed more toward these feckless and uninspired SPD politicians than toward the generals themselves, the real source of the reaction. The hostility of the generals to the revolution is a given; they are the incarnate resistance to any change toward a more just and peaceful social order. But it is Ebert and the others who betray their supposed ideals and the trust of the people. He and the temporizing USPD leaders are presented as largely responsible for the failure of the revolution and thus for the social and political deterioration leading to the rise of the Nazis. They commit a "crime against the nation and world peace" (*November* 4:318; Woods 2:279). It is a double crime, because they have both bungled the opportunity to begin a new and just society in Germany and laid the foundation for the much greater conflagration of the next war:

> Today they would drive the nails from which they would hang the carcass of the mighty, floundering, bloodthirsty creature that wore a spiked helmet on its head and a monocle in its cynical, ugly face.
> But as it turned out, the judges and executioners would stumble into the very trap they had laid, would get wrapped up in the noose they had tied. And the perpetrator of the crimes, believing that his own last hour had come, would use this moment to leap forward and tie the noose tight about the neck of his judge and executioner and string up his struggling victim—his victim once again—with all the energy in his practiced hands, string him up, and all with the assistance of the friends of the court. The court was made up of the current republican government, put in office by the revolution, of the ruling Social Democrats whom later generations would curse. The German revolution would hang by its own rope, and with it, though invisibly, millions of other people living in Europe, Asia and Africa."[24]
>
> (*November* 4:305–6; Woods
> 2:267–68)

In contrast to the treatment of the SPD politicians, Quartermaster General Groener and the other officers at the General Headquarters in Kassel are presented in the manner of the "new objectivity." The narrator primarily lets their own dialogue characterize them. They emerge as cold, cynical calculators, exploiting Ebert to preserve as much of their power as possible, waiting for the moment when they can crush the radical workers. Here is Major Kurt von Schleicher discussing Ebert with Colonel Haeften:

> "He's a reasonable man. He's been out mixing with people for decades and knows what's what."
> Schleicher sniffed and replied, "Hm. Curious fellow. Saw him once in Spa with some other Reichstag fogeys who all wanted to get in to have a look at the grand motor-works as it were. Guided tours Mondays from

five to six, the management is not responsible for injury in case of accident."

Haeften: "You know him then."

Von Schleicher, a man in his mid-thirties, passed his hand over his bald head, his very lively eyes laughed. "Like the back of my hand. We appear to have made an almost sinfully good catch with him. I'm told two of his sons fell in the war. He's a sly, respectable fellow and he's got the socialists tied up in his sack. The good Lord heard our prayers after all. Lost the war, but won Herr Ebert."

(November 2:164–65; Woods
1:132)

The embodiment of this elite ruling caste is the old countess in Kassel, the "sibyl true to the Kaiser" as the narrator calls her, who presides over a salon for the officers of the General Headquarters. Now eighty-five years old, she was a member of the court of Kaiser Wilhelm I and his Kaiserin. The officers relate the legend that she refused to receive Napoleon III after the Battle of Sedan in 1870. She is no provincial Francophobe, however: "She told of the World Exposition in Paris in 1878. She had come across pictures of it today. What a city, Paris. What a wonderful charm it had. She had been there for the last time exactly twenty years before" (*November* 2:173–74; Woods 1:139). This incarnation of the traditions of the German nobility cannot forgive the officers their betrayal of the Kaiser nor their cooperation with Ebert and his colleagues, whose very name she cannot bear to speak: "I beg you to do me the kindness and explain to me what you feel when dealing with—those people" (*November* 2:178; Woods 1:143). She is much more idealistic than her younger guests, absolute in her loyalty to the imperial order and her contempt for the lower classes. In response to von Schleicher's *Realpolitik* regarding the need for the Kaiser to abdicate in order to preserve the Reich, she admonishes him: "Do not believe that the Reich is more important than the Kaiser, and that the Kaiser should perish if only the Reich may endure. The Reich has no life of its own without the Kaiser. The Reich grew with the Kaiser. Do not forget him there in Holland while you dirty your hands dealing with those people. I am afraid for you" (*November* 2:179; Woods 1:143).

It becomes clear, however, that this woman is no mere dusty fossil but in fact a "sibyl," a prophetess, when she reappears later in *A People Betrayed*. She demands a new Wallenstein, a leader who will violently and ruthlessly put down the radical rabble of the Left and reestablish the old order. She mocks the vacillating and demoralized generals who are not hungry enough for power: "You are all courageous in battle, but afterward you're ninnies. . . . Power is no enticement. Your watchword is subordination" (*November* 2:265–66; Woods 1:200). Here the narrator probes to the center of the authoritarian ideology of the German ruling class by letting its own representatives articulate it. For all her scorn for the generals, the countess too makes herself an advocate of subordination by her call for a powerful leader. Von Schleicher's unspoken reaction to the countess's attack anticipates the advent of Hitler, who will ride to power on the ideology of subordination: "Von Schleicher sat there silent. A Wallenstein, someone who would make a grab for the imperial crown? Hindenburg? A mute paladin, at best a surrogate for someone else" (*November* 2:266; Woods 1:200).

A remarkable passage follows immediately upon this conversation, a passage that deepens the probe into the ruling ideology by exposing its psychosexual origins. After von Schleicher leaves, the countess retires to her bedroom where she drops her shawl over her face in order to induce a bloody, Dionysian vision, in anticipation of which she "rubbed her narrow lips together in excitement":

> A battle of goats, black against a gray background, now and again a flash of lightning. The animals danced, leaped, shot past one another, collided in midair, locked horns, went at one another with their forelegs waving and rubbed brows together. They bleated and snorted. . . . The battle developed—now on the ground, now in the air—into a savage frenzy, the animals' horns grew with the pace, their black bristly bodies grew smoother. They slapped together like meat when they touched each other. They wallowed on the ground. Many of them lay there motionless. A stream of blood flowed from them.
> (*November* 2:267; Woods 1:201)

Here Döblin makes use of a sudden shift of narrative style to great advantage. Up to now, the countess has been presented from objective distance as an irreproachably urbane *grande dame* and spiritual inspiration to the officers who frequent her salon. Now we suddenly see her from within, as she takes sexual delight in her private vision of orgiastic violence. She pants "enraptured" along with the goats, and as the sexual connotations of the vision become more and more explicit (the phallic horns grow in size, the bodies become smoother and slap together like meat), she achieves a sort of climax:

> With great delight the old woman wadded up the cloth before her eyes, which now gave off only a blurred white gleam.

She was very weak, smiled and gazed at the shadowy wall. "Go to sleep now. You have played." Her nostrils were dilated.

She let herself fall limply against the high arm of the easy chair, breathing wearily. When she rang for the housekeeper and let herself be helped up out of the chair, her features were once more those of a delicate, attentive, serious old woman.

A charming smile illumined her face as she trembled there on the arm of her nurse.

(*November* 2:267−68; Woods 1:201−2)

It is the only passage in the novel where the narrator uncovers the hidden recesses in the psyche of a member of the ruling elite, and what he discovers there are the subconscious roots of its outwardly cold, calculated power politics: a sexual pleasure in violence and blood for their own sake. The passage thus is intimately connected to the violence of the suppression of the revolution and the brutal murders of Rosa Luxemburg and Karl Liebknecht in the fourth volume. The countess and the generals, in their cold and haughty menace, are beyond the reach of satire.

What of the initiator and motor of the revolution, the common people—soldiers and workers—whose main motivation was not to establish a socialist state, but to end the war and rid themselves of the yoke of militarism and exploitation? From his first volume, Döblin includes in his cast of characters members of the working class for whom the revolution initially means only the great relief that the war is over. The narrator at one point articulates their virtues: they are "solid, independent, skeptical, gregarious" (*November* 2:349; Woods 1:250).[25] The first common soldier presented extensively is Bottrowski, a housepainter from Berlin who encounters his former company commander, Lieutenant von Heiberg, during the first, chaotic days of the revolution in Strasbourg. Bottrowski bears no resentment toward his former officer, but neither does he show him any particular respect. He likes him personally, but von Heiberg remains for him a representative of the officer corps. Bottrowski quite naturally adopts the familiar *du*, an unheard-of affront under the old regime, and invites von Heiberg into a tavern. There he explains his conception of the significance of the revolution:

"You officers have lost the war and ruined the people. Watch us or walk on by: you've got nothing more to say, so keep your mouth shut. That's the safest thing you can do. Otherwise we'll have to go about this in a different way. You wonder why, Heiberg. That's because you're young and don't know anything. If I ask my daughter, who's twelve years old, why we don't eat meat or send Mom to the country in the summer, because she needs it, then she just laughs at me, 'Dad, you must be crazy.' She thinks that's how things have got to be. When the war started, we housepainters and plasterers kept our mouths shut and went to the front when it was our turn, because there was nothing else we could do, and a lot of our union members were killed or are hobbling around with missing limbs and won't be climbing ladders any more. But now the war is over and you've lost the game. You, Heiberg. Because you belong with them, just like my daughter belongs with me, Heiberg, and now we can run things differently and things are going to change."

He turned his unshaven face toward Heiberg. He didn't look angry, just very determined, stern. Heiberg was almost bursting with suppressed fury.

(*November* 1:34)

The passage is a marvelously compressed reflection of the mood of the majority of the German army at the end of the war.[26] Initially willing to be drafted (because after all, their representatives in the SPD also backed the war), they now realize how badly they were misled. The war was waged for the benefit of the elite and lost by the elite, at a terrible cost in death and suffering for the common troops. But now the revolution has ended the war, and it is up to the old ruling class to simply disappear. Their hour is past. Instead of camaraderie with his former officer, Bottrowski feels class solidarity with his daughter and his fellow workers. His dialogue is wonderful in its honesty and simplicity, but also tragic in its political naiveté. Heiberg hides his fury, but he will later join the mercenary Freikorps who continued fighting against the Bolsheviks in Poland and the Ukraine and would be used by Noske against the revolutionaries in Berlin itself.

Bottrowski is one of the very few working-class characters who figures prominently in *Soldiers and Citizens*. In this first volume, attention is focused on the largely bourgeois and petit-bourgeois population of the small town in Alsace. They are by and large fickle hypocrites who scramble to transfer their loyalties to the French when they realize that the Germans have been defeated. It is in the second novel, *A People Betrayed,* that the archetypical German proletarians are introduced in the persons of the Imker family, "Proles Among Themselves," as the chapter subtitle announces.[27] Their family name suggests virtuous industry (*Imker* means "beekeeper"), and it is clear that Döblin is at pains to make them both exemplary members of the proletariat and representative of the split within the socialist camp between the majority SPD and the radical Left. The father is a long-time SPD member and favors Ebert's plans for a constituent assembly and a democratic republic. The daughter and oldest child, Minna, has been radicalized by the revolution and favors the left wing of the dissident Independent Socialist Party (USPD) or Spartakus. The older brother wants to emigrate to South America. The younger brother, Ede, has just returned from the front with the Iron Cross second class and partial loss of his hearing. Like most of the returning troops, he is a blank slate politically, ready to be swayed either right or left. He sees no sense in the dispute between majority and radicals, can see no further than that the war is over: "We need peace and something on our plates. All the rest is trash. . . . As far as I'm concerned, I'm going to go get the civvies they're handing out on discharge and my fifty marks. And then I'll watch to see what everybody else is doing. At any rate I'm going to stash my rifle here at home" (*November* 2 : 80−81; Woods 1 : 61).

The Imkers are also typical of the ironies inherent in a war that had been supported by the SPD and a spontaneous revolution that took it by surprise. The family have had steady work during the war and have put their savings into war bonds. The end of the war, however, has brought economic hardship. Only the father is still working full time. Nevertheless, they are all glad the war is over and place their hopes for the future in the "socialist republic." Minna tells her brother Ede about a rally in the Circus Busch, a rally at which Ebert and Liebknecht could still appear together on the same podium: " 'I—I cried, it was so beautiful. Someone said that no matter what peace may turn out to look like, it's better than going on with mass slaughter. Ed, I can still hear how they shouted and sang for a quarter of an hour, and the meeting couldn't even go on. . . .' Even their father nodded, and the mother's face showed she was touched" (*November* 2 : 77; Woods 1 : 58).

Here, if anywhere, is the *verratenes Volk* of the second volume's title, the people who will be "betrayed" by the political leadership. The narrator presents them with straightforward realism and obvious sympathy, and uses them throughout the remainder of the tetralogy as a standard of decency against which other characters can be measured. How narrow a piece of ground this standard occupies, however, is also clear from the beginning. In the chapter in which they first appear, the Imkers' narrative is framed by two other subsections that suggest their isolation.[28] The chapter begins with a speech by Eduard Bernstein, a "gentle theoretician" (*November* 2 : 73; Woods 1 : 55), the revisionist and gradualist par excellence against whom Rosa Luxemburg wrote *Sozialreform oder Revolution*. He argues that socialization will not be possible until the economy has recovered from the ruinous war, that is, the socialists must resign themselves to cooperation with the capitalist system for "years, perhaps decades" (*November* 2 : 74; Woods 1 : 56). Then follows the section in which the Imkers are introduced, and the chapter closes with a section that begins the narration of the robbery and murder of a money lender by two homosexual prostitutes. One of them is a demobilized soldier who will eventually escape capture by joining the Freikorps troops training outside the city. The Imkers are implicitly an island of hope and decency, threatened on one side by a temporizing leadership and on the other by a criminal *Lumpenprole-tariat* eager to serve as troops for the counterrevolution.

Indeed, there is a general sense that while the revolution is being betrayed by its leadership, it is also foundering on the egoism and corruptibility of the "little people" with their eyes solely on their own advantage. The revolution is repeatedly parodied in the first volume as a "revolution in miniature," a pretext for greed, revenge, and passion. A soldier appropriates the apartment of his peacetime boss and installs himself as the new master; an old porter's wife plunders the abandoned barracks; an officer's widow has an amorous fling; profiteers calculate how much they can make from the revolution; deserters seize occasions for theft; a woman wants to marry a blinded soldier for his full pension (*November* 1 : 74–79, 140–41, 176–77, 244ff., 261, 266–67).

In *A People Betrayed*, there is an entire chapter devoted to such "Private Revolution" (*November* 2 : 99; Woods 1 : 77). Within it, there is a comic, grotesque section subtitled "Travelers' Ration Books," in which a Berlin couple and their son, a demobilized soldier, conspire to steal invalid ration books and sell them on the black market. We are reminded of the couple in *Berlin Alexanderplatz*, living in the building where Franz Biberkopf has retreated on his alcoholic binge, who become accomplices to a band of burglars (*BA* 159–69, EJ 190–205). In both cases, a lower-middle-class couple succumbs to the temptation of economic gain and commits a criminal act against a large, anonymous institution. The difference is that in *November 1918*, the couple hypocritically justify their behavior as a revolutionary act:

They knew that this was their great chance. Both of them were revolutionaries, as only befits laid-off munitions workers, and they wanted nothing more than to make shreds of capitalism. Couldn't everyone plainly see how the war profiteers were getting fat, how they were taking the skin right off the backs of the great mass of the people? Their lives of luxury were notorious, and they managed it by making use of a brilliantly organized black-market, with the cooperation of the farmers. And others were supposed to hold back? No, not for a moment. And the bellicose pair advised their son to do his part to help dying, putrid, staggering capitalism to its final collapse. He should look to see if he could get hold of those travelers' ration books. They would take care of the rest. "How?" Max asked. "By selling them." They wanted to supply the black marketeers with them, offering them either to the black marketeers or selling them directly to the rich. They weren't at all troubled by the contradiction inherent in their behavior. It can't hurt, they said slyly, for the parasites to swell up even more, that way they'll finally explode, and their rottenness will stink to high heaven. They would be contributing to the revolution.

(*November* 2: 104; Woods 2: 81)

The narrator of *Berlin Alexanderplatz* refrains from judging his miscreants. Their feckless attempt to improve their lot through criminality serves as a spur to Franz Biberkopf to reenter the world and try again, with more cynicism, to live his life. In *November 1918*, by contrast, the couple's "revolutionary" hypocrisy is the object of narrative sarcasm. The entire incident becomes a grotesque and bitter joke, another example of why the revolution is doomed from the beginning.

Indeed, throughout the tetralogy the suggestion recurs that the revolution ultimately founders on the German character itself. This opinion is to be expected from the French historical figures who appear especially in the first volume, men like Maurice Barrès and Marshal Foch. They clearly see that the German generals will attempt to obscure their responsibility for the lost war and let the civilian politicians take the blame for the capitulation, that the "revolution" is only a smokescreen to placate the entente. They provide the most pitiless, devastating summing up of the German character: "That's how the Germans are. . . . The aristocrats at the top hard as glass, cold as ice, servants of the King, the working masses willing, pliable, sentimental, susceptible to brutality, the middle class educated and cowardly to the point of servility" (*November* 1: 312). One assumes that it was partly because of such passages that the French censors in postwar occupied Germany refused permission to republish *Soldiers and Citizens* as part of the tetralogy.

A similar analysis, albeit only of the German socialists, comes from the opposite end of the political spectrum, from Karl Radek, the emissary sent by Lenin to advise Liebknecht and the Spartacists. As he watches the revolutionary opportunity slip away and the forces of reaction assemble, Radek reflects bitterly:

> For the Germans Marxism is apparently a new sort of Middle Ages. Yet another attempt to build St. Augustine's City of God here on earth. And naturally a flimsy one at that.
>
> But they still don't see the main thing, and are so blind they'll probably never see it, that the history of mankind is a morass of such attempts. That's why they can find no Lenin. And that's why there is only one solution for them: somewhere or other, if need be even in Russia, to find them a dictator and assign him to them, a Robespierre who'll drain that swamp and educate them to realism. Heads will have to roll, and no quarter will be shown. A Robespierre, and if I had anything to say in the matter, if I were their dictator now, the first head I would see roll is that of that die-hard pacifist Liebknecht.
>
> (*November* 3 : 274–75; Woods
> 1 : 497)

Radek, like the countess in Kassel, is an absolutist of power and decisive action surrounded by indecisiveness. Just as she calls for a Wallenstein to restore the old order, he calls for a Lenin or a Robespierre to ruthlessly carry out the revolution. He echoes the pitiless leitmotif of *Men without Mercy:* "No quarter will be shown" (*kein Pardon darf gegeben werden*). Here Döblin's recurrent theme of action versus passivity has been generalized and even nationalized. The hesitation bred into the German character creates the opportunity—even the necessity—for a ruthless charismatic leader, a Wallenstein or a Hitler, to step in and take command.

If Leibknecht is indecisive, it is because even he doubts the character of his followers, the most radical of the proletariat: "You said our party developed in such a way that, I hate to say it, Ebert fit right in. You're right, damn it. I see it every day, in the barracks, everywhere. Where are the proletarians? The proles? They're all petit bourgeois, bourgeoisie with no property, who want a parlor. That's their motive. That's why there's supposed to be a revolution" (*November* 3 : 354; Woods 1 : 560). But what really worries Liebknecht, "the core of his reflections," is the underside of this petit-bourgeois mentality: the mindless brutality ready to serve any master, the penchant for violence that has been born by the war:

"Everywhere I go I see strange fellows, I'm literally surrounded by them. They're soldiers, warriors, of a sort I never saw before, or only now and then. How should I describe them for you? Human refuse. Sometimes I can talk myself into believing they've been sent to us by the enemy to disrupt us, to disconcert us. But they can't have been sent. There are too many of them. They come on their own. They are everyday, average Germans, people from that same lower middle class we were just talking about, but some from further up the social ladder too, some of them educated, soldiers and workers. They have an odd way about them. The way they stand there, sit there. They don't honestly listen, they simply stare at you. They have a mean look, the snarling teeth of a wolf. Mostly they just sit there silently, sometimes they laugh with scorn. The war has brutalized people, wrecked them. They leave me with the impression that they are beasts of prey. You can expect most anything from them."
(*November* 3 : 357–58; Woods
1 : 563)

There are tragically few Ede Imkers among these returning soldiers. The difference between Radek and Liebknecht is that the latter refuses to make use of such men to further the cause of revolution. Like Radek, Ebert and Noske have no such scruples, and so this "human refuse" will be used to put down the Spartacist uprising and to murder its leaders Liebknecht and Rosa Luxemburg. It is also made abundantly clear that Lenin would have had no such scruples. Throughout the tetralogy, the leader of the Bolshevik revolution is held up as a model of unhesitating decisiveness, especially by Radek. At one point, he describes how Lenin rode over the objections of hesitating party members and ordered the beginning of the armed revolution:

"Lenin, the spirit of the revolution, our teacher, the perfect Marxist. He led with absolute assurance right on past all mere observation and pseudo-objectivity. And if there is a snare for Marxists, then it is the delusion that in some way one can be 'objective,' that somehow one can stand outside the situation. That's where Lenin was absolutely sure of himself. He had broken through this error of objectivity on a psychological level as well, saw it as a screen thrown up by bourgeois, academic irresolution. . . ."
The Russian[29] knew how deeply each of these remarks struck his German comrade, given as he was to musings, weighing everything, torn back and forth by his scruples. . . . These Germans were terrible gnawers of their own guts. . . . How had such a people given birth to Karl Marx, Radek asked himself.
(*November* 2 : 357; Woods 1 : 256)

Ultimately the narrator himself shares this doubt in the German character. Halfway through the second volume, "the author takes stock" of his story and his own feelings toward it: "So far no actual revolutionary masses have come into view. This might be considered sufficient reason for reproaching someone who has set out to describe a revolution. But it is not our fault. This is, after all, a German revolution" (*November* 2:242; Woods 1:186). Here is the title of the entire tetralogy, revealed for the first time in all its irony.[30] Beneath the historical fact of the failure of the German revolution, there is a deep narrative skepticism that a revolution would have been possible in Germany under any circumstances. Certainly this pessimism is a function of the bitterness of Döblin's exile, an example of the retrospective impact of subsequent events on the way the narrator treats the events of 1918–19. It is strongly reminiscent of Stalin's wartime *bon mot*, reported by Milovan Djilas: " 'In Germany you cannot have a revolution because you would have to step on the lawns.' "[31]

Whether the narrator's mode is the satire of the SPD leadership, the irony with which he treats the self-serving "miniature revolutions" of the common people, the cold objectivity with which he views the generals, or the sympathetic realism of his portrait of the Imkers, there lies over it all a feeling of weary inevitability in the gradual extinction of revolutionary hope during the slightly more than two months covered by the tetralogy. This inevitability is a function of the framework of historical fact itself: the narrator cannot undo the historical record of revolutionary failure. What he does, however, is to provide the story of Friedrich Becker as a counterpoise and commentary on the aborted revolution.

☐

Becker is a teacher of classics in a Berlin high school who has fought in the war as a first lieutenant and been seriously wounded. He returns to Berlin after the cease-fire in November 1918. There his convalescence is repeatedly disturbed by the political turmoil of the city, by the claims of friendship and love, and ultimately by the devil himself. Becker is saved from suicide by conversion to Christianity, but his subsequent actions as an engaged Christian so alienate him from his society that he gradually sinks into fanaticism and dies a vagabond.

Friedrich Becker is in some ways very different from the other central heroes we have encountered in the course of this study. He is a *Gymnasium* teacher and intellectual, an archetypical member of the educated middle class, precisely the class Döblin had scourged in most of his works, although himself a member of it. Another character calls Becker "the most German thing I know" (*November* 4 : 178; Woods 2 : 153), an apt description if "German" implies the tradition of bourgeois German culture since Goethe. Becker is by training and inclination both a repository of that tradition and, as a school teacher, its promulgator to the next generation. This is all the more remarkable in view of Döblin's own school experiences and scorn for the institution of the Prussian *Gymnasium*. But it must be remembered that even in the scathing attack in "First Glance Back," there were certain teachers whom Döblin admired and who managed to be human in spite of the system in which they worked.

It is also in keeping with the traditions of the German middle class that Becker considers himself and is in fact deeply apolitical. He is a perfect example of the typical German junior officer as he is described by the historian Arthur Rosenberg: "men who in their peace-time avocations as students, shopkeepers, teachers, &c., would never have been reckoned among the aristocratic ruling class and who were prepared on the conclusion of the war to return to their humble callings. But with the officer's commission was bound up the aristocratic exclusiveness that in Prussia separated an officer from his men." [32] We have seen that by the time Döblin wrote *Berlin Alexanderplatz,* he was consciously shaping his characters as exemplary figures. But Karl in *Men without Mercy* and, to an even greater degree, Friedrich Becker are exemplary in a much more sociological and political way than is Biberkopf.

Before the war Becker had been happy in his work and something of a playboy, along with his colleague, the science teacher Dr. Krug. But Becker's experiences in the war, and especially his near-fatal wound, have wrought a profound change in him. In volume 1, *Soldiers and Citizens,* he is in intense physical pain, still recuperating from the "terrible hole" a piece of shrapnel has torn in his sacrum during the fighting on the Somme (*November* 1 : 105).

But Becker's mental anguish at the mass suffering and death caused by the war tortures him even more than his wound. He is now revolted by the society whose exemplar he is, and revolted at himself for having entered the war so insouciantly and, as an officer of the kind described by Arthur Rosenberg, sent his men to their deaths in what he now perceives to have been a senseless conflict. Above all, he feels personal responsibility for not having taken action to try to prevent the war. He is haunted by the recurring memory of young soldiers being marched off and into cattle cars at the beginning of the war—young soldiers who have in the meantime all died: "I went along. Which means I was stupid, wicked and evil" (*November* 3:79; Woods 1:354). Of all the characters in the novel, only Friedrich Becker feels such intense personal responsibility for the war. Revolutionaries like Karl Liebknecht and Rosa Luxemburg have opposed the war all along. Working-class soldiers like Bottrowski have realized that they were being duped. Average citizens are simply glad that the war is over, while the ones responsible for the disaster, the German elite embodied in the officer corps, are scrambling to avoid responsibility and retain their power.

Becker's guilt and self-loathing lead him to a tortured and intense scrutiny of his life and its meaning. Upon his return to Berlin from the military hospital in Alsace, he nails shut his bookcase and removes from his walls the pictures and busts of his intellectual mentors Sophocles, Kleist, Kant, and Goethe, symbolically wiping clean his spiritual slate. His emotional slate, by contrast, appears to need little cleaning, and here one senses the abstractness of a *héros à thèse* whom Döblin has cleansed of the intense personal problems characteristic of his other heroes. Becker is an only child who dispenses with his deceased father in one depreciating sentence, never to mention him again: "My father was nothing special, a customs official, I can't remember him very well, he died early, he had brought my mother here from the Rhineland" (*November* 1:166). For this work, Döblin has resolutely left to one side the entire personal complex engendered by the flight of his own father, including his deeply ambivalent feelings about his mother.

Becker's mother, with whom he lives in Berlin, is the diametrical opposite of the mother in *Men without Mercy*. She is a sweet and pious woman who spends her days caring for her convalescent son and doing charitable work among the urban poor as a member of the "Patriotic Women's Circle" (*November* 3:176; Woods 1:423). There is not the slightest hint of conflict between them, except for a certain reticence on Becker's part to talk about his spiritual anguish with her. His conversion to practicing Christianity in the second half of the work only brings them closer together.

Thus the development of Friedrich Becker's character does not proceed from familial conflict, as is the case with Karl in *Men without*

Mercy. Personal change is instead thrust on Becker by the catastrophe of war and is structured by narrative reference to three literary-mythical antecedents: Faust, Antigone, and Christ. *November 1918* is an example of what Theodore Ziolkowski calls "postfigurative" modern fiction, novels whose "action is 'prefigured' in a familiar mythic pattern."[33] Döblin had used mythic references beginning as early as *The Black Curtain,*[34] and we have seen the references to the House of Atreus in *Wadzek's Battle with the Steam Turbine.* The mythic references in *Berlin Alexanderplatz,* both to the Agamemnon myth and to the Bible, are of course legion, but they do not become prefigurative in the sense that they constitute a palimpsest underlying the structure of the modern story. Instead, as Otto Keller emphasizes, by being presented in montage, the mythic references invite critical comparison with the modern story, "the mythic figure is removed from a static realm, is placed into time, is humanized."[35] One need only think of the comparison between Biberkopf and Orestes at the end of the second book of *Berlin Alexanderplatz* (*BA* 103–10, EJ 121–30).

In *November 1918,* by contrast, Friedrich Becker is fitted with three successive mythic prefigurations. If his life does not ultimately conform perfectly to any of them, they nevertheless provide a key to his spiritual development.[36] Rather than being used, like the Agamemnon myth in *Berlin Alexanderplatz,* as an ironic and critical contrast to the contemporary plot, they underlie, without a trace of irony, the existential crises of Becker's life in order to infuse them with meaning and purpose. Moreover, the order in which the mythic postfigurations come is significant. Becker moves from Faust's hubris, to Antigone's defense of the individual conscience against the dictates of the state, to Christ's redemptive sacrifice of self.

The least explicit of these postfigurations is of the Faust legend. The references to it occur mainly in the third novel, *The Troops Return.*[37] Early in the novel, Becker jokingly calls his friend Maus "my Mephisto" for taking him to a political rally (*November* 3:29; Woods 1:325). Maus's furious condemnation of Becker's inaction finally brings the latter to the point of despair at which an actual "Mephisto" appears to him. There are several more or less explicit references to the Faust legend in the course of Becker's three confrontations with the devil. Becker's study, the room in which he conjures Satan, is called his "laboratory," and the word is placed between suggestive quotation marks (*November* 3:219; Woods 1:454). The devil at one point sar-

castically calls Becker "Herr Becker, Friedrich Becker, doctor of phi-
lology, doctor of the highest wisdom," echoing the opening monologue in Goethe's *Faust:* "Heisse Magister, heisse Doktor gar, / Und
ziehe schon an die zehen Jahr' / Herauf, herab und quer und krumm /
Meine Schüler an der Nase herum / Und sehe, dass wir nichts wissen
können!" (They call me Magister, even Doctor / and for almost ten
years now / back and forth, up and down / I've been leading my students by the nose / and I see that we can't know anything). The Goethe
passage echoes Becker's anguish at having "misled" his soldiers. The
Alsatian nurse Hilde, who has sought out Becker in Berlin to offer him
her love, is compared to Gretchen (*November* 1 : 3 3 4). Finally, in the
banal love story whose episodes alternate with those of Becker's temptation, the writer Erwin Stauffer quotes the last line of Goethe's monumental drama to himself after his long-lost love has "given herself to
him": "Das Ewigweibliche zieht uns hinan" (The Eternal Feminine
leads us onward) (*November* 3 : 227).[38]

These explicit allusions to Goethe's *Faust* are the outward signposts
of the affinity between Becker and Faust. Their similarity is one of both
character and situation. Becker, like Faust, is a scholar who finds himself in radical spiritual isolation. The problematic that emerges is familiar from Döblin's other works but here more clearly Faustian because of Becker's learnedness: his lonely search for meaning and the
right path is also a form of hubris. Johannes Tauler, the Alsatian
mystic of the fourteenth century who appears to Becker in dreams
throughout the tetralogy, calls him a "good man" but also "hard and
proud, a great soul, a high mountain" (*November* 1 : 147). Like Faust,
he is a searcher after absolutes in a world of compromise, and it is this
spiritual hubris by which Satan hopes to ensnare him.

The fundamental difference between Becker and Faust lies in the
origin of their isolation; Faust is isolated by his contempt for the inadequacy and ignorance of other men, whereas Becker's isolation
springs from his guilt and self-contempt for his unthinking participation in the mass slaughter of the war. Thus when Satan offers Becker
first political power over other men and then unlimited sensual grati-
fication, both temptations to which Faust succumbs, Becker rejects
them out of hand (*November* 3 : 206 – 7; Woods 1 : 448 – 49). He
counters Satan's offer of unlimited power and freedom for his ego, of
total solipsistic self-affirmation, with the question, "Who is served by
it?" (*November* 3 : 209; Woods 1 : 450), thereby reintroducing into the

debate the source of his crisis, the dimension of social responsibility that Satan tries to ignore. With his tutelary genius Johannes Tauler at his shoulder, he is finally able to articulate the "precedent" for right action he seeks: it is "the conscience" (*November* 3 : 226; Woods 1 : 459). But the debate is not over yet. In a brilliant twist of satanic casuistry, the devil demonstrates that "conscience" is nothing more than the dictatorial superego, the societal conditioning imposed by parents, teachers, pastors, and the state, and is thus the very authority that led Becker to participate so unquestioningly in the war in the first place. Becker has no further counterargument and in despair tries to hang himself from a hook in his study wall. He is saved from death only by accident; the knot in his noose does not hold. The nurse Hilde arrives too late to be the instrument of his rescue, but when Becker regains his consciousness, the sight of her weeping and praying very quickly effects his conversion to Christianity.

Faust too is saved from suicide by the intervention of religion.[39] In his case only the memory of the naive faith of childhood holds him back from the fatal step; it is not enough to prevent him from entering into the pact with Mephisto. For Becker, however, the acknowledgment of the divinity of Christ ends his hubristic search for meaning solely within himself, and so ends the Faust parallel: "There I stood in front of my ego, searching for my self, for my ego, and I shook my ego, told it to give me something, and it could give me nothing because how could there be anything there that could tell me my duties, determine my path, if it were not already planted there by Him" (*November* 3 : 290; Woods 1 : 510).

Becker has tried to hang himself from the hook that held his bust of Sophocles, and Antigone succeeds Faust as his guiding prefiguration. Becker's conversion to Christianity, while freeing him from his solipsistic and suicidal despair, does not make his path totally smooth. It provides the ultimate basis for decisions about life in the world, but the decisions must still be made. That is why the Antigone story now becomes operable: it is the central mythic prefiguration of the text (providing the title for book 3 of *Karl and Rosa*) precisely because it embodies the central problem of the responsibility of the individual in the face of the demands of the state.[40]

The Antigone parallels are more carefully elaborated than those to Faust and to Christ. Döblin uses Sophocles' work as both an explicit and implicit model within the novel. On the first day Becker returns to his teaching post at the Berlin *Gymnasium,* the assigned text happens to be Sophocles' play. A few days after discussing *Antigone* with his students, he himself is forced by the dictates of his new-found faith to play the part of Antigone in the course of an ugly scandal involving the school principal.[41] *Antigone* is thus also the novel's primary demonstration of the importance of literature for life, an intensely important conviction for the German exiles in their social and linguistic isolation.

Becker is not simply returning to his profession after his long convalescence. His teaching post has become a sacred trust because of the war. As he explains to his class the concept of the sins of the fathers being visited on the sons, its relevance is made clear: "They were the children, the heirs, grown older now while others had been out there engaged in war. They had assumed the guilt of those older than they— and they knew nothing of it" (*November* 4:193; Woods 2:167). What disturbs Becker is not that these boys are suffering the consequences of the lost war for which they were not responsible, but rather that they have wholly adopted the unreconstructed jingoism of their middle-class parents: "They come here with old, rotten ideas, from homes that did not experience the war. These aren't young men at all, they are men from 1900 or 1910" (*November* 4:220; Woods 2:190).

Most of the fifteen students in Becker's class contemptuously reject Antigone as a heroine. In their eyes, she betrays her country in time of war. The best student, spokesman for the class, also makes clear the connection of their opinion to the current political situation: "Antigone really doesn't have our sympathy. One of her brothers bravely fought for his native city; he fell in battle and was buried with honors. As it should be. The other brother was a traitor who had assembled a great hostile army to attack his home. That would be the same as if now the Spartacists were to invite France to send troops here to do Germany in" (*November* 4:196; Woods 2:169). The students do not consider the ancient play irrelevant to their lives, but they derive precisely the wrong lesson from it. They are on the side of Creon, in favor of the absolute authority of the state over the individual. They reject Antigone as a model in favor of that most Prussian of heroes, Kleist's Prince Friedrich von Homburg, who accepts his death sentence for disobeying an order in spite of having won the battle.

Becker tries in vain to get them to see that the ultimate conflict in

Antigone is not "the political rights of the oppressed over against tyrants," as the one socialist in the class maintains (*November* 4:198; Woods 2:171), nor even more abstractly "emotion versus duty . . . but rather, 'How is the world of the living to treat the world of the dead?'" (*November* 4:224; Woods 2:194). The conviction that our being is not circumscribed by birth and death, and that we owe respect and love to the dead, underlies Becker's actions. It is a religious rather than a political conviction, but if acted on, it has political consequences, as Becker is about to discover. He has made himself the advocate of those who fell in the war, whom he so insouciantly watched being marched off to their deaths. In his thoughts, he explicitly draws the parallel with Antigone: "Just as Antigone takes up the cause of her dead brother, so have I taken up that of the many who fell" (*November* 4:224; Woods 2:194). In Becker's case, this advocacy means doing everything he can to insure that senseless war does not recur.

But the death that provokes the postfiguration of the Antigone story, in which "life emerges from the books," as a chapter title has it, has nothing to do with the mass dying that haunts Becker. What has added an element of hostile tension to the classroom discussion is the gradually emerging fact that the principal of the *Gymnasium* is romantically involved with Heinz Riedel, a student from the class. The principal is a classically educated, finely cultivated but self-indulgent man who, like the "little people" discussed above, uses the revolution as a pretext—in his case, to be more open about his homosexuality. Becker finds the man repellant and self-deceiving, but also calls him "my poor brother" (*November* 4:227; Woods 2:197). With the encouragement of his mother, he sees it as his human duty to intervene in the affair. It is the first real test of his new faith, a kind of miniature echo of his missed opportunity at the beginning of the war. His mother says, "Friedrich, you're making yourself an accessory if you don't intervene" (*November* 4:213; Woods 2:185). Becker persuades the principal to take a leave of absence.

At this point in the story, the novel's third book ends. The fourth and fifth books are devoted almost entirely to the aborted Spartacist uprising that began on January 5, 1919, and to Noske's gradual assembling of the troops who will suppress it. Against this background of political crisis and threatening reactionary violence, the thread of the Antigone postfiguration is taken up once again. The principal cannot resist trying to arrange another assignation with Heinz Riedel. The boy's brutal, alcoholic father finds his note, seeks the principal out, and beats him up so badly that he dies several days later.

Becker, who by this time has been denounced to the school authorities for what he said in the classroom discussion of *Antigone,* is perceived by the students and their reactionary parents as at best an accomplice of the principal, at worst a homosexual or revolutionary himself. He compounds their suspicion by taking Heinz Riedel under his wing and by visiting the morgue with him to arrange for the principal's funeral. In a chapter entitled "In the Footsteps of Antigone," so that no doubt about the reenactment of the myth can remain, two members of the school's parent council pay Becker a visit in order to warn him not to attend the principal's funeral. In protofascist turns of phrase, they explain that they want "to cleanse our school of all manifestations of decadence and decay" and admonish Becker "to go have a look at Alexanderplatz right at this moment, where civil war was in full swing" (*November* 4:430; Woods 2:347). They consider a demonstrative refusal to attend the funeral to be Becker's duty to the school and the state, and again the *Antigone* parallel is explicitly drawn:

> "We want to serve the general public. I repeat. For that purpose we can demand that each individual make his sacrifice and suppress even the most notable of his personal feelings."
> Becker (I'm slipping completely into *Antigone.* King Creon will be here soon to have me arrested): "There is neither a public nor a general interest that could deter me from showing a poor man the last token of my affection."
> (*November* 4:432; Woods 2:348)

Becker arranges the funeral, at which a priest refuses to officiate. The only others in attendance are Heinz Riedel, Becker's mother, and his colleague Dr. Krug. Their pictures are snapped at the graveside by two press photographers, and the affair becomes public knowledge. Becker is called before a chief school inspector, a latter-day Creon who chats amiably with him, praises his principles, and as soon as Becker leaves his office, has him removed from his teaching post. Thus ends the postfiguration of the Antigone story.

Unlike his prototype, Becker is not put to death by the state. But he is now driven into a kind of social death. He can no longer practice his profession. It should be emphasized again that Becker's initial actions as a Christian are, like Antigone's burial rites for her brother, acts of individual piety that have no intentional political dimension. His attempt to rescue Heinz Riedel from among the Spartacists in the besieged police headquarters is superficially a repetition of Karl's crossing over to the revolutionaries at the end of *Men without Mercy*, but there are two important differences. First, Becker is literally under divine guidance, for a vision tells him that Heinz is in the headquarters (*November* 4:483; Woods 2:393). Second, his motive is not political or social conviction, but rather personal responsibility. And although he takes up the cause of the revolutionaries after seeing the body of Minna Imker being carried by, his solidarity is based on sympathy for their plight, not agreement with their convictions: "These are poor human beings. They're searching for help. They don't know what else to do. And whatever they do, whether they're mistaken or not, they are my brothers and sisters, they are like me, and I am no better a man than they" (*November* 4:502; Woods 2:410). The principal had been called his "brother"; now they are his "brothers and sisters." After having served three years in prison for participating in the occupation of police headquarters, rather than join the Communists or any other political party, Becker enacts an *imitatio Christi*, a sacrifice of self for the salvation of his fellow men.

□

Eighteen hundred pages into the tetralogy and fifty pages before its end, the reader unexpectedly encounters Friedrich Becker being released from prison. The narrator mentions offhandedly that he has voluntarily turned himself in and has served three years for participating in the Spartacist uprising. The sudden gap in narrated time and the echo of the beginning of *Berlin Alexanderplatz* make one feel that a whole new novel is beginning at this point, and this feeling is reinforced in subsequent pages, where the precise chronology of the rest of the tetralogy—the two months of the revolution—is replaced by an elastic time that stretches imprecisely into months and years. The relationship of narrated time to narrative time is suddenly stood on its head.

We also get a new physical description of Becker, something largely lacking in the rest of the tetralogy: "a tall, grave, slightly bent man with a full brown beard" (*November* 4:612; Woods 2:503). In the following pages, this description is twice repeated, with the addition of the adjective "gentle" (*November* 4:613, 647; Woods 2:504, 534). This reiterated description is a warning that we are confronted with a new Friedrich Becker. But more than that, it hints at the coming imitation of Christ that will occur within the hazy, almost legendary time frame.

Prison has changed him, making him even more isolated from the world than before. His friends have either died or moved away. Even his mother is about to move out of Berlin. Becker has lost his position at the *Gymnasium,* and his attempts to teach at private schools end in characteristic failure; he becomes too involved with his students: "There were long conversations in the classroom between him and his students. He spent some of his private time with them, even got involved in their own home life. This resulted in certain difficulties, and he had to be let go" (*November* 4:618; Woods 2:508). He sets off on wanderings through the Germany of the Weimar Republic—"durch die deutschen Gaue" (through the provinces of Germany; *November* 4:641; Woods 2:529) in the consciously archaic language of the narrator—and continues to attract followers, or disciples if one will, among young people and students.

He preaches humility, poverty, and obedience to the will of God, in a conscious imitation of Christ: "Just as Jesus yielded himself when they tore the clothes from his body and even ripped the skin from his body with their whips before nailing him to the highest cross, that is how we must strip away all the weakness and wickedness, and our pride and vanity above all, so that we can present ourselves before God. We must present ourselves not just in words, but in everything we do. Surrender is the word" (*November* 4:625; Woods 2:514). In his wanderings, Becker continues to be accompanied not only by his tutelary saint Johannes Tauler, but also by Satan, who lays three "snares" for him. Although they are not the same temptations presented to the young Christ in the Wilderness, the number three certainly evokes the New Testament story (besides echoing the three visits of Satan to Becker/Faust).

Becker is tempted first by "woman" (*das Weib; November* 4:618ff.; Woods 2:508ff.), becoming involved in vaguely described affairs with the female relatives of some of his students. After being called to order by Tauler, he falls into the next snare, fanatical religious absolutism. He pillories the hypocrisy of established Christianity and enters village churches in order to reprimand the preacher for "chewing around on the word of God Sunday after Sunday, even though he knew better. They were the most corrupt capitalists in the world, because they exploited the most sacred thing man had" (*November* 4:648; Woods 2:535). For this echo of Christ's attack on the money changers in the temple (John 2:13–16), Becker is repeatedly jailed. The press dubs him the "Red Parson" (*November* 4:648; Woods 2:535), although he allies himself with no political group. When he tries to speak in a nationalist political convention, he is hounded away as a "stupid idiot" (*dummer August; November* 4:650; Woods 2:537), the same epithet with which the suspicious Spartacists in police headquarters greeted his arrival (*November* 4:490; Woods 2:400). For both ends of the political spectrum, he is the figure of God's fool, the holy idiot: "He was shaken by fanaticism" (*November* 4:650; Woods 2:537).

He does not so much avoid this temptation as sink even further into it in the third and final snare: a wager concluded with Satan in a Hamburg bar "near the close of the twenties" (*November* 4:647; Woods 2:537). It is not insignificant that Becker, here at the end of the tetralogy, is brought into close chronological proximity with Franz Biberkopf, and a Biberkopf-like figure, a coarse "fat bargeman with a red face," becomes the object of their wager (*November* 4:651; Woods 2:538). Friedrich bets Satan that he can find some redeeming quality in him, and Satan actually "slipped the other fellow's soul into [Becker's] breast, and something like a mangy dog was jumping around inside him, and he would have to live with it" (*November* 4:653; Woods 2:540). The alien and unredeemable soul forces Becker into drunkenness, whoring, theft, and blasphemy, and when the bargeman drowns, he can no longer rid himself of his soul. He is badly wounded during a robbery with some companions, and as he lies in a garage, dying among thieves and as a common criminal like Christ, there is a celestial battle over the final disposition of Becker's soul between Satan and Antoniel, the guardian angel assigned to him by Tauler. As is to be expected, Antoniel and two fiery lions in the end drive away Satan in the shape of a great "horse of hell," just as in *Berlin Alexanderplatz* Death drives off the Whore of Babylon. In a final parallel to the life of Christ, Becker's body disappears, albeit not miraculously:

> Afterward they had one damnable time with the body. Because they didn't want any police there in the shed—and what should they do with it?
> They waited till the day had passed, and that evening they loaded

their dead pal onto a vegetable cart under some crates and drove him
down to the docks. They stuffed him in a coal sack and put him into a
little motorboat, and in the dark they made a little tour of the harbor,
during which they eased the sack down into the water, with no one the
wiser.

(*November* 4 : 662; Woods 2 : 547)

Thus ends the postfiguration of the life of Christ as well as the entire
tetralogy. It is one of the most anticlimactic of Döblin's many anticlimactic endings, hearkening back in both its tone and imagery to the
story "On Heavenly Mercy." But that story's absolute separation of
bleak, everyday reality from the possibility of transcendence and redemption has now been replaced by a complete interpenetration of the
two levels. Just before the ending quoted above, the angel Antoniel has
assured the dying Becker that God "shall wipe away all tears, and
there shall be no more death, neither sorrow, nor crying, neither shall
there be any more pain" (*November* 4 : 661; Woods 2 : 547). The absolute faith of the narrator suffuses the final, outwardly bleak para-
graphs. This is merely Becker's body being disposed of. His soul, even
besmirched with the soul of the bargeman, has been saved.

□

The first snare Satan lays for Becker in the final *imitatio Christi* is the
snare of woman: sex and sensuality. Although he briefly succumbs to
this "disease" (*November* 4 : 619; Woods 2 : 509), he realizes that the
women he is with are "lovely and exciting little creatures, nothing
more" who want to degrade him to the status of a "male of the species" (*Männchen*).[42] Johannes Tauler has little trouble convincing him
to abandon this path. In fact, Becker's notable lack of sensuality
throughout the tetralogy makes this first temptation, as even the narrator is constrained to admit, "quite improbable" (*November* 4 : 618;
Woods 2 : 508). Why, then, does he include it?

Although the sight of a weeping woman, Hilde, finally converts
Becker to Christianity, and the sight of a dead woman, Minna Imker,
to active advocacy of the poor, when the final, legendary *imitatio
Christi* requires a schematic presentation of woman's role in his life,
she automatically becomes pure sensuality, *das Weib*, a temptation to
be overcome. The two most important women in *November 1918* are
the nurse Hilde and Rosa Luxemburg, one a private, fictional charac-

ter, the other an important historical figure, one of the most brilliant women of the twentieth century. Hilde and Rosa are the embodiments of the two great themes of the novel: religion and revolution respectively. Yet both of them show the stamp of sensuality characteristic of the women in Döblin's other works.

Hilde is presented as an ideal of Germanic womanhood: tall, full-bosomed, blond, a "Brünhilde figure" (*November* 1 : 116) as the narrator calls her, or "like Germania" as another character says (*November* 2 : 92; Woods 1 : 71). One wonders whether, in creating this character, Döblin was refusing to cede to the Nazis proprietary rights to such qualities. But it is not just her physical characteristics that make her an ideal. We first see her as a volunteer nurse in the military hospital in volume 1, selflessly caring for the wounded and dying, in love with the fatally wounded pilot Richard. We also discover that she is a devout Catholic; one of the first things she does upon returning home to Strasbourg is visit the cathedral and offer a prayer of thanks to the Virgin. She has fallen in love with Becker just before the evacuation of the hospital and follows him to Berlin, where she helps take care of him through his crisis and ultimately facilitates his conversion.

Yet there is also a dark side to this character, a side that has to do with her sensuality. For in fact, in spite of her piety and the virginal white of her nurse's uniform, Hilde is a sensualist.[43] We learn that she is serving as a nurse in order to escape a sadomasochistic love affair. Amid the confusion of the evacuation of the hospital in Alsace, Hilde is raped by Becker's roommate Lieutenant Maus, who is hopelessly in love with her. The rape runs a course familiar from *Berlin Alexanderplatz*. Hilde resists at first, but "his kisses became more and more ardent, and he called her pet names. She did not answer and let him do what he wanted. As she lay in his embrace, her convulsive trembling stopped, and she lost consciousness in a dreadful ecstasy" (*November* 1 : 112). In the final novel of the tetralogy, Hilde forgives Maus, whom she is about to marry, for having raped her, and makes it sound as though it had been her fault: "I'm a human being, Hans, a sinful human being. You know that. I've lain in your arms once before" (*November* 4 : 176; Woods 2 : 151). In her native Strasbourg after the cease-fire, Hilde soon resumes the sadomasochistic affair with Bernhard, her father's assistant. Her decision to go to Berlin in order to seek Becker is really a decision to tear herself away from Bernhard, and when she does, he commits suicide. Here, as in her attraction to the dying pilot Richard in the novel's opening pages, Hilde the ministering angel becomes Hilde the angel of death. The narrator once describes her as a "bright Valkyrie" (*November* 2:91; Woods 1:71).

Hilde is attracted to Becker at least partly because of his terrible suffering and the possibility of death. There is a curious duality in their relationship: she is in part a motherly, almost sexless caregiver, in part a sensual woman offering him love. Having left Bernhard to his despair and suicide, she comes to Becker in the role of a nurse of virgin purity: "she sank back into her loam, into maidenly gentleness" (*November* 3:21; Woods 1:318). But she also is presented as the female of the species, sizing up Becker as a mate (*Männchen,* the same word used by Becker at the end of the novel to describe the status he has sunk to in his experiments with women). Hilde is "the watchful mother, the doe, and she regarded the male animal leaping before her. I want to build upon you, will you assist me in the building of my nest? If you will protect me when the young are born, then I will let you be the father of my children, I will have you" (*November* 3:25; Woods 1:321).

Becker ultimately forgoes Hilde because she distracts him from his search for meaning in life, for she herself cannot be that meaning. While Becker, just before his three satanic visions, flays himself with guilt over his participation in the war, Hilde wants only to cure him so they can begin their life together: "How can I tear him away from these ghastly notions. He's making wonderful progress physically. If he wanted to, he could be a healthy man again in four weeks—and we could begin a new life" (*November* 3:179; Woods 1:425). Becker asks her, "How can I bring God to me when I cling to you so?" (*November* 3:192; Woods 1:437). It is clear that the dichotomy, which informs the early novel *The Black Curtain,* of man as metaphysical seeker and woman as sensual, "natural" being survives basically unchanged into the last phase of Döblin's career. The only difference is that Hilde, because she is a believer, can acknowledge the scope of Becker's struggle and the danger she represents to him. As soon as she has provided the impetus for his conversion, she voluntarily renounces him as her chosen mate: "She had become terribly aware of just how fond she was of Becker—and that she was not good enough to love him. No, she didn't want to do it. She didn't want to ruin this man too" (*November* 3:276; Woods 1:498). She chooses instead Hans Maus, the man who raped her. By the time Becker is released from prison, Maus has left Noske's armed forces ("his heart was no longer in it"; *November* 4:628; Woods 2:518) and he and Hilde have married, moved to Karlsruhe (where Maus is studying engineering), and had a child. In other words, Hilde at the end of the novel enters an apotheosis of upper-middle-class life. She, Maus, and the child constitute a kind of bourgeois holy family, and Becker the wandering fanatic gives his stamp of approval to Hilde's natural, sensual piety during an unexpected visit: "Enjoy the blessing of the child, Hilda. It will not fall into these pagans' hands, because it is your child" (*November* 4:631; Woods 2:520).

□

Hilde enters the novel as a rape victim and leaves it as a middle-class madonna, married to her rapist. Rosa Luxemburg, along with Becker the central figure of the fourth volume, *Karl and Rosa,* similarly comes full circle in the course of the novel. At the beginning of *Karl and Rosa,* in January 1918, she is a political prisoner in Breslau, where she helplessly witnesses a soldier brutally beating his team of Rumanian oxen. In the end this same soldier, the rifleman Runge, assassinates her. This deft tying together of beginning and end is a good example of how Döblin, the master *monteur,* can integrate particles of historical reality into his fiction.[44] The historical Rosa Luxemburg indeed witnessed such a scene and was deeply disturbed by it. Döblin makes use of her letter to Sonja Liebknecht in his recreation of the scene in the novel.[45] The soldier Runge was indeed Rosa's murderer.[46] The only thing Döblin has added is to make him also the driver of the oxen, so that his brutality toward them is an anticipation of his brutality toward Rosa. At the moment of her murder, recognizing Runge and recalling the beautiful beasts, she is herself identified as a sacrificial animal. He recognizes her, too ("Where have I seen that waddling duck with the white hair before?"; *November* 4:591; Woods 2:489).

But such economical and effective novelistic license in the use of the historical record is far outweighed by Döblin's misuse of it in the case of Rosa Luxemburg. Although clearly sympathetic to her, his very sympathy leads him into gross distortion; Döblin's compulsively recurring image of women determines even his portrait of this extraordinary intellectual. In the first hundred pages of *Karl and Rosa,* the imprisoned Luxemburg is so hysterical with grief over the death on the eastern front of her lover, Hans Düsterberg (actually Diefenbach), that

she hallucinates him visiting her in her cell. Her cell becomes "my den of
iniquity" (*November* 4 : 30; Woods 2 : 20) where they celebrate "marriage." In a particularly distasteful passage, Hannes "enters" her as an
icy coldness: "it had taken hold deep within her, this icy cold, down into
her bowels. She moaned, 'Hannes, oh, you are cold'" (*November* 4 : 36;
Woods 2 : 25). These hysterical hallucinations of the revolutionary suffering under her enforced inactivity are alternated in bitter irony with a
narration of Lenin's decisive leadership in the Bolshevik revolution.

But even after her release from prison "in the midst of the fray"
(*November* 4 : 103; Woods 2 : 85), Rosa still yearns for Hannes. In her
grief for him and her despair at the emerging failure of the revolution,
she sees the devil as the dominant reality. Her visitations by Hannes
resume, but he himself turns out to be Satan in disguise, a devil of sensuality who seduces and makes love to her:

> It was their wedding, a real marriage this time, and how very different
> from the first one in prison with the icy shade who wanted to warm
> himself on her, with that poor broken warrior. This man was warm, hot
> and bewitchingly handsome, and gave of himself, nor did she hold her-
> self back.
> The ecstasy, the intoxication robbed her of consciousness.
> (*November* 4 : 297; Woods 2 : 260)

When she is able to interpret him as a revolutionary like herself, Rosa
even goes so far as to declare allegiance to Satan (*November* 4 : 385;
Woods 2 : 312). But after the actual revolution has been suppressed by
Noske's troops, after the fall of the *Vorwärts* building and the police
headquarters, after Luxemburg and Liebknecht have gone into hiding
together, Rosa is visited by a celestial messenger from Hannes, a cherub
who tells her how Hannes has found peace through suffering and repen-
tance. Although Rosa initially rejects this message and allows Satan in
the form of Hannes to make love to her "before the mute, blushing,
mournful cherub" (*November* 4 : 547; Woods 2 : 450), the latter finally
chases Satan away and converts Rosa. She must give up her "proud
soul" and repent. At the moment of her murder, her assassin Runge
turns into Satan just before bludgeoning her to death, thus connecting
her violent death to her sensuality.

There is very little basis in fact for Rosa Luxemburg's private life as
it is presented in *November 1918*, and none at all for her conversion.[47]
Certainly it is true that Luxemburg was a passionate woman who did
not deny her sensuality and who had a series of lovers in the course of

her life.[48] It is also true that she was devastated by the death of Hans Diefenbach, the last of her lovers. One can even point to the sentence in one of her letters from prison that probably gave Döblin the idea for his hypertrophic development of her hysterical visions: "I feel so good, in spite of my pain for Hans. . . . For I live in a dream world in which he has not died at all. For me he still lives and often, when I think of him, I smile at him."[49]

To plead poetic license in Döblin's defense is to beg the question. Why did Döblin choose to portray Rosa Luxemburg in this way? One does not have to look far for the answer: the parallels to Friedrich Becker fairly cry out. Of all the characters in the novel, only Becker and Luxemburg are visited by Satan, for they are the strivers after absolutes, Becker in the spiritual and Luxemburg in the social realm. They both incorporate an alien soul and struggle terribly with it. Both are saved at the end by the intervention of an angel who drives Satan away. They die similarly ignominious deaths, and their bodies are cast into the water.

But the differences between the two are as illuminating as the similarities. Rosa's incorporation of the soul of Hans Düsterberg, as well as her visits from Satan, are above all struggles with her sensuality. She is presented primarily not as a political figure but as a private woman. Although Rosa Luxemburg was certainly a clearer head and greater thinker than Karl Liebknecht, for instance, it is Liebknecht whom we see most often in the fray of daily plans and debates with Radek. To be sure, Döblin does not totally neglect Rosa the thinker, especially in her criticism of Lenin's resort to terror and repression in Russia. He quotes, for instance, the famous prophetic passage from her pamphlet "The Russian Revolution": "Without general elections, without unhampered freedom of the press and assembly, without free debate of opinions, life will die out in every public institution. It will only seem to live, while only one single effective pulse of life will remain—the bureaucracy" (*November* 4 : 92; Woods 2 : 75).[50] But such passages are more the exception than the rule, and they drift incongruously amid the tides of her ecstatic and sensuous visions.

Becker, the monkish aristocrat of the spirit, is tempted by intellectual egoism and absolutism. Luxemburg, the passionate woman of the world, although just as much of an intellectual as Becker, is tempted by her sensuality. They both must learn humility and submission from their guardian angels before they can be saved and then killed. In order to connect religion and revolution, Döblin needs to make first a sinner and then a convert of Rosa Luxemburg. Although this is surely a tribute from the author who had converted to Christianity, it so distorts the historical Rosa Luxemburg that it seriously compromises her credibility as a fictional character.

The historical Rosa Luxemburg, like the German Revolution itself, had long since been sacrificed on the altar of history when Döblin wrote his novel. His narrator operates in opposition to this incontrovertible knowledge, like Becker who in *Soldiers and Citizens* refuses to accept the collapse of his world: "'I don't care if it's written or printed. It doesn't exist. It doesn't exist'" (*November* 1:109). Rosa's last-minute conversion, to say nothing of the final years of Friedrich Becker, represents the narrator's desperate attempt to raise his story out of the realm of history, to suggest a transcendent alternative that focuses on the individual soul rather than a society in turmoil.

☐

If Rosa Luxemburg is the parallel figure that connects Becker to the realm of revolutionary politics, then the *littérateur* Erwin Stauffer is the parallel figure who connects Becker to the narrator and ultimately to Döblin himself. The Stauffer narrative is the most puzzling of the parallel strands that accompany and reflect upon Becker's narrative. On its surface, Stauffer's story, which spans all four novels of the tetralogy, resembles nothing so much as a serialized romance in a women's magazine. It is a story of betrayal, revenge, near suicide, and a love affair resumed after a twenty-year interruption, set in elegant apartments, Swiss castles, and grand hotels. The writing is at times almost embarrassingly kitschy and conventional, and it is at first difficult to see why Döblin included this story, since it goes on too long to be a parody of this kind of writing. John Woods, the translator of *November 1918* into English, left out the entire Stauffer narrative. Yet a close reading of it suggests the intended purpose of its inclusion.

Stauffer is a variation on Friedrich Becker (and on the author himself), but at a trivialized level. They are both intellectuals, men of the word. Late in the fourth volume, the narrator compares them explicitly: "[Stauffer] wanted to purify his spirit. He did it not with the vehemence of a Friedrich Becker . . . but with the caution and sensitivity appropriate to the temperate climate of his education and past" (*No-*

vember 4:606). Both undergo a conversion upon being brought into contact with the "Geisterreich" (spirit realm), but while this word means for Becker literal temptation by satanic forces, for Stauffer it is nothing more than a bit of costume drama in the Swiss castle before he consummates his reunion with his long-lost true love. The conventional machinery of gothic romance gradually falls away, however, to be replaced by sobering reality: Lucie, for Stauffer a casual affair of twenty years ago whom he had completely forgotten, turns out to be alcoholic and manic-depressive, while Stauffer himself is shown to be a middle-aged writer who has lost his inspiration. The two have become "dis-enchanted" (*entzaubert*) by the end of the tetralogy (*November* 4:404). They depart for America and a comfortable middle-class future in which Stauffer gives up writing entirely. In his final appearance, he quotes the mystic Suso on the virtues of a contemplative withdrawal from active participation in life: "If you desire to help all creatures, then turn away from all creatures" (*November* 4:611). He has renounced all public activity and declares himself unable to reach "either a political or an intellectual or a religious conviction" (*November* 4:611). Here is another major character who, like Hilde, opts for middle-class respectability.

It is unclear whether the five lines set as free verse at the end of this final episode in the Stauffer narrative are by Stauffer himself or by the narrator. The lack of clarity on this point is all the more disturbing because they reflect a deep pessimism about the possibility of any meaningful action in the face of the impending war. If they are Stauffer's words, they are out of character because of their ominous seriousness; if the narrator's, then they cast his entire project, guided by the "partisanship of the active person," into question:

> Something dark was looming in Europe.
> Loneliness became oppressive.
> Nothing had stability, nothing grew, nothing prospered.
> Year by year, life became more sinister.
> People shivered and wanted to hide.
>   (*November* 4:612)

The ambiguous origin of these final lines in the Stauffer story points to its other function. Besides being a trivialized parallel to the hero Friedrich Becker, Stauffer also serves as an ironic mirror of the author Alfred Döblin, or at least of the part of himself that he saw as frivolously literary, whose books "deserved to be burned" (*Briefe* 207). It is no accident that Stauffer bears some resemblance to the author's father Max Döblin: he is artistically gifted in a rather superficial way, abandons his child, and moves to America. In *November 1918*, writers are consistently satirized as helpless in a revolutionary situation. There is no more mordant satire within the tetralogy than the presentation of the "Intellectual Workers' Council," where we first meet Erwin Stauffer late in the first volume, *Citizens and Soldiers:* "Since they were only intellectual workers, they didn't have to worry about the petty details or even about how to get things done. That was the business of politics and the parties—the parties whom they either rejected out of hand or attacked with abandon" (*November* 1:297). Döblin himself had been similarly touched by the fever of idealistic hope at the end of the First World War and made similar unrealizable demands in the essay "Die Vertreibung der Gespenster" ("Exorcising the Ghosts," 1919; *SPG* 71–82).

Stauffer represents not just Döblin's criticism of his own past, but also his doubts about the project at hand, *November 1918*. It is no accident that the brief section entitled "The Author Takes Stock" (*November* 2:242–44; Woods 1:186) occurs in the midst of the Stauffer narrative. As we have already seen, the "author" first makes it clear that the entire narrative is to be understood as satirical. But the impossibility of a revolution in Germany—the narrator's and the reader's privileged knowledge that the German revolution is doomed from the beginning—also leads the narrator to a stylized ennui. Whether Ebert outwits the generals or vice versa does not much matter, he says: "We could close our book right now for lack of interest—on our part. A serious matter when the lack of interest in a book already begins with the author" (*November* 2:244; Woods 1:187). What keeps him going is the possibility, existing only in his fiction, that out of the incontrovertible historical fact of failure something unforeseen may emerge: "For instance, it could be that two men get into a fight, in the course of which a kerosene lamp is knocked over and the house burns down, while in the building next door, which just happens to be a menagerie, the lion caged there escapes and runs loose in the city. So no pretext of philosophy. *Allons*, to work!" (*November* 2:244; Woods 1:187–88). But this metaphorical lion points away from the possibility of radical social change and back toward the religious center of the book: it is in

the form of a lion that Satan appears to Becker, and two flaming lions
drive Satan away in Becker's final apotheosis and death.

□

Becker's conversion is certainly meant to be the spiritual center of the
novel, mirroring as it does Döblin's own spiritual crisis and conversion
in the midst of the composition of the tetralogy.[51] At the same time, it is
the most problematic aspect of the novel. For it represents a kind of
absolute and transcendent solution to the problems that beset not only
Becker but society at large. It is a final basis of judgment from which
there neither can nor need be any further appeal. It means that in spite
of the failed revolution, in spite of the Second World War that Friedrich
Becker predicts and the narrator knows at firsthand, in spite of Becker's
apparent defeat at the hands of Satan, ultimate peace and forgiveness
are assured on the metaphysical level, if one is only willing to sacrifice
one's ego and submit to God's will. In "Epilog," the late essay in which
Döblin retrospectively reinterprets all his works in the light of his
Christian faith, he writes of *November 1918:* "Up to this point, all my
epic works had been tests. Now there was nothing left to 'investigate'"
(*AzL* 396). In the last volume, *Karl and Rosa,* the narrator pronounces
an epitaph for the occupiers of the *Vorwärts* building. All of them, including the novel's archetypical good proletarian Ede Imker, will be
beaten to death by Noske's Freikorps troops:

> They were fanatical men and women, young and old, all deeply touched
> by the great rousing call of the revolution, gladly willing to fight for the
> sake of humanity and to sacrifice themselves. There were strangely ex-
> cited and intense figures among them, believers: believers in this world
> and utopians who dreamed of eternal peace. And though they were
> weak and they were few, they towered miles above the miserable figures
> of the little philistine Ebert and the wooden Noske with his mercenaries,
> who would soon raise their cudgels and smash them.
> (*November* 4:466−67;
> Woods 2:378−79)

It is the narrator's tribute to the anonymous men and women of what
he deems the real revolution, the poor and oppressed whose desire is
peace. But it is also a pious wish fulfillment, skewing these men and
women into line with Friedrich Becker and the converted Döblin him-

self. They are fanatics, believers, "gladly willing . . . to sacrifice themselves." Here is sad evidence of the progressive writer's despair in his helpless exile in Los Angeles: the only possibility for action he discerns beyond Karl's spontaneous identification with the oppressed at the end of *Men without Mercy* is the fanatical self-sacrifice of Friedrich Becker and these doomed revolutionaries.

Conclusion

Alfred Döblin is a writer with a deep sense of unease about himself and his place in society, and about modern man and society in general. His novels arise from and reflect that unease, both in form and content. None of them has the structural coherence and polished finish that characterize the works of a more aesthetically inclined and commercially successful contemporary like Thomas Mann. Manfred Auer has written that for Döblin, style is always in the service of socially relevant content, never of aestheticism.[1] Mann's artist-heroes are set apart from society by their aesthetic and philosophical sensibilities, whereas Döblin's characters, whether they come from the working class or the bourgeoisie, are plunged directly into a hostile and chaotic environment.

Even works like *The Three Leaps of Wang-lun* and *Mountains Seas and Giants*, ostensibly narratives of distant times and places, reflect modern dilemmas, as their introductory dedications make clear. But in his Berlin novels, Döblin confronts most directly the problems of contemporary society. The modern metropolis is the focal point of those problems; the city *is* the modern world for the Berliner Döblin.

The central problematic in Döblin's Berlin novels is the relation of the individual to society, delimited by the polarity of activity and passivity, rebellion and submission, that informs all his work. From "Modern" to *November 1918*, Döblin's progressive, rebellious political instinct is in conflict with an emotional pathology—evident in his image of women—that demands submission as the price of redemption.

We have seen how Döblin's treatment of the city shifts along with his conception of the individual and his role in society. In the essayistic story "Modern," the young writer uncritically embraces August Bebel's Marxist analysis of the capitalist city and presents the fictional account of Bertha as a case study of its effect on an individual. In the early lyrical novels *Galloping Horses* and *The Black Curtain*, however, the psychological torment of the central characters occupies

Döblin's interest to the almost complete exclusion of their social context. The story "On Heavenly Mercy" reflects another radical change in Döblin's treatment of character, a change that allows the reintroduction of the city. The fiercely objective narrator completely ignores any possibility of inner life in the *lumpen* city dwellers who are his characters, but allows their bleak environment to emerge as an implicit correlative to the absent inner level. The interpolated bird songs and the lyrical metaphor for death more obviously suggest other levels of experience but remain unsettling intrusions, radically divorced from the main narrative. At the same time, they anticipate the vastly more complex use of montage in *Berlin Alexanderplatz*.

Although Döblin's first Berlin novel, *Wadzek's Battle with the Steam Turbine*, has a quintessentially urban figure, an industrialist, as its central character, the Berlin in which he lives is an indistinct backdrop. The novel's title is curiously misleading, for its central "battle" is between the ideas of heroic rebellion and submission to fate rather than between man and technology, and it is fought out in Wadzek's private life rather than in the public sphere of commerce and technology. Wadzek's failure to keep his family life separate from his business life, the realm of the heart from the realm of ideas, is parallel to Döblin's failure to write the futuristic novel of technology and urban life he had originally planned. Wadzek's overtly pathological character makes him seem more closely related to the grotesque protagonists of satirical stories like "The Murder of a Buttercup" or "Astralia" than to Franz Biberkopf or Karl or Friedrich Becker. Alfred Döblin's own psychopathology is near the surface in *Wadzek's Battle with the Steam Turbine*. This is the city novel in which his polarized image of women expresses itself most clearly in the dichotomy between the monstrous, solipsistic Pauline and the self-sacrificing, victimized Gaby. At its end the novel suggests an escape from obsessive behavior in the ideology of flexibility, and from the dichotomy of rebellion and surrender in the flight to America with Gaby. Neither of these escapes, however, is fully convincing. They have the effect of the interpolations in "On Heavenly Mercy" by suggesting other levels of experience without integrating them into the main narrative.

In the years following the First World War, during the Weimar Republic, Döblin's political and social activity increased as his basic unease gradually focused more sharply on the relation of the individual and society. Dissatisfied with the Marxist orientation of "Modern" on the one hand and explorations of individual psychopathology on the other, he developed a biological metaphor in his works of speculative philosophy that allowed him to integrate both the individual and human society into a universal continuum. The metaphor of the coral colony, which in *Wadzek* still expressed the alienation of man within the city, is now positively reinterpreted; man is seen primarily as a social and collective being.

Social engagement and the balance between the individual and the collective, the biological metaphor, and the theme of the metropolis all converge in Döblin's greatest work, *Berlin Alexanderplatz*. The montage that informs the novel from beginning to end is the formal expression of its positive image of the individual within the multitudinousness of the city. Franz Biberkopf and his environment ultimately complement each other, and by the end of the novel, he is ready to reenter society as a new man. The montage facilitates reconciliation on another level of the novel as well, allowing Döblin's opposed images of woman to be presented on different levels of reality. Woman as vampire has become the apocalyptic Whore of Babylon, the embodiment of evil finally vanquished by Death in the metaphysical battle for Biberkopf's soul. On the level of the plot, only the image of woman as self-sacrificing victim remains, embodied in Mieze, the most sacred of Döblin's sacred prostitutes. Her sacrificial death precipitates the final catastrophe through which Biberkopf is transformed into a new man, but conveniently leaves him alone at the end of the novel. This open end, so characteristic of Döblin, is perhaps the clearest example of the writer's continuing ambivalence toward the problem of activism versus passivity. Biberkopf is left hovering on the brink of social engagement, but what form that engagement will take, and the significance of the masses marching past his window, remain unclear.

This prescient image and the dilemma it expresses became acutely real with the triumph of National Socialism four years after the publication of *Berlin Alexanderplatz*. In *Men without Mercy*, a novel written in exile, Döblin attempts to explain—to himself as well as his readers—the origins of repression. In the person of his hero, Karl, Döblin suggests the interdependence of psychological repression within the family and political and economic repression in the social order. In the character of Karl's mother, Döblin confronts most directly the sources of his own view of women. Like Franz Biberkopf, Karl undergoes a positive transformation at the end of the novel. Like Biberkopf, he is also alone, having rid himself of both mother and wife. Unlike Biberkopf, however, he takes the next step beyond that transformation by attempting to join the rebellion. In spite of the fact that Karl dies in the attempt and the rebellion is crushed, the narrator, near the end of the novel, expressly holds out hope for its ultimate success.

Yet that hope seems to fade into insubstantiality on the novel's closing pages, when the narrator leaves the question of social liberation to return to the private sphere of the family. Here the novel's formal characteristics, unique within Döblin's oeuvre, become problematic. *Men without Mercy* is the novelist's only work that is formally closed. The recapitulation of the opening scene—figures clothed in mourning, waiting on a station platform—brings the novel full circle and ends the history of Karl's family where it began—ends it, but does not resolve it. Karl's younger brother Erich disappears into a life of inconsequentiality, while the central figure of the mother is still terrible and unbending, unable to cry, not even aware that Karl has died in rebellion against society rather than in its defense. For a writer like Thomas Mann, whose great theme is the interaction of art and life, there is a measure of comfort to be derived from the perfection of form, even when a family like the Buddenbrooks is extinguished. For Döblin in *Men without Mercy,* formal balance seems ultimately pessimistic and even sterile.

There is also a kind of sterility in Döblin's decision to make the city in *Men without Mercy* an anonymous metropolis. It never becomes a real city, for its schematized geography—the royal palaces and museums on their hill, gazing down on the proletarian quarters—is too obviously symbolic. In trying to universalize the significance of his story, Döblin loses the documentary immediacy of the city in *Berlin Alexanderplatz.* Biberkopf is so convincing a character because his surroundings are convincing. The characters in *Men without Mercy* are in danger of becoming as schematic as their city; even the figure of the revolutionary Paul does not escape that fate. The essence of *Berlin Alexanderplatz*'s power is its contemporaneity for both reader and author, underlined by its use of present as the primary tense of narration. Franz Biberkopf can progress no further than his author, there can be no bridge to the "further shore" of activism, as Döblin described it in his letter to Julius Petersen, if the author himself cannot discern such a bridge.

Five years later, from his exile in France, Döblin saw the consequences of the failure to act, and so he has Karl take the last desperate step into action. But this act, both for Karl and for his author, is a gesture, not a program, a fatalistic resolve to join the oppressed in their defeat. The defeat itself, in spite of the hope-filled rhetoric of the narrator, is a foregone conclusion, no longer an open question as it still is in *Berlin Alexanderplatz.*

In Döblin's last Berlin novel, *November 1918,* the ideological organization of the city is more precisely focused by being tied to the real historical crisis of the German revolution. As in *Men without Mercy,* the city is no longer the heterogeneous microcosm of *Berlin Alexanderplatz.* It has been reduced to unambiguous, emblematic significance as the location of repression and exploitation, the home of the "gigantic beast of public life." In this sense, Döblin has come full circle as a writer. The negative Berlin of "Modern," where Berta yearns for the sentimental love she reads about in cheap novels but is forced toward prostitution, is also the Berlin of *November 1918,* whose inhabitants "went to the movies and the screen showed them love, beauty and adventure. In the streets they were confronted with prostitution" (*November* 1:259). The utopia of free love and socialism that is "Modern's" answer has become the Christian utopia of the heavenly Jerusalem. The solution to the hostile confrontation of individual and society in *November 1918* is no longer sought, as it is at the end of *Berlin Alexanderplatz,* in the reconciliation of man and city. Rather, the solution has now been found in Christian salvation—a salvation that points away from the real city toward the heavenly one. *Berlin Alexanderplatz* seeks the universal meaning concealed within the particulars of its montage. In *November 1918,* the universal has already been found, and the particulars are reduced in value.[2]

Once the conversion to Christianity is accomplished—both by Döblin himself and by his hero Friedrich Becker—the passive pole of the active/passive dichotomy is invested with Christian meaning. It now signifies surrender not to the flux of nature but to divine guidance and the assurance of final salvation through Christ. Not that the practicing Christian Friedrich Becker disengages himself from the struggle against oppression. On the contrary, it is his faith that literally leads him into that struggle in the police headquarters. The depreciation of the idea of fate in *Wadzek* gives way to the acceptance of divine intervention in *November 1918.* But this is a highly problematic resolution of the dichotomy of rebellion and submission. For although submission to God now leads to action, it does not lead to any practical vision of a just society. Instead, Becker sinks into fanaticism. The ambiguity of this solution is evident in the late essay "Christentum und Revolution" (Christianity and Revolution; 1950), in which Döblin reflects on *November 1918*. While espousing solidarity with the victims of capitalism and war, he is still caught between Scylla and Charybdis: "Not armed revolution and not the black lifelessness of Pascal" (*AzL* 381). The essay ends with the same helplessness that spoke from the final pages of *Know and Change!*: "Let no one begin with 'deeds' of which the world has seen more than enough in recent centuries. Truly, we have need of something else. A good tree will surely bear good fruit" (*AzL* 383).

Novelists are not politicians, of course, and it is unfair to expect from them a practical formula for social reform. Döblin, however, always thrusts his heroes into abrasive conflict with society, thereby himself raising the question of what is to be done. The question never gets answered, not even after his conversion. On the one hand, he is too honest to escape into a private idyll. For Döblin, the private realm of the heart can never exist independently of the public realm of ideas. This explains his lifelong hostility to the realistic novel of bourgeois life. It also explains why his own characters who attain that life in conventional marriage (Julie and José, Hilde and Maus, Stauffer and Lucie) become bland stereotypes. On the other hand, he also cannot escape into a social or religious utopia. Friedrich Becker converts, but dies an obscure and ignominious death all the same.

Döblin presents no solutions, but at his best, in *Berlin Alexanderplatz* and sections of *November 1918,* he structures the confrontation between the individual and society with an intensity of vision, a depth of sympathy, and a radicality of form that place him among the great novelists of the century.

Notes

Introduction

1. See Walter Laqueur, *Weimar: A Cultural History 1918–1933* (New York: G. P. Putnam's Sons: 1974), pp. 41–77. Laqueur corrects the popular one-sided view of Weimar culture as purely leftist by also analyzing the right-wing intellectuals (pp. 78–109), but the only imaginative writer of any stature he can adduce on the Right is Ernst Jünger.

2. Alfred Döblin, in his afterword to the reprint edition of *Berlin Alexanderplatz* ("Nachwort zu einem Neudruck," *BA* 509). All translations are mine unless otherwise indicated.

3. "Krisis des Romans: Zu Döblins 'Berlin Alexanderplatz,'" *Die Gesellschaft* 7 (1930), pp. 562–66. Now in Walter Benjamin, *Gesammelte Schriften*, vol. 3, ed. Hella Tiedemann-Bartels (Frankfurt: Suhrkamp, 1972), pp. 230–36.

4. Jost Hermand and Frank Trommler see in pre–World War I Expressionism the roots of the utopianism common in the early years of the Republic. *Die Kultur der Weimarer Republik* (Munich: Nymphenburger Verlagshandlung, 1978), 36–40.

5. The German title actually means "No Quarter Given." See below, Chapter 4, n. 1.

6. See Heidi Thomann Tewarson, *Alfred Döblin: Grundlagen seiner Ästhetik und ihre Entwicklung, 1900–1933* (Bern: Peter Lang, 1979), pp. 58 and 83–84, for an intelligent exposition of the implicit parallels between *Wang-lun* and *Wallenstein* on the one hand and Wilhelmian Germany before and during the war on the other.

7. See Helmut Kiesel, *Literarische Trauerarbeit. Das Exil- und Spätwerk Alfred Döblins* (Tübingen: Max Niemeyer, 1986), pp. 207–9.

1. The City Theme in Döblin's Early Works

1. Louis Huguet calls this "Döblin's fundamental experience." See his Jungian interpretation of Döblin's early writings in "L'Oeuvre d'Alfred Döblin ou la Dialectique de l'Exode, 1878–1918," Diss. Paris-Nanterre, 1970, p. iii.

2. Peter Gay, *Weimar Culture: The Outsider as Insider* (New York: Harper and Row, 1968), pp. 102–18.

3. Heidi Thomann Tewarson writes that in Döblin's early works, "Interpersonal relations are almost exclusively based on physical attraction, while psychic—i.e., intellectual or emotional—sympathy is as far as possible eliminated. Thus all relationships take on erotic characteristics, not just those be-

tween a man and a woman, but also those between two men or two women."
Tewarson, *Alfred Döblin*, pp. 69–70.

4. He could have written this sketch, in which he is "approaching forty"
(*SLW* 14), between January and his birthday in August.

5. See the excellent "Döblin-Chronik" in Jochen Meyer, ed., *Alfred Döblin
1878–1978*, catalogue of the exhibit at the Deutsches Literaturarchiv, Marbach am Neckar, June 10–December 31, 1978 (Marbach: Deutsche Schillergesellschaft, 1978), pp. 15–21.

6. On the characterization of Döblin's marriage, see Robert Minder, "Begegnungen mit Alfred Döblin in Frankreich," *Text + Kritik* 13/14 (June 1966),
p. 59. Bertolt Brecht writes of Döblin's "life with an uncommonly stupid and
philistine woman"; Brecht, *Arbeitsjournal*, ed. Werner Hecht, vol. 2 (Frankfurt: Suhrkamp, 1973), p. 605.

7. Armin Arnold, "Les styles, voilà l'homme! Döblins sprachliche Entwicklung bis zu 'Berlin Alexanderplatz,'" in *Zu Alfred Döblin*, ed. Ingrid
Schuster (Stuttgart: Ernst Klett Verlag, 1980), pp. 41–56, disagrees. He finds
"Modern" an exercise in schoolboy rhetoric; only the theme is unusual
(pp. 41–42).

8. August Bebel, *Die Frau und der Sozialismus (Die Frau in der Vergangenheit, Gegenwart und Zukunft)*, 10th ed. (Stuttgart: Dietz, 1891).

9. *Die literarische Welt* 2 (May 21, 1926), p. 6, quoted by Klaus Müller-
Salget in *Alfred Döblin: Werk und Entwicklung* (Bonn: Bouvier Verlag,
1972), p. 95.

10. See Heidi Thomann Tewarson, "Von der Frauenfrage zum Geschlechterkampf: Der Wandel der Prioritäten im Frühwerk Alfred Döblins," *The German Quarterly* 58 (Spring 1985), pp. 208–22.

11. See Anthony Riley, "Nachwort des Herausgebers," *JR* 293–94.

12. Döblin mentions this setting explicitly along with the youth of the hero
(and implicitly also of the author) in the essay of 1927, "Stille Bewohner des
Rollschrankes" (Silent Inhabitants of My Desk Drawer): "At the beginning,
the hero is in youthful, rural narrowness" (*AzL* 357).

13. See Monique Weyembergh-Boussart, *Alfred Döblin: Seine Religiosität
in Persönlichkeit und Werk* (Bonn: Bouvier Verlag, 1970), pp. 88–89.

14. Tewarson, *Alfred Döblin*, pp. 21–22, contrasts the progressive position of Bebel to the antifeminist position of a writer like Strindberg, whom
Döblin admired. Döblin, she writes, is basically antifeminist in his imaginative writings, though he occasionally espouses a progressive position in his
journalism.

15. The influence of Italian Futurism on the *Sturm* circle and other Expressionists confirms Walter Laqueur's insistence that a good deal of what we consider "Weimar culture" was already fully developed before the First World
War. Laqueur, pp. 110–13.

16. *Der Sturm* 104 (March 1912), p. 829; also quoted in Christa Baumgarth, *Geschichte des Futurismus* (Reinbek bei Hamburg: Rowohlt, 1966),
p. 28.

17. See Marianne W. Martin, *Futurist Art and Theory 1909–1915* (New
York: Hacker Art Books, 1978), p. 40: "Marinetti originally wavered between
Dynamism and Futurism as names for his incipient movement."

18. *Der Sturm* 103 (March 1912), p. 823; also in Baumgarth, p. 182.

19. "Die Bilder der Futuristen," *Der Sturm* 110 (May 1912), pp. 41–42.
Republished in *Zeitlupe* 7–11.

20. See Baumgarth, pp. 166–71 for the "Technical Manifesto"; pp. 171–73 for the "Supplement"; and pp. 250–51 for "Battle: Weight + Smell," the French version of which was appended to the "Supplement" in *Sturm* 150/151 (March 1913), p. 280.

21. See Tewarson, *Alfred Döblin*, p. 54, who shows that Döblin's 1910 essay on the aesthetics of music, "Gespräche mit Kalypso. Über die Musik," already had established many of the aesthetic positions attributed in the secondary literature to the influence of Futurism.

22. *Der Sturm* 133 (October 1912), p. 195; Baumgarth, p. 168.

23. *Der Sturm* 133, p. 194; Baumgarth, p. 166.

24. *Der Sturm* 133, p. 194.

25. This point is also made by Winfried Georg Sebald, *Der Mythus der Zerstörung im Werk Döblins* (Stuttgart: Ernst Klett, 1980), pp. 129–30.

26. On the importance of *Sachlichkeit*, see Tewarson, *Alfred Döblin*, pp. 47ff.

27. Compare the similar remarks of the Russian Constructivist Naum Gabo apropos the Futurists: "Ask any Futurist how he imagines speed, and on the scene will appear a whole arsenal of raging automobiles, rumbling stations, tangled wire, the clang, bang, noise and ring of the whirling streets. . . . This is not at all required for speed and its rhythms. . . . Look at a ray of sun—the quietest of the silent strengths—it runs three thousand kilometers in a second. Our starry sky—does anyone hear it?" Quoted by Linda Shearer, "Beyond Futurism: The Winston/Malbin Collection," in *Futurism: A Modern Focus* (New York: The Solomon R. Guggenheim Museum, 1973), p. 14, from *Gabo-Pevsner* (New York: The Museum of Modern Art, 1948), pp. 18–19.

28. *Der Sturm* 150/151 (March 1913), p. 280. Cf. Baumgarth, p. 251: "general-little island" and "bodies-watering cans heads-football scattering."

29. Tewarson, *Alfred Döblin*, p. 53, and Judith Ryan, "From Futurism to 'Döblinism,'" *German Quarterly* 54 (1981), p. 415, suggest that it was *Mafarka* that Döblin was criticizing in the "Open Letter." A close reading shows, however, that "Bataille" rather than the earlier novel was the object of his attack.

30. See Baumgarth, p. 63.

31. *Der Sturm* 104 (March 1912), p. 828; Baumgarth, p. 26.

32. Armin Arnold, *Die Literatur des Expressionismus: Sprachliche und thematische Quellen* (Stuttgart: Kohlhammer, 1966), pp. 62–69.

33. The connections between Futurism and fascism have been perhaps most convincingly argued by James Joll, *Intellectuals in Politics: Three Biographical Essays* (London: Weidenfeld and Nicolson, 1960), pp. 133–78. See Giovanni Lista, *Futurisme: Manifestes—Proclamations—Documents* (Lausanne: L'Age d'Homme, 1973), pp. 22–33, for an informed apologia for the protofascist elements in Futurism. The resurgence of interest in Futurist painting and sculpture during the past twenty-five years, particularly at major exhibits in America (the Museum of Modern Art in 1961, the Guggenheim in 1973, the Philadelphia Museum of Art in 1980, the Yale University Art Gallery in 1983), and most recently at the Palazzo Grassi in Venice in 1986, has been accompanied by a tendency to minimize fascist or protofascist elements. There is some justification for this tendency in the case of the Futurist painters, since the original group—Boccioni, Carrà, Russolo, Severini, Balla—did not often glorify war or violence in their works. This phase of Futurism, called *il primo futurismo*, was in any event over by 1916, the artists having either died in the

war or left the movement (see Martin, *Futurist Art*, pp. xxx–xxxi). The tendency is to blame the younger postwar Futurists (*il secondo futurismo*), still led by Marinetti, for succumbing to fascism, as in this statement by Anne Coffin Hanson: "For many years full consideration of the movement has not been encouraged because of its late historical links to Italian Fascism. While early Futurist writings include elements which are not universally acceptable today, it is manifestly unsound to read history backwards and to invest the optimistic aspirations and energies of the first Futurists with the sinister overtones of events which had not yet occurred"; *The Futurist Imagination: Word + Image in Italian Futurist Painting, Drawing, Collage and Free-Word Poetry* (New Haven: Yale University Art Gallery, 1983), p. iii. (Why "manifestly unsound," by the way, unless one rejects historical causality and the ability of ideas to influence subsequent events?)

34. *Der Sturm* 104 (March 1912), p. 828; Baumgarth, p. 26.

35. *Der Sturm* 104, p. 829; Baumgarth, p. 28.

36. *Der Sturm* 104, p. 829; Baumgarth, p. 26.

37. Marinetti, "Tod dem Mondenschein! Zweites Manifest des Futurismus," in Baumgarth, p. 240.

38. F. T. Marinetti, *Mafarka le Futuriste: Roman Africain* (Paris: E. Sansot, 1909), pp. viii–ix. This and all subsequent translations from *Mafarka* are mine.

39. This manifesto also mitigates the absolutism of the stylistic prescriptions in the "Technical Manifesto" and the "Supplement" and may have been meant as a reply to Döblin's "Open Letter," which appeared in *Der Sturm* in the same March issue that contained the "Supplement."

40. Umbro Apollonio, ed., *Der Futurismus: Manifeste und Dokumente einer künstlerischen Revolution 1909–1918* (Cologne: M. DuMont Schauberg, 1972), p. 120. The German text has "fünfzigprozentige Gleichberechtigung" for "full equality."

41. See Lista, *Futurisme*, p. 327.

42. French original reprinted in Lista, pp. 329–32. For more information on Valentine de Saint-Point, a grandniece of Lamartine, see Lista, pp. 51–57.

43. Baumgarth, pp. 237–39, emphasis in original.

44. *Mafarka le Futuriste*, pp. 30–31.

45. Ibid., p. 31.

46. Ibid., p. 147.

47. Ibid., pp. x, xi.

48. Ibid., pp. 281–82.

49. Friedrich Nietzsche, *Werke in zwei Bänden*, vol. 1 (Munich: Hanser, 1967), p. 588.

50. *Mafarka le Futuriste*, p. 302.

51. Cf. Müller-Salget, pp. 29–31.

52. Leo Kreutzer, *Alfred Döblin: Sein Werk bis 1933* (Stuttgart: Kohlhammer Verlag, 1970), p. 21. It is Kreutzer who first drew attention to the suppressed first chapter of *Wang-lun* (now to be found in E 96-113, with the title "Der Überfall auf Chao-Lao-Sü"), which is much more overtly political than the alternate version that Döblin eventually chose. See Kreutzer, pp. 47–48.

53. *Die Kultur der Weimarer Republik*, p. 81. They go on to show how the popular culture of the Weimar Republic exploited the cliché in the variation of vamp and boyish *femme enfant*. Walter Laqueur, in his more narrative ac-

count of Weimar culture, seems to accept this stereotype as reality when he generalizes about Weimar women, "half vamp and half Gretchen," in *Weimar*, p. 32.

54. "Grün ist der Mai. Mit mancherlei schönen Blümelein gezieret sind Berg und Tal. Viele kalte Brünnlein rauschen, darauf wir Waldvögelein lauschen."

55. "Des Menschen Gemüt, hoch aufgeblüht, soll sich nun auch ergötzen zu dieser Zeit, mit Lust und Freud sich an dem Maien letzen. Und bitten Gott gar eben, er wolle weiter Gnade geben."

56. Ernst Ribbat, *Die Wahrheit des Lebens im frühen Werk Alfred Döblins* (Münster: Verlag Aschendorff, 1970), p. 24.

57. Klaus Theweleit's study of the literature of the prefascist Freikorps movement following the First World War sheds much light on this phenomenon. Theweleit shows how proletarian women are automatically regarded as prostitutes, and that violence toward them is violence toward female sexuality in general. Theweleit, *Male Fantasies*, vol. 1: *Women, Floods, Bodies, History*, trans. Stephen Conway (Minneapolis: University of Minnesota Press, 1987), pp. 63–70, 171–204.

2. Wadzek's Battle with the Steam Turbine

1. See Ingrid Schuster and Ingrid Bode, *Alfred Döblin im Spiegel der zeitgenössischen Kritik* (Bern: Francke Verlag, 1973), pp. 52–61.

2. Ibid., p. 61.

3. Bertolt Brecht, *Tagebücher 1920–1922. Autobiographische Aufzeichnungen 1920–1954* (Frankfurt: Suhrkamp, 1975), p. 48.

4. Judith Ryan has addressed one such problem, that of the multiperspective narrative, in her article "From Futurism to 'Döblinism,'" *German Quarterly* 54 (1981), pp. 415–26.

5. See Werner Stauffacher, "'Komisches Grundgefühl' und 'scheinbare Tragik': Zu 'Wadzeks Kampf mit der Dampfturbine,'" in Werner Stauffacher, ed., *Internationale Alfred Döblin-Kolloquien (= Jahrbuch für Internationale Germanistik*, ser. A, vol. 14) (Bern: Peter Lang, 1986), p. 170.

6. Matthias Prangel, *Alfred Döblin* (Stuttgart: Metzler, 1973), p. 33.

7. The final text of the novel does not clearly state why Gaby demands an introduction to Wadzek's daughter as the price of her aid in his stock maneuvers, but earlier manuscript versions show that Döblin conceived the relationship as a homoerotic one (see W 349, note to p. 39).

8. Brecht, *Tagebücher 1920–1922*, p. 48.

9. Otto Keller, *Döblins Montageroman als Epos der Moderne* (Munich: Fink Verlag, 1980), p. 205.

10. Although it is not explicitly stated, Wadzek's outward reactions (which are all the narrator gives us) suggest clearly that the "critical point" is the realization of his machine's inferiority: "The paper fell from his hand, he half fainted" (W 30).

11. Keller, pp. 72ff. and 143ff., has drawn attention to the anticipatory parables in *Wang-lun* and *Berlin Alexanderplatz*. The past history of Schneemann, although not explicitly parabolical, occupies a similar position at the beginning of the novel and serves a similar purpose.

12. See for example Müller-Salget, p. 88.

13. See Theodore Ziolkowski, *Fictional Transfigurations of Jesus* (Princeton: Princeton University Press, 1972), pp. 6–8.

14. See *W* 349–50, note to p. 40, on Döblin's frequent allusions to the Agamemnon story in his works.

15. He is thus interpreted by Hansjörg Elshorst, "Mensch und Umwelt im Werk Alfred Döblins," Diss., Munich, 1966, p. 27.

16. Kiesel, pp. 201–29, contains a thoroughly researched chapter on the meaning of psychopathology for Döblin's work. Kiesel writes of Döblin's "pathophilia" (p. 224) and asserts that his narrative style often imitates delusionary psychotic states in order to gain insight or "illumination."

17. Schuster and Bode, p. 61.

18. Klaus Schröter is undoubtedly right when he criticizes the novel for a surfeit of undigested symbolism in "Die Vorstufe zu *Berlin Alexanderplatz.* Alfred Döblins Roman *Wadzeks Kampf mit der Dampfturbine,*" *Akzente* 24 (1977), p. 571. This also means a field day for a Jungian critic like Huguet, whose interpretation of the novel depends on the possession of detailed information about Döblin's private life.

19. For Roland Links, the broken mirror shows the "doubtfulness" of Wadzek's existence as a "completely rootless, alienated petit bourgeois, crushed by capitalist competition"; "The unbroken mirror image is a lie. Only in the shards lies the truth"; *Alfred Döblin: Leben und Werk* (Berlin: Volk und Wissen, 1980), pp. 59 and 60. Hansjörg Elshorst calls the mirror scene the "central point" of the novel and interprets its symbolism as showing that Wadzek and Schneemann are "interchangeable": "There is in reality no unmistakable, concrete individuality" (Elshorst, p. 25). Louis Huguet writes that Wadzek breaks the mirror and wounds himself as self-punishment for incestuous and patricidal wishes (Huguet, p. 711) although there is no mention of Wadzek's parents in the novel. I agree with Ernst Ribbat, who writes that Wadzek identifies with Schneemann's defeat in Stettin and in breaking the mirror "destroys his previous self" (Ribbat, p. 177).

20. See Kimberly Sparks, "Drei schwarze Kaninchen: Zu einer Deutung der Zimmerherren in Kafkas 'Die Verwandlung,'" *Zeitschrift für deutsche Philologie* 84 (1965), Sonderheft *Moderne deutsche Dichtung,* p. 78.

21. See Stauffacher, p. 179.

22. See the excellent notes in Anthony Riley's new edition of the novel, *W* 359.

23. Judith Ryan, pp. 419–20, shows how another urban description from *Wadzek* is a "correlative for the emotional state of the central character." That does not seem to be the case in the passage under discussion.

24. Links, *Alfred Döblin,* p. 60.

3. Berlin Alexanderplatz

1. See Kreutzer, pp. 71–81, 134–47; and Sebald, pp. 14–58. During Döblin's exile in Paris, Arthur Koestler and Manès Sperber are reported to have called him the "Konfusionsrat" (Counselor of Confusion). See J. Strelka, "Der Erzähler Alfred Döblin," in *The German Quarterly* 33 (1960), p. 209, quoted in *SPG* 509.

2. See Sebald, p. 22, and Kreutzer, p. 76.

3. See Kreutzer, p. 82.

4. The *Ausgewählte Werke in Einzelbänden,* begun in 1960 by the Walter-Verlag with new volumes still being added, is the standard edition of Döblin's works. Under its current editor, Anthony Riley, it is approaching the status of a complete edition.

5. See Müller-Salget, pp. 12–15.

6. This is reminiscent of a passage about engineers in Robert Musil's *The Man without Qualities:* "Why do they like to stick tie-pins adorned with stags' teeth or small horseshoes in their ties? Why are their suits constructed like the motor-car in its early stages? And why do they seldom talk of anything but their profession? Or if they ever do, why do they do it in a special, stiff, out-of-touch, extraneous manner of speaking that does not go any deeper down, inside, than the epiglottis?" Musil, *The Man without Qualities,* vol. 1, trans. Eithne Wilkins and Ernst Kaiser (New York: Capricorn Books, 1965), p. 38.

7. In January 1924, Döblin became a member of the "Gesellschaft der Freunde des Neuen Russland" (Society of Friends of the New Russia). See Meyer, p. 25.

8. See Burton Pike, *The Image of the City in Modern Literature* (Princeton: Princeton University Press, 1981), p. 8. Pike writes that the city has always been an image of extreme ambivalence in Western culture, but that the scales tipped toward a negative image during the rise of industrialism in the nineteenth century. Döblin's essay attempts to counteract this negative image.

9. Pike, p. 88, points out that the topos of the city versus the country, conventional since Vergil, declines in importance in the nineteenth and twentieth centuries. The city becomes the primary setting of modern man.

10. See Sebald, pp. 140–41.

11. Biberkopf also represents an implicit critique of the bourgeois urban aesthete who is the typical hero of the nineteenth-century city novel, including Dostoyevsky's Raskolnikov. See Pike, p. 100.

12. Quotations from *Berlin Alexanderplatz* will be referenced to both the German edition (= *BA*) and to the English translation *Alexanderplatz Berlin: The Story of Franz Biberkopf,* trans. Eugene Jolas (New York: Frederick Ungar, 1976) = EJ. In some cases, it has been necessary to make changes in the Jolas translation.

13. Volker Klotz, *Die erzählte Stadt. Ein Sujet als Herausforderung des Romans von Lesage bis Döblin* (Munich: Carl Hanser Verlag, 1969), p. 397, manages to compress the plot into one—albeit fairly complex—sentence.

14. Theodore Ziolkowski, *Dimensions of the Modern Novel: German Texts and European Contexts* (Princeton: Princeton University Press, 1969), pp. 128–29, points out the probable travesty of Friedrich Hebbel's play "Gyges and his Ring," based on the legend of Gyges and Candaules in Herodotus.

15. Keller, *Döblins Montageroman,* analyzes the montage technique in *The Black Curtain* and *Wang-lun* as well as in *Berlin Alexanderplatz.*

16. Ekkehard Kaemmerling, "Die filmische Schreibweise," in Matthias ·Prangel, ed., *Materialien zu Alfred Döblin. "Berlin Alexanderplatz"* (Frankfurt: Suhrkamp, 1975), p. 185. Pike, p. 9, writes that it is natural to perceive a city as "a cacophony of impressions."

17. Werner Welzig in his survey of the twentieth-century German novel arranges his material thematically and treats under the rubric "City Novel," his most meagerly represented category, only one work besides *Berlin Alexander-*

platz, Wolfgang Koeppen's *Tauben im Gras* (1951). Welzig, *Der deutsche Roman im 20. Jahrhundert,* 2nd ed. (Stuttgart: Alfred Kröner, 1970), pp. 111–20.

18. Pike, *The Image of the City,* p. 132, writes of the "stubborn spatiality of the city."

19. This important distinction in point of view has been made by Müller-Salget, p. 295, and again by Keller, p. 145. The overwhelmingly chaotic impression of the first chapter has misled many commentators into treating it as the novel's primary mode for viewing the city.

20. See Keller, pp. 143–52. Keller sees in the story the Jews tell Biberkopf a parable of central importance for the novel.

21. Döblin's pronouncement in "The Structure of the Epic Work" that "It makes no difference and is a purely technical question, whether the epic author writes in present, preterite, or perfect tense" (*AzL* 111) means only that choice of tense cannot be legislated and has no effect on the epic's "presence." Technique, of course, has a decisive influence on meaning. Müller-Salget, p. 120, points out the importance of the only narrative sentence in present tense in the whole of *Wang-lun.*

22. To my knowledge, the only time Döblin uses the word "montage" is in a 1947 letter to Paul Lüth (*Briefe* 377).

23. Dietrich Scheunemann, *Romankrise: Die Entstehungsgeschichte der modernen Romanpoetik in Deutschland* (Heidelberg: Quelle & Meyer, 1978), pp. 167–74, 182–83.

24. Benjamin, *Gesammelte Schriften,* vol. 3, pp. 230–36. The two passages quoted below occur on pp. 232 and 233.

25. Scheunemann, p. 176.

26. While passages from this chapter are often cited in the secondary literature, it is treated systematically, to my knowledge, only by Klotz, pp. 375–80. In many cases, I have come to similar conclusions, but with differences in emphasis significant enough to warrant a second look. Müller-Salget, pp. 335–39, analyzes the montage at the beginning of book 5 as exemplary of all the others, because his main concern is to show how closely the "big city episodes" are related through theme, motif, imagery, and anticipation or recapitulation to the rest of the novel. Breon Mitchell, *James Joyce and the German Novel 1922–1933* (Athens, Ohio: Ohio University Press, 1976), pp. 131–50, argues convincingly that Döblin's reading of *Ulysses* influenced his technique in *Berlin Alexanderplatz.* On pages 138–39, Mitchell shows how Döblin changed book 2, chapter 1, after reading *Ulysses.*

27. Müller-Salget, p. 121, points out the comparable natural rhythms of season in *Wang-lun.*

28. Mitchell, p. 139, suggests that Döblin borrowed this device from *Ulysses.* Cf. James Joyce, *Ulysses* (New York: The Modern Library, 1961), p. 116.

29. Marilyn Sibley Fries, "The City as Metaphor for the Human Condition: Alfred Döblin's *Berlin Alexanderplatz* (1929)," *Modern Fiction Studies* 24 (Spring 1978), p. 44, notes this natural choice of a square to concentrate a fictional presentation of a city, while Klotz, p. 377, calls it "simultaneously the point of departure, arrival, and transfer."

30. There are several feuilletons and short essays from the twenties in which Döblin treats this eastern quarter of Berlin. Their tone is consistently celebratory of the diversity and energy of its life, while not denying its darker side. One often encounters here motifs from reality which were later incorporated into the fictional city of the novel. Thus, in "Berlin und die Künstler"

(Berlin and the Artists) from the *Vossische Zeitung*, No. 180 (April 16, 1922): "in the Brunnenstrasse, the AEG: a delight!" (now collected in *Zeitlupe* 59). See also "Östlich um den Alexanderplatz" (In the East around the Alexanderplatz; 1923) in *Zeitlupe* 60–63, which includes as important a motif as a young man singing "Heil dir im Siegerkranz" in a back courtyard, as well as "Großstadt und Großstädter" (The Big City and its Inhabitants), *Zeitlupe* 225–44.

31. They are not "pictorial symbols of the main facets of commerce in the city," as Mitchell calls them in *James Joyce and the German Novel*, p. 138.

32. Klotz, pp. 375–76, calls them "a summary of the total city" and comments, "the epically organized city legitimizes itself through the officially organized city." Keller, p. 145, calls the city here "a thoroughly ordered whole . . . a community formed by the human spirit . . . a living alliance."

33. Fries, pp. 46–47, seems to suggest that the list provides an arsenal of metaphor for the novel, and Klotz, p. 375, overstates the case when he says that the list "includes all possible institutions of this urban community." The emblem which seems most out of place both in the list and the novel, the Greek head symbolizing "Art and Culture," plays a humorously modest role when Biberkopf's friend Meck makes fun of him for joining a peddlers' association although he has nothing to peddle. Meck says he may as well sell mouse traps or "plaster heads" and Franz answers, why not? (*BA* 63, *EJ* 68).

34. Again, connections can be made to Biberkopf. The building permit is related to the constant demolition and construction going on throughout the novel, and the license to hunt wild rabbits in the Fauler Seepark anticipates the refrain "The chase, the pursuit, the damned pursuit" (*BA* 442–43, *EJ* 559–61) that runs through Franz's head just before his arrest.

35. Biberkopf is later shown studying similar announcements on a Litfass pillar on the Alexanderplatz (*BA* 186, *EJ* 226).

36. Jürgen Stenzel, "Mit Kleister und Schere. Zur Handschrift von *Berlin Alexanderplatz*," *Text + Kritik* 13/14 (June 1966), p. 43. Cf. Mitchell, pp. 137–38.

37. Klotz, p. 379, asserts that the narrator here adopts his "omniscient role," but it is only a virtuoso pretense of omniscience, presented with a good deal of tongue-in-cheek.

38. Christopher Isherwood, *Goodbye to Berlin* (New York: New Directions, 1954), p. 1.

39. Fritz Martini, *Das Wagnis der Sprache. Interpretationen deutscher Prosa von Nietzsche bis Benn* (Stuttgart: Ernst Klett, 1954), p. 360.

40. Ekkehard Kaemmerling undertakes to show specific cinematic techniques utilized by Döblin in *Berlin Alexanderplatz*, even claiming—without supporting evidence—that Döblin was directly indebted to the montage theories of Eisenstein and Pudovkin (Kaemmerling, p. 191). He says that only a "reader-cineaste" can fully understand all the cinematic techniques used in the novel (pp. 197–98). In contrast, Erich Kleinschmidt, the editor of Döblin's collected dramas, radio plays, and film scripts, has written that "for his epic theory, the formal possibilities of film had a fruitful, if not a decisive effect" (Kleinschmidt, "Nachwort," *DHF* 653).

41. Klotz, pp. 381–82, states incorrectly that the chapter "ends with the conversation of two failures in a corner pub."

42. Cf. Kaemmerling, p. 196, who describes a similar passage (*BA* 267–

68, EJ 333) as "referring to its origin in a filmscript," without showing why it couldn't just as well have come from a playscript.

43. Mitchell, pp. 138–39, argues convincingly through analysis of the *Berlin Alexanderplatz* manuscript that the chapter originally consisted of only section 3, and that sections 1 and 2 were added after Döblin read Joyce's *Ulysses*.

44. Timothy Joseph Casey, "Alfred Döblin," in *Expressionismus als Literatur. Gesammelte Studien*, ed. Wolfgang Rothe (Bern: Francke, 1969), pp. 637–55, calls the novel "decidedly ordered by statistics" (p. 647).

45. Klotz, p. 382, breaks off his analysis of this chapter after what I have called the second section, but treats the narrator extensively elsewhere.

46. See *SLW* 142–70.

47. Casey, p. 646, injects a word of caution: "The teacher has thrown out the baby with the bathwater, has denied the Furies of guilt along with those of fate." True, but Krause is also clearly posturing in this statement, and admits to having felt enough guilt to try to commit suicide.

48. Hans-Peter Bayerdörfer, "Der Wissende und die Gewalt. Alfred Döblins Theorie des epischen Werkes und der Schluss von *Berlin Alexanderplatz*," in Prangel, ed., *Materialien zu Alfred Döblin*, p. 169. Cf. *UD* 418.

49. Döblin is here quoting the text of a socialist song, "*Das sind wir Arbeitsmänner, das Proletariat.*"

50. Martini; Welzig; Erich Hülse in *Möglichkeiten des modernen deutschen Romans*, ed. Rolf Geissler (Frankfurt: Moritz Diesterweg, 1962), pp. 45–101. Roland Links presents a specifically Marxist variation on this interpretive line by defining Berlin as a capitalist metropolis (*Alfred Döblin*, p. 124) and charging that the end of the novel, although urging solidarity with the marching masses, does not become sufficiently Communist in its call (p. 126).

51. Klotz; Müller-Salget; and Casey. Albrecht Schöne, "Döblin: *Berlin Alexanderplatz*," in Benno von Wiese, ed., *Der deutsche Roman. Vom Barock bis zur Gegenwart*, vol. 2 (Düsseldorf: August Bagel, 1963), pp. 291–325, represents an exception to the general rule. Although strongly emphasizing the "great theme of submission" to one's fate (p. 308), he contests Martini's assertion that the world of the novel is fragmented (p. 316).

52. Bayerdörfer, p. 163, accepting the thesis of the city as chaos, nevertheless asserts that by the end of the novel, Biberkopf has achieved a *political* consciousness equal to that of the narrator. I would argue that urban and political consciousness reinforce each other. A politically aware Biberkopf will also be alive to the social potential of the city.

53. Benjamin, pp. 235–36, implies that Biberkopf's loss of "fate" represents an aesthetic faltering which in the end degrades Biberkopf to the status of a hero in a bourgeois *Bildungsroman*.

54. Keller, p. 144, interprets all the figures who appear in book 2, chapter 1, as parallel to Biberkopf in the sense that they are also trying to "conquer the city." This seems to me to go too far. It is only Biberkopf who has vowed to be decent and to survive on his own. If all these figures are "battlers, conquerors and failures," then the gesture of "conquering the city," which Keller interprets as Biberkopf's basic hubris and weakness, is reduced to simply an equivalent for "living."

55. See Prangel, *Materialien*, p. 54. While Döblin may not have written the dust jacket copy, he used the same phrase in an interview: Franz learns "that what's important is not to be a so-called decent person, but to find the proper comrade" (*SLW* 180).

56. At the same point in the novel, Death calls him "Pope Biberkopf" (*BA* 479, EJ 605).

57. Robert Minder, "Alfred Döblin," in Hermann Friedmann and Otto Mann, eds., *Deutsche Literatur im zwanzigsten Jahrhundert* (Heidelberg: Wolfgang Rothe Verlag, 1954), p. 295.

58. Cf. Ziolkowski, *Dimensions*, pp. 120–31.

59. See Sebald, pp. 89–91, who interprets the bread-baking metaphor as a mythical initiation into social conformity.

60. See Müller-Salget, p. 310.

61. See Kathleen Komar, "Technique and Structure in Döblin's *Berlin Alexanderplatz*," *The German Quarterly* 54 (May 1981), pp. 322–23, on the echoes of Ecclesiastes 4:9–12 in this last paragraph. As Komar notes, the biblical parallel tends to universalize rather than particularize the call for solidarity.

62. James H. Reid, "*Berlin Alexanderplatz*—A Political Novel," *German Life and Letters* 21 (April 1968), p. 221.

63. Bayerdörfer, pp. 156–65.

64. Bayerdörfer, p. 163.

65. Bayerdörfer, pp. 163–64. It seems wrong, however, to say that "In the final chapter Döblin has gone out of his way to make the constellation of contemporary political parties visible to the eye of the reader" (p. 164). This is precisely what he has not done, and it is the reason that the final chapter has caused such confusion.

66. Minder, "Alfred Döblin," p. 295.

67. Keller, p. 149.

68. Links, *Alfred Döblin*, p. 115; Müller-Salget, p. 315; Keller, pp. 165 and 174.

69. Ziolkowski, *Dimensions*, p. 129.

70. Helmut Kiesel dubs these female figures "with a dual 'disposition' to erotic and religious redemption" *Madonna Lisa*, a phrase he borrows from Rilke (in the poem "Und du erbst das Grün" in the *Stunden-Buch*). "The most complete realization of this type in Döblin's work, the synthesis of saint and whore from which all contradiction has been eliminated, is . . . Emilie Parsunke from *Berlin Alexanderplatz*" (Kiesel, p. 469).

71. About Biberkopf's childhood we learn only that with his mother and siblings, he pasted decorations onto painted eggs to earn money (*BA* 267, EJ 332).

72. I have had to revise the Jolas translation considerably in this passage to make it conform to Döblin's original. Jolas follows Revelation 17:1–6 in the King James Version too closely and Döblin not closely enough. See Helmut Schwimmer, *Alfred Döblin. Berlin Alexanderplatz* (Munich: R. Oldenbourg Verlag, 1973), pp. 117–18, for a comparison of this passage with the Luther translation. Döblin's main changes are a switch from first to second person and from preterite to present.

4. Men without Mercy

1. All quotes from the novel will be referenced to both the translation (*MWM*) and the German original in the *Ausgewählte Werke* edition (*P*). The novel's German title is *Pardon wird nicht gegeben* (No Quarter Given). The decision to change it in the English translation is unfortunate, since the title phrase becomes a leitmotif in the novel. It has occasionally been necessary to make changes in the translation.

2. Manfred Auer, *Das Exil vor der Vertreibung: Motivkontinuität und Quellenproblematik im späten Werk Alfred Döblins* (Bonn: Bouvier, 1977), p. 33, writes of a "reduction in the realms of structure, narrative technique, style and theme."

3. Auer, p. 33, argues that the basic theme is the "battle of the individual for self-affirmation" (p. 33), principally in the private sphere of the family, and that the connection between familial and political struggle is not causal (p. 37), but only "figurative" (p. 33).

4. See Prangel, *Alfred Döblin*, p. 81; and Klaus Schröter, *Alfred Döblin in Selbstzeugnissen und Bilddokumenten* (Reinbek bei Hamburg: Rowohlt Taschenbuch, 1978), p. 123.

5. "Nachwort des Herausgebers," *P* 373.

6. Kiesel, p. 58, characterizes it as a "document of poetic resistance to psychoanalysis *and* of the dubious value of 'writing as therapy.'"

7. See David W. Morgan, *The Socialist Left and the German Revolution: A History of the German Independent Social Democratic Party, 1917–1922* (Ithaca: Cornell University Press, 1975), pp. 232–36.

8. "Wo gehobelt wird, fallen Späne" (When you plane you get shavings): Noske's words at the Social-Democratic Party convention in June 1919 in defense of the mass executions in Berlin. See *WV* 291, note to p. 23.

9. See *SPG* 92.

10. Kiesel, p. 56, says the passage is "psychologically understandable, but politically and morally indefensible." This is a particularly strong statement from Kiesel, whose thesis is that Döblin's central motif since 1918 is "sorrow at destruction and man's lust for destruction" (p. 17).

11. Kiesel, p. 56.

12. See Tewarson, *Alfred Döblin*, pp. 99–111.

13. Quoted in *SPG* 488–89.

14. See Kreutzer, pp. 134–47, for a good account of the controversy.

15. See *Briefe* 476, and Klaus Petersen, *Die "Gruppe 1925": Geschichte und Soziologie einer Schriftstellervereinigung* (Heidelberg: Winter, 1981).

16. See *DHF* 616–17 and 625.

17. Müller-Salget, p. 360.

18. See Kreutzer, pp. 134–62.

19. See Wulf Koepke, "Alfred Döblin's Überparteilichkeit. Zur Publizistik in den letzten Jahren der Weimarer Republik," in Thomas Koebner, ed., *Weimars Ende: Prognosen und Diagnosen in der deutschen Literatur und politischen Publizistik 1930–1933* (Frankfurt: Suhrkamp, 1982), pp. 321–23. Koepke sees in *Know and Change!* the influence of Karl Mannheim's analysis of the intelligentsia in *Ideology and Utopia*.

20. Kreutzer, p. 146.

21. Heinz Graber, "Nachwort des Herausgebers," *WV* 313.
22. Cf. *UD* 473.
23. Auer, p. 33, says the familial battle is a "paradigm for the entire society."
24. Auer, p. 33, calls the mother-father conflict a "dominating leitmotif."
25. Typical of the latter approach is his socio-criminological study of an abused proletarian wife who, together with her female lover, poisoned her husband, *Die beiden Freundinnen und ihr Giftmord* (Berlin: Verlag Die Schmiede, n.d. [1925]), reprinted as vol. 289 of the Bibliothek Suhrkamp (Frankfurt: Suhrkamp, 1971).
26. Walter Muschg speaks of the novel's "heathen tragedy of fate" and "the air of Greek tragedy" surrounding the mother (*P* 380); Roland Links writes that Karl's destiny "is fulfilled with the logic of a Greek tragedy," *Alfred Döblin*, p. 157.
27. "The seducer's name is José, of course" (Müller-Salget, p. 371).
28. The Blewitt translation is misleading in this passage. It should read: "And if he had formerly left his flat in the evenings to wander about the streets, to vanquish José and Julie and to exalt himself above them . . . he was now impelled towards something that was called Paul."
29. This point is also made by Walter Muschg in his afterword to the German edition of the novel (*P* 379).
30. Links, *Alfred Döblin*, pp. 162–63, suggests that this broad appeal reflects the antifascist front Döblin could see forming in Paris in 1934, but of course the blurring of the distinction between workers and middle class was already central to *Know and Change!*
31. Kiesel, pp. 288–90, remarks insightfully that Döblin's idea of a "partisan" historiography owes more to Nietzsche's essay "Vom Nutzen und Nachteil der Historie für das Leben" than it does to Marx. Kiesel sees Nietzsche's category of a "monumental history" appropriate to "active and striving men" reflected in the figures of Rosa Luxemburg and Woodrow Wilson in *November 1918*. Döblin presents them in a pathetic style that sometimes deteriorates into colportage.
32. Links, *Alfred Döblin*, p. 163, says he "sometimes acts like a caricature of Nietzsche's Superman."
33. Manfred Auer disagrees, interpreting the sociopolitical aspect of the novel as of minor importance. He seems to miss the mark when he says that "it is never a question of Karl making a basic choice between the bourgeoisie and the proletariat" (Auer, p. 36). We have seen that Döblin rejects these Marxist categories. Karl certainly does make a choice between the more general categories of the oppressed and the oppressors, joining the latter as a successful businessman and returning to the former at the end of the novel.
34. A garbled version of this English proverb is introduced into the conversation in which Wadzek uses the metaphor of the ship (*W* 237).
35. The Blewitt translation of this passage is inaccurate.
36. The Blewitt translation of this passage is inaccurate.
37. E.g., Links, *Alfred Döblin*, p. 161; and Klaus Schröter, *Alfred Döblin*, p. 123, where he also calls the novel "the high point in Döblin's imaginative writing."
38. See Auer, p. 35: the circularity of the plot is carried out "ad absurdum."

5. November 1918: A German Revolution

1. Because of the complicated history of its composition and publication, there is disagreement about whether the work should be called a trilogy or a tetralogy. Auer, pp. 57–63, argues persuasively that Döblin conceived it as a trilogy (cf. *Briefe* 231) and only divided the middle part in two volumes because of its length. Heinz Osterle, the editor of the new edition (Munich: Deutscher Taschenbuch Verlag, 1978), argues for the designation "tetralogy" (cf. *Briefe* 318). Since his edition is in four volumes, I will refer to *November 1918* as a tetralogy. In any case, it should be understood that the "trilogy" published between 1948 and 1950 (Munich: Verlag Karl Alber) is *not* the complete *November 1918*. *Bürger und Soldaten* (Soldiers and Citizens), the first volume published in Amsterdam in 1939 and Döblin's last work to be published until after the Second World War, could not be included in the Karl Alber edition. The censors of the French occupying forces refused permission to publish it, apparently because of its setting in Alsace, and it was reduced to a "prelude" to *Verratenes Volk* (A People Betrayed). The recent English translation by John Woods regrettably deletes the first novel without comment and even without the prelude from the postwar Munich edition.

2. This is sometimes implicitly regarded as the official "end" of the novel's time frame. See Anthony W. Riley, "The Aftermath of the First World War: Christianity and Revolution in Alfred Döblin's *November 1918*," in Charles N. Genno and Heinz Wetzel, eds., *The First World War in German Narrative Prose* (Toronto: University of Toronto Press, 1980), p. 95.

3. Hermann Broch, in the last novel of his trilogy *The Sleepwalkers*, also chose a small-town setting to help give coherence to his multistranded narrative of the war's end.

4. Quotations from the tetralogy will be referenced first to the German edition (*November 1–4*), then to the English translation (*Woods 1 and 2*). The following chart shows the relation of the German edition to the Woods translation:

1. *Bürger und Soldaten*	(not included; translations my own)
2. *Verratenes Volk* ⎫	1. *A People Betrayed*
3. *Heimkehr der Fronttruppen* ⎭	
4. *Karl und Rosa*	2. *Karl and Rosa*

5. See Auer, pp. 65–68.
6. See Kiesel, p. 297.
7. Auer, p. 69.
8. Auer, p. 68.
9. Cf. the section of *Unser Dasein* entitled "Einer liest Zeitung" (A Man Reads the Newspaper), where newspapers are already regarded as symptoms of an inauthentic and enslaving modern society (*UD* 426–30). Döblin had thus come to this conclusion by the early thirties.
10. In the original *der Staat* (the state).
11. The "Monologue of the Spree" was also possibly inspired by one of the few fictional, nondocumentary scenes in Walter Ruttman's 1927 film "Berlin,

Symphonie einer Großstadt," in which a wild-eyed suicide flings herself from a bridge into the river.

12. John Woods translates "vieles, was dazu passte" as "many things that fit his mood," but the only real antecedents for *dazu* are the "schönes Bild" and its metaphor, the ant colony.

13. Keller, pp. 142–44.

14. See Komar, p. 321. Komar writes that the old Jew is referring to Biberkopf, not to Berlin, when *he* quotes from Jeremiah (*BA* 19, EJ 13). In *November 1918*, it is clearly the frivolous city being indicted through the words of the prophet.

15. See Kiesel, pp. 275 and 331.

16. Cf. Kiesel, p. 291.

17. See Roland Links, "Mit Geschichte will man etwas. Alfred Döblin: 'November 1918,'" in Sigrid Bock and Manfred Hahn, eds., *Erfahrung Exil: Antifaschistische Romane 1933–1945* (Berlin: Aufbau-Verlag, 1979), p. 340. Links says Döblin's purpose in this passage is to "alienate" the reader from the action in order to establish an "agreement" between reader and narrator.

18. See Kiesel, pp. 341–42, who calls the three basic narrative modes satirical, ironical, and passionate (*pathetisch*). His assignment of these modes to different groups of characters is somewhat problematic. Not all historical figures, for instance, are treated satirically.

19. This realism was noted by an early reviewer. See Schuster and Bode, p. 409.

20. See Auer, pp. 65–70, for Döblin's tendentious use of documentary material.

21. See Gay, pp. 8–13, on this common pattern of enthusiasm and disappointment. See also Auer, p. 66.

22. Sebastian Haffner, *Die verratene Revolution: Deutschland 1918/19* (Bern: Scherz Verlag, 1969).

23. See Links, "Mit Geschichte will man etwas," p. 345.

24. Ebert's measure of guilt continues to be debated even today among historians and within the ranks of the contemporary German SPD (see, for instance, Brigitte Brandt's review of Heinrich August Winkler's history of the German workers' movement from 1918 to 1924 in *Der Spiegel*, May 27, 1985, pp. 34–43). The consensus among Western historians seems to be that Ebert and Noske were correct in their aims (to curb left-wing rebellion in order to stabilize both internal and external politics) but misguided in their means (cooperating with reactionary generals and allowing the formation of Freikorps). Cf. for example Arthur Rosenberg, *A History of the German Republic*, trans. Ian F. D. Morrow and L. Marie Sieveking (London: Methuen, 1936), pp. 50–51 and 80–83; Gay, p. 19; Morgan, p. 216. On the other side there is Haffner, p. 10: "The German Revolution of 1918 was a Social Democratic revolution that was suppressed by the Social Democratic leaders, a unique occurrence in the history of the world."

25. The English translation fails to include the first adjective in the series: *langsam* (slow).

26. See Arthur Rosenberg, *Imperial Germany: The Birth of the German Republic 1871–1918*, trans. Ian F. D. Morrow (Boston: Beacon Press, 1964), p. 270: "The chief aim of the military revolution was to assure peace by abolishing the power of the officers."

27. See Links, "Mit Geschichte will man etwas," p. 342 and Kiesel, pp. 280–81.

28. See Auer, pp. 70ff., for another instance of such indirect narrative comment through juxtaposition.

29. Actually, Radek was a Polish Jew, born Karl Sobelsohn in Lvov in 1885.

30. A contemporary reviewer of the first volume had already noted the irony of the title: "One would never speak of 'a French revolution'; people will always say 'the French Revolution,' and will not only know which one is meant, but also what it meant." A. M. Frey, quoted in Schuster and Bode, p. 369.

31. Milovan Djilas, *Conversations with Stalin* (Harmondsworth: Penguin, 1963), p. 66.

32. Rosenberg, *Imperial Germany*, pp. 93–94.

33. Ziolkowski, *Fictional Transfigurations*, p. 7.

34. See Keller, pp. 51–52.

35. Keller, p. 52.

36. It should be noted that only the Antigone story is a genuine prefiguration in Ziolkowski's strict sense, i.e., an ancient story that provides a "pattern of events" for a modern story. The parallels with Faust and Christ are less fully developed, more oblique. See Ziolkowski, *Fictional Transfigurations*, pp. 8–10.

37. Heinz Osterle, "Alfred Döblins Revolutionsroman," afterword to Alfred Döblin, *Karl und Rosa* (Munich: Deutscher Taschenbuch Verlag, 1978), p. 685, locates the "Faust parody" at the end of the entire tetralogy. As will be shown below, I interpret the end as a postfiguration of the story of Jesus rather than of Faust.

38. The entire Stauffer narrative has been deleted in the English translation.

39. See J. W. Goethe, *Faust*, Part I, lines 720–807.

40. On the influence of Kierkegaard's Antigone-recreation in *Either/Or*, see Riley, pp. 104–5; Kiesel, pp. 475–76; and Heinz D. Osterle, "Auf den Spuren der Antigone: Sophokles, Döblin, Brecht," in Stauffacher, ed., *Internationale Alfred Döblin-Kolloquien*, pp. 96–97.

41. George Steiner, *Antigones* (New York: Oxford University Press, 1984), pp. 188–90, treats the classroom discussion, but does not mention the postfigurative recreation.

42. This is one of the very few times when the Woods translation seems wrong, translating *Männchen* as "a kept man." "Male of the species" is more accurate, and corresponds to the word *Tierchen* ("little animal") used for the women.

43. In her combination of purity and sensuality, Hilde conforms to the image of the "weisse Krankenschwester" (white nurse) in the prefascist Freikorps novels analyzed by Theweleit, pp. 90–100. See also Kiesel, pp. 465–69.

44. See Auer, p. 78.

45. Compare *November* 4 : 13–15, Woods 2 : 5–7, with Rosa Luxemburg, *Briefe aus dem Gefängnis* (Berlin: Verlag Junge Garde, 1920), pp. 37–38.

46. There is a photograph of him celebrating among the officers at the Eden Hotel after the murder. It was printed in the Spartacist newspaper *Rote Fahne* as part of its futile campaign to bring the murderers to justice. See J. P. Nettl, *Rosa Luxemburg*, vol. 2 (London: Oxford University Press, 1966), pp. vii, 762.

47. J. P. Nettl, in the commentated bibliography appended to his ex-

haustive two-volume biography of Luxemburg, calls *Karl and Rosa* "a not insensitive but gaudy dramatization of Rosa Luxemburg's prison years . . . the story departs substantially from the truth and grossly over-emphasizes her love-life" (Nettl, vol. 2, p. 918).

48. See Nettl, vol. 1, p. 25, and Elżbieta Ettinger, introduction to *Comrade and Lover: Rosa Luxemburg's Letters to Leo Jogiches* (Cambridge, Mass.: MIT Press, 1981), pp. xvi–xviii.

49. Luxemburg, *Briefe aus dem Gefängnis*, p. 35. There is lively critical debate on the plausibility of Döblin's portrayal of Luxemburg. Müller-Salget, p. 378, and Heidi Tewarson, "Alfred Döblins Geschichtskonzeption in 'November 1918. Eine deutsche Revolution,'" in Stauffacher, ed., *Internationale Alfred Döblin-Kolloquien*, pp. 64–75, are critical. Riley, pp. 99–103; Links, "Mit Geschichte will man etwas," pp. 348–49; Auer, pp. 76–77; and Kiesel, pp. 401–2, defend Döblin's portrayal.

50. How astute Döblin was in choosing Luxemburg as the great representative figure of the German revolution, and how relevant she remains today for dissident Marxists in Eastern Europe, can be measured by the fact that the East German poet and performer Wolf Biermann quoted precisely this passage at the beginning of his concert in Cologne in 1976. Following the concert he found himself expatriated and denied reentry into the German Democratic Republic. See also Ettinger, p. xxxiii: "She alone among her contemporaries made a comeback in the 1960s as tanks rolled and shots were fired and people were fighting again for government 'with a human face.'"

51. Döblin himself, like Becker, saw a "weeping woman" in the cathedral of Mende, France, where his religious crisis occurred (*ASLA* 189).

Conclusion

1. Auer, p. 160.

2. How foreign Döblin's Christianity was to his friends in exile is captured in Bertolt Brecht's bitterly satirical poem "Peinlicher Vorfall" (Embarrassing Incident), written after Döblin had hinted at his conversion at a Hollywood party for him on his sixty-fifth birthday in 1943: "the celebrated god . . . / Fell lewdly to his knees and shamelessly / Struck up a saucy hymn, thus offending / The irreligious sentiments of his listeners, some of them / Mere youths" (Brecht, *Gesammelte Werke*, vol. 10 [Frankfurt: Suhrkamp, 1967], p. 862). How foreign Döblin's Christianity would be to younger German writers can be measured by Hans Mayer's characterization of postwar German literature—East and West—as a literature "without faith" (Mayer, "Literatur heute im geteilten Deutschland," in Werner Link, ed., *Schriftsteller und Politik in Deutschland* [Düsseldorf: Droste Verlag, 1979], p. 127).

Works Cited

Works of Alfred Döblin

For all of Döblin's works that have been reprinted, citations in the text are to the reprinted edition.

Alexanderplatz Berlin: The Story of Franz Biberkopf. Translated by Eugene Jolas. New York: Viking Press, 1931. Reprint. New York: Frederick Ungar, 1976.

Aufsätze zur Literatur. Olten: Walter-Verlag, 1963.

Autobiographische Schriften und letzte Aufzeichnungen. Olten: Walter-Verlag, 1980.

Die beiden Freundinnen und ihr Giftmord. Berlin: Verlag Die Schmiede, 1925 (= Rudolf Leonhard, ed. *Aussenseiter der Gesellschaft—Die Verbrechen der Gegenwart,* vol. 1). Reprint. Frankfurt: Suhrkamp, 1971.

Berge Meere und Giganten. Berlin: S. Fischer Verlag, 1924. Reprint. Olten: Walter-Verlag, 1978.

Berlin Alexanderplatz. Die Geschichte vom Franz Biberkopf. Berlin: S. Fischer Verlag, 1929. Reprint. Olten: Walter-Verlag, 1961.

Briefe. Olten: Walter-Verlag, 1970.

Der deutsche Maskenball von Linke Poot. Berlin: S. Fischer Verlag, 1921. Reprint. *Der deutsche Maskenball von Linke Poot. Wissen und Verändern!* Olten: Walter-Verlag, 1972.

Drama. Hörspiel. Film. Olten: Walter-Verlag, 1983.

Die drei Sprünge des Wang-lun. Chinesischer Roman. Berlin: S. Fischer Verlag, 1915. Reprint. Olten: Walter-Verlag, 1960.

Erzählungen aus fünf Jahrzehnten. Olten: Walter-Verlag, 1979.

Gespräche mit Kalypso: über die Musik. Edited by Bernd Jentzsch. Olten: Walter-Verlag, 1980.

Das Ich über der Natur. Berlin: S. Fischer, 1927.

Jagende Rosse, Der schwarze Vorhang, und andere frühe Erzählwerke. Olten: Walter-Verlag, 1981.

Men Without Mercy. Translated by Trevor and Phyllis Blewitt. London: Victor Gollancz, 1937. Reprint. New York: Howard Fertig, 1976.

Minotaurus: Dichtung unter den Hufen von Staat und Industrie. Edited by Alfred Döblin. Wiesbaden: Franz Steiner Verlag, 1953.

November 1918: A German Revolution. Vol. 1, *A People Betrayed;* vol. 2,

Karl and Rosa. Translated by John E. Woods. New York: Fromm International Publishing Corp., 1983.

November 1918: Eine deutsche Revolution. Vol. 1, *Bürger und Soldaten;* vol. 2, *Verratenes Volk;* vol. 3, *Heimkehr der Fronttruppen;* vol. 4, *Karl und Rosa.* Munich: Deutscher Taschenbuch Verlag, 1978.

Pardon wird nicht gegeben. Amsterdam: Querido Verlag, 1935. Reprint. Olten: Walter-Verlag, 1960.

Reise in Polen. Berlin: S. Fischer Verlag, 1926. Reprint. Olten: Walter-Verlag, 1968.

Schriften zu Leben und Werk. Olten: Walter-Verlag, 1986.

Schriften zur Politik und Gesellschaft. Olten: Walter-Verlag, 1972.

Der schwarze Vorhang. Roman von den Worten und Zufällen. Berlin: S. Fischer Verlag, 1919. Reprint. *Jagende Rosse, Der schwarze Vorhang, und andere frühe Erzählwerke.* Olten: Walter-Verlag, 1981.

Unser Dasein. Berlin: S. Fischer Verlag, 1933. Reprint. Olten: Walter-Verlag, 1964.

Wadzeks Kampf mit der Dampfturbine. Berlin: S. Fischer Verlag, 1918. Reprint. Olten: Walter-Verlag, 1982.

Wissen und Verändern! Offene Briefe an einen jungen Menschen. Berlin: S. Fischer Verlag, 1931. Reprint. *Der deutsche Maskenball von Linke Poot. Wissen und Verändern!* Olten: Walter-Verlag, 1972.

Die Zeitlupe. Kleine Prosa. Olten: Walter-Verlag, 1962.

Secondary Works

Apollonio, Umbro, ed. *Der Futurismus: Manifeste und Dokumente einer künstlerischen Revolution 1909–1918.* Cologne: M. DuMont Schauberg, 1972.

Arnold, Armin. *Die Literatur des Expressionismus: Sprachliche und thematische Quellen.* Stuttgart: Kohlhammer Verlag, 1966.

———. "Les styles, voilà l'homme! Döblins sprachliche Entwicklung bis zu 'Berlin Alexanderplatz.'" In Ingrid Schuster, ed., *Zu Alfred Döblin.* Stuttgart: Ernst Klett Verlag, 1980. Pp. 41–56.

Auer, Manfred. *Das Exil vor der Vertreibung: Motivkontinuität und Quellenproblematik im späten Werk Alfred Döblins.* Bonn: Bouvier Verlag, 1977.

Baumgarth, Christa. *Geschichte des Futurismus.* Reinbek bei Hamburg: Rowohlt, 1966.

Bayerdörfer, Hans-Peter. "Der Wissende und die Gewalt: Alfred Döblins Theorie des epischen Werkes und der Schluß von *Berlin Alexanderplatz.*" In Matthias Prangel, ed., *Materialien zu Alfred Döblin. "Berlin Alexanderplatz."* Frankfurt: Suhrkamp, 1975. Pp. 150–85.

Bebel, August. *Die Frau und der Sozialismus (Die Frau in der Vergangenheit, Gegenwart und Zukunft).* 10th ed. Stuttgart: Dietz, 1891.

Benjamin, Walter. "Krisis des Romans: Zu Döblins 'Berlin Alexanderplatz.'" In Hella Tiedemann-Bartels, ed., *Gesammelte Schriften,* vol. 3. Frankfurt: Suhrkamp, 1972. Pp. 230–36.

Benn, Gottfried. *Gesammelte Werke 4: Reden und Vorträge.* Wiesbaden: Limes Verlag, 1968.

Brandt, Brigitte. "'Führernaturen fallen nicht vom Himmel.'" *Der Spiegel,* May 27, 1985. Pp. 34–43.

Brecht, Bertolt. *Arbeitsjournal.* Edited by Werner Hecht. 2 vols. Frankfurt: Suhrkamp, 1973.

———. *Gesammelte Werke,* vol. 10 (*Gedichte 3*). Frankfurt: Suhrkamp, 1967.

———. *Tagebücher 1920–1922. Autobiographische Aufzeichnungen 1920–1954.* Frankfurt: Suhrkamp, 1975.

Casey, Timothy Joseph. "Alfred Döblin." In Wolfgang Rothe, ed., *Expressionismus als Literatur: Gesammelte Studien.* Bern: Francke, 1969. Pp. 637–55.

Djilas, Milovan. *Conversations with Stalin.* Harmondsworth: Penguin, 1963.

Elshorst, Hansjörg. "Mensch und Umwelt im Werk Alfred Döblins." Diss., Munich, 1966.

Ettinger, Elżbieta, ed. and trans. *Comrade and Lover: Rosa Luxemburg's Letters to Leo Jogiches.* Cambridge, Mass.: MIT Press, 1981.

Fries, Marilyn Sibley. "The City as Metaphor for the Human Condition: Alfred Döblin's *Berlin Alexanderplatz* (1929)." *Modern Fiction Studies* 24 (1978), pp. 41–64.

Gay, Peter. *Weimar Culture: The Outsider as Insider.* New York: Harper & Row, 1968.

Goethe, J. W. *Goethes Faust. Der Tragödie erster und zweiter Teil. Urfaust.* Hamburg: Christian Wegner Verlag, 1963.

Graber, Heinz. "Nachwort des Herausgebers." In Alfred Döblin, *Der deutsche Maskenball von Linke Poot. Wissen und Verändern!* Olten: Walter-Verlag, 1972. Pp. 305–18.

Haffner, Sebastian. *Die verratene Revolution: Deutschland 1918/19.* Bern: Scherz Verlag, 1969.

Hanson, Anne Coffin, ed. *The Futurist Imagination: Word + Image in Italian Futurist Painting, Drawing, Collage and Free-Word Poetry.* New Haven: Yale University Art Gallery, 1983.

Hermand, Jost and Frank Trommler. *Die Kultur der Weimarer Republik.* Munich: Nymphenburger Verlagshandlung, 1978.

Huguet, Louis. "L'Oeuvre d'Alfred Döblin ou la Dialectique de l'Exode, 1878–1918." Diss. Paris-Nanterre, 1970.

Hülse, Erich. "Alfred Döblin. 'Berlin Alexanderplatz.'" In Rolf Geissler, ed., *Möglichkeiten des modernen deutschen Romans.* Frankfurt: Moritz Diesterweg, 1962. Pp. 45–101.

Isherwood, Christopher. *Goodbye to Berlin.* New York: New Directions, 1954.

Joll, James. *Intellectuals in Politics: Three Biographical Essays.* London: Weidenfeld and Nicolson, 1960.

Joyce, James. *Ulysses.* New York: The Modern Library, 1961.

Kaemmerling, Ekkehard. "Die filmische Schreibweise." In Matthias Prangel, ed., *Materialien zu Alfred Döblin. "Berlin Alexanderplatz."* Frankfurt: Suhrkamp, 1975. Pp. 185–98.

Keller, Otto. *Döblins Montageroman als Epos der Moderne: Die Struktur der Romane "Der schwarze Vorhang," "Die drei Sprünge des Wang-lun" und "Berlin Alexanderplatz."* Munich: Fink Verlag, 1980.

Kiesel, Helmut. *Literarische Trauerarbeit. Das Exil- und Spätwerk Alfred Döblins.* Tübingen: Max Niemeyer, 1986.

Kleinschmidt, Erich. "Nachwort des Herausgebers." In Alfred Döblin, *Drama. Hörspiel. Film.* Olten: Walter-Verlag, 1983. Pp. 579–669.

Klotz, Volker. *Die erzählte Stadt: Ein Sujet als Herausforderung des Romans von Lesage bis Döblin.* Munich: Carl Hanser Verlag, 1969.

Koepke, Wulf. "Alfred Döblin's Überparteilichkeit. Zur Publizistik in den letzten Jahren der Weimarer Republik." In Thomas Koebner, ed., *Weimars Ende: Prognosen und Diagnosen in der deutschen Literatur und politischen Publizistik 1930–1933.* Frankfurt: Suhrkamp, 1982. Pp. 318–29.

Komar, Kathleen. "Technique and Structure in Döblin's *Berlin Alexanderplatz.*" *The German Quarterly* 54 (May 1981), pp. 318–34.

Kreutzer, Leo. *Alfred Döblin: Sein Werk bis 1933.* Stuttgart: Kohlhammer Verlag, 1970.

Laqueur, Walter. *Weimar: A Cultural History 1918–1933.* New York: G. P. Putnam's Sons: 1974.

Links, Roland. *Alfred Döblin: Leben und Werk.* Berlin: Volk und Wissen, 1980.

———. "Mit Geschichte will man etwas. Alfred Döblin: 'November 1918.'" In Sigrid Bock and Manfred Hahn, eds., *Erfahrung Exil: Antifaschistische Romane 1933–1945.* Berlin: Aufbau-Verlag, 1979. Pp. 328–51.

Lista, Giovanni. *Futurisme: Manifestes—Proclamations—Documents.* Lausanne: L'Age d'Homme, 1973.

Luxemburg, Rosa. *Briefe aus dem Gefängnis.* Berlin: Verlag Junge Garde, n.d. [1920].

Marinetti, F. T. "Die futuristische Literatur: Technisches Manifest." Translated by Jean-Jacques. *Der Sturm* 133 (October 1912), pp. 194–95.

———. *Mafarka le Futuriste: Roman Africain.* Paris: E. Sansot, 1909.

———. "Manifest des Futurismus." Translated by Jean-Jacques. *Der Sturm* 104 (March 1912), pp. 828–29.

———. "Supplement zum technischen Manifest der Futuristischen Literatur." Translated by Jean-Jacques. *Der Sturm* 150/151 (March 1913), pp. 279–80.

———. "Tod dem Mondenschein! Zweites Manifest des Futurismus." Quoted in Christa Baumgarth. *Geschichte des Futurismus.* Reinbek bei Hamburg: Rowohlt, 1966. P. 240.

Martin, Marianne W. *Futurist Art and Theory 1909–1915.* New York: Hacker Art Books, 1978.

Martini, Fritz. *Das Wagnis der Sprache: Interpretationen deutscher Prosa von Nietzsche bis Benn.* Stuttgart: Ernst Klett, 1954.

Mayer, Hans. "Literatur heute im geteilten Deutschland." In Werner Link, ed., *Schriftsteller und Politik in Deutschland.* Düsseldorf: Droste Verlag, 1979. Pp. 115–29.

Meyer, Jochen. "Döblin-Chronik." In Jochen Meyer, ed., *Alfred Döblin 1878–1978*. Marbach: Deutsche Schillergesellschaft, 1978. Pp. 10–57.

Minder, Robert. "Alfred Döblin." In Hermann Friedmann and Otto Mann, eds., *Deutsche Literatur im zwanzigsten Jahrhundert*. Heidelberg: Wolfgang Rothe Verlag, 1954. Pp. 283–303.

———. "Begegnungen mit Alfred Döblin in Frankreich." *Text + Kritik* 13/14 (1966), pp. 57–64.

Mitchell, Breon. *James Joyce and the German Novel 1922–1933*. Athens, Ohio: Ohio University Press, 1976.

Morgan, David W. *The Socialist Left and the German Revolution: A History of the German Independent Social Democratic Party, 1917–1922*. Ithaca: Cornell University Press, 1975.

Müller-Salget, Klaus. *Alfred Döblin: Werk und Entwicklung*. Bonn: Bouvier, 1972.

Muschg, Walter. "Nachwort des Herausgebers." In Alfred Döblin, *Pardon wird nicht gegeben*. Olten: Walter-Verlag, 1960. Pp. 371–84.

Musil, Robert. *The Man without Qualities*, vol. 1. Translated by Eithne Wilkins and Ernst Kaiser. New York: Capricorn Books, 1965.

Nettl, J. P. *Rosa Luxemburg*. 2 vols. London: Oxford University Press, 1966.

Nietzsche, Friedrich. *Werke in zwei Bänden*. Munich: Hanser Verlag, 1967.

Osterle, Heinz D. "Alfred Döblins Revolutionsroman." In Alfred Döblin, *Karl und Rosa*. Munich: Deutscher Taschenbuch Verlag, 1978. Pp. 665–95.

———. "Auf den Spuren der Antigone: Sophokles, Döblin, Brecht." In *Internationale Alfred Döblin-Kolloquien* (*see* Stauffacher, ed.). Pp. 86–115.

Petersen, Klaus. *Die "Gruppe 1925": Geschichte und Soziologie einer Schriftstellervereinigung*. Heidelberg: Winter, 1981.

Pike, Burton. *The Image of the City in Modern Literature*. Princeton: Princeton University Press, 1981.

Prangel, Matthias. *Alfred Döblin*. Stuttgart: Metzler, 1973.

———, ed. *Materialien zu Alfred Döblin. "Berlin Alexanderplatz."* Frankfurt: Suhrkamp, 1975.

Reid, James H. "*Berlin Alexanderplatz*—A Political Novel." *German Life and Letters* 21 (1968), pp. 214–23.

Ribbat, Ernst. *Die Wahrheit des Lebens im frühen Werk Alfred Döblins*. Münster: Verlag Aschendorff, 1970.

Riley, Anthony. "Nachwort des Herausgebers." In Alfred Döblin, *Jagende Rosse, Der schwarze Vorhang, und andere frühe Erzählwerke*. Olten: Walter-Verlag, 1981. Pp. 281–326.

———. "The Aftermath of the First World War: Christianity and Revolution in Alfred Döblin's *November 1918*." In Charles N. Genno and Heinz Wetzel, eds., *The First World War in German Narrative Prose*. Toronto: University of Toronto Press, 1980. Pp. 93–117.

Rosenberg, Arthur. *A History of the German Republic*. Translated by Ian F. D. Morrow and L. Marie Sieveking. London: Methuen, 1936.

———. *Imperial Germany: The Birth of the German Republic, 1871–1918*. Translated by Ian F. D. Morrow. Boston: Beacon Press, 1964.

Ryan, Judith. "From Futurism to 'Döblinism.'" *The German Quarterly* 54 (1981), pp. 415–26.

Scheunemann, Dietrich. *Romankrise: Die Entstehungsgeschichte der modernen Romanpoetik in Deutschland*. Heidelberg: Quelle & Meyer, 1978.

Schöne, Albrecht. "Döblin: Berlin Alexanderplatz." In Benno von Wiese, ed., *Der deutsche Roman: Vom Barock bis zur Gegenwart*, vol. 2. Düsseldorf: August Bagel, 1963. Pp. 291–325.

Schröter, Klaus. *Alfred Döblin in Selbstzeugnissen und Bilddokumenten*. Reinbek bei Hamburg: Rowohlt, 1978.

———. "Die Vorstufe zu *Berlin Alexanderplatz*: Alfred Döblins Roman *Wadzeks Kampf mit der Dampfturbine*." *Akzente* 24 (1977), pp. 569–75.

Schuster, Ingrid, ed. *Zu Alfred Döblin*. Stuttgart: Ernst Klett Verlag, 1980.

Schuster, Ingrid, and Ingrid Bode, eds. *Alfred Döblin im Spiegel der zeitgenössischen Kritik*. Bern: Francke Verlag, 1973.

Schwimmer, Helmut. *Alfred Döblin: Berlin Alexanderplatz*. Munich: R. Oldenbourg Verlag, 1973.

Sebald, Winfried Georg. *Der Mythus der Zerstörung im Werk Döblins*. Stuttgart: Ernst Klett Verlag, 1980.

Shearer, Linda. "Beyond Futurism: The Winston/Malbin Collection." In *Futurism: A Modern Focus*. (Exhibition catalogue.) New York: The Solomon R. Guggenheim Museum, 1973. Pp. 9–16.

Sparks, Kimberly. "Drei schwarze Kaninchen: Zu einer Deutung der Zimmerherren in Kafkas 'Die Verwandlung.'" *Zeitschrift für deutsche Philologie* 84 (1965), Sonderheft *Moderne deutsche Dichtung*, pp. 73–82.

Stauffacher, Werner, ed. *Internationale Alfred Döblin-Kolloquien* (= *Jahrbuch für Internationale Germanistik*, ser. A, vol. 14). Bern: Peter Lang, 1986.

———. "'Komisches Grundgefühl' und 'scheinbare Tragik': Zu 'Wadzeks Kampf mit der Dampfturbine.'" In *Internationale Alfred Döblin-Kolloquien* (*see* Stauffacher, ed.). Pp. 168–83.

Steiner, George. *Antigones*. New York: Oxford University Press, 1984.

Stenzel, Jürgen. "Mit Kleister und Schere: Zur Handschrift von *Berlin Alexanderplatz*." *Text + Kritik* 13/14 (1966), pp. 41–44.

Strelka, J. "Der Erzähler Alfred Döblin." *The German Quarterly* 33 (1960), pp. 197–210.

Tewarson, Heidi Thomann. *Alfred Döblin: Grundlagen seiner Ästhetik und ihre Entwicklung, 1900–1933*. Bern: Peter Lang, 1979.

———. "Alfred Döblins Geschichtskonzeption in 'November 1918. Eine deutsche Revolution.'" In *Internationale Alfred Döblin-Kolloquien* (*see* Stauffacher, ed.). Pp. 64–75.

———. "Von der Frauenfrage zum Geschlechterkampf: Der Wandel der Prioritäten im Frühwerk Alfred Döblins." *The German Quarterly* 58 (1985), pp. 208–22.

Theweleit, Klaus. *Male Fantasies*. Vol. 1. *Women, Floods, Bodies, History*. Translated by Stephen Conway in collaboration with Erica Carter and Chris Turner. Minneapolis: University of Minnesota Press, 1987.

Welzig, Werner. *Der deutsche Roman im 20. Jahrhundert*. 2nd ed. Stuttgart: Alfred Kröner Verlag, 1970.

Weyembergh-Boussart, Monique. *Alfred Döblin: Seine Religiosität in Persön-lichkeit und Werk*. Bonn: Bouvier Verlag, 1970.

Ziolkowski, Theodore. *Dimensions of the Modern Novel: German Texts and European Contexts*. Princeton: Princeton University Press, 1969.

———. *Fictional Transfigurations of Jesus*. Princeton: Princeton University Press, 1972.

Index

Compositor: G & S Typesetters, Inc.
Text: 10/13 Sabon
Display: Sabon
Printer: Braun-Brumfield, Inc.
Binder: Braun-Brumfield, Inc.